Another Saturday & Sweet F.A

By

Calvin Wade

Dear Tucker,

Hope you enjoy the book!

Best wishes,

Calvin Wade

4-6-14.

ACKNOWLEDGEMENTS

As detailed within this book, I have had a testing period of my life since leaving banking in February 2012. Lots of people have been incredibly supportive over the last couple of years, but the following people deserve a special mention.

My wife, Alison, for her enduring love, no matter what circumstances we face and her ongoing emotional support. My Nan always said if she could have picked a wife for me, she would have picked Alison, she was a smart woman.

My Mum and Dad, Jacquie and Richie, for the pride, love and belief they have always had in me. It has been more than a pleasure to go through this F.A Cup adventure with my Dad.

The following people have also helped in one way or another to keep my spirits high and/or my bank manager at bay (most of the time).

Neil Smith, Chris Ayres, Andrew Elkington, Lee Rankin, Jamie Lowe, Shaun and Jo McManus, Barry & Paula Walker, Lindsay Stones, Robert Bulloch, Marc Harrison, Jon Gildea, Carl McGovern, Lee Rankin, Nick Woodward, Mark Sunderland, Des Platt, Joy & Dereck Stagg, John Earnshaw, John Harper, Bill & Karen Cecil, Andy Sykes, Lisa & Vin Vernon, Jen & Jon Askew, Gill & Dave Hughes, Michael Walsh, Anna Ponting, Steve Heighway, Keith Brian, Ed Payne, Russ & Steph Watkins, Sean &Kellie O'Donnell, Cathie Hunter, Julian Tittershill, Vikkie Ditchburn, Garry Gibbons, Gary Westhoff-Lewis, Chris Joy, Keith Brian, Liz Ling, Andy Pealing & Kit Loughlin.

Thanks also to Tamsin & Paul Hawkins, Phil & Joanne Holmstrom, Jay & Debbie Davy, Andrew & Yvonne Berry, Graeme & Jackie Gregory and Andrew & Sarah Moss for their longstanding friendships.

Huge thanks also to all the kindhearted people who follow me on Twitter and have managed to spread the word about my previous books.

The F.A Cup 2013-14 was very much about the journey not purely the destination. Thanks to all the following people who made that journey not only possible but incredibly pleasurable too.

Alan 'The Casual Hopper' Oliver – 'my fellow ever present'. I hope this book helps you raise a brilliant amount for 'The Christie'.

Richard Wade, Phil Cooper and Jordan Oliver – 'the regulars'.

Ken Haigh, Steve Mulligan, Tom Boycott, Nick Boycott, Peter Abel, Matthew Nayler, Joel Wade, Alex Santos, "Santos", Keith Brian (thanks for bringing the camera and taking some brilliant photos too, Keith), Sanjay Gupta, Steve Uttley (Doncaster Rovers FC), Toby Robinson, Paul Wharton, Jacquie Wade, John & Carol Neill and Brad Wade – 'those that joined us along the way'.

Finally, thank you to all the following people who helped us get tickets when it seemed impossible to do so.

Andy Pountney, Steve Hyde (Stourbridge FC), Paul Cooper, Paul Fairclough, Clive Abrey (Stevenage FC), Sanjay Gupta, Alan McDermott, Dave Horsman, Mitch Pomfret, Mel Pomfret, Joe Royle, Ed Jones (Wigan Athletic), Gordon Johnson and Steve Bruce.

It's amazing what you can do with a bit of teamwork!

Think that's enough thank yous now – really sorry if I forgot anybody, I'm sure somewhere along the line I will have done!

Foreword by Joe Royle

When Gareth Southgate missed the penalty that ended England's European Championship dreams at the Semi Final Stage, at Wembley, back in 1996, I was watching on television with Calvin, his Dad, Richie and several of their family and friends. We were at the Wincot Restaurant in Aughton, to celebrate the Golden Wedding Anniversary of Calvin's maternal grandparents, Ernie and Elsie McGrae, who were lifelong friends of my Mum and Dad, Joe (Senior) and Irene.

The friendship that my Mum and Dad had with Ernie and Elsie has led to my wife, Janet and me becoming great friends with Jacquie and Richie, Calvin's parents and I have known Calvin and his sister, Lisa, throughout their lives. Since he was a little boy, Calvin has always been a huge football fan, inheriting his father's passion for the game. Both Richie and Calvin are big Evertonians, but even more than that, they are lovers of our great game. Having read his very entertaining fictional books, I am really looking forward to reading 'Another Saturday & Sweet F.A'. I am sure it will be a fascinating read.

JOE ROYLE – April 2014

Sunday 30th June 2013– 3.30 a.m – In The Beginning There Was Darkness

The story wasn't supposed to start here. It was obviously supposed to start at the beginning, but it wasn't supposed to start at half three in the morning in June. The starting point should have been the Extra Preliminary Round draw for the F.A.Cup, which I have been told, (via email by the F.A) will take place in early July.

I am a writer, a part-time writer with lofty ambitions to be a full-time writer. I am currently 80% of the way through completing my second book and the idea was that the third book would be a non-fictional one about the 2013-14 footballing season, primarily about the F.A.Cup - a hands-on experience of the F.A Cup from beginning to end. I would pick a game from the Extra Preliminary Round draw and then follow the winners of each subsequent game through to the F.A Cup Final. Begin with the spawn and follow it all the way through to next May when one of the big, fat ugly toads lifts the Cup. If that big, fat ugly toad happens to be Everton, as an Everton fan I can stomach that, but Liverpool winning would be a bit of a nightmare and if one of the rich clubs that don't really care about the competition wins, then that wouldn't be great either. Start with the tiny amateur clubs with players playing for the love of it and watch the competition evolve round by round, until you reach the latter stages with teams made up of massive squads of millionaires.

I don't just want this to be about the ninety minutes of football on the pitch though. An afternoon of going to a football match has never just been about the game itself. It is about the journey to the game, the time spent in the pub, the half-time drinks, the journey home, the pre-match discussions, the banter during the game, the post-match analysis, the ref, his assistants, the stadium, the people and a whole lot more. I want this book to be about life, about the people I meet and to an extent about me. One of the reasons I want to write this book, is to analyse whether the F.A. Cup makes anyone happy any more. It is certainly not the creature it was, up to around twenty years ago. I'm 42 now. I will be 43 by the time this book is finished. As a child, the F.A Cup was a dream competition that every professional footballer dreamt of playing in and every fan of an English team wanted their club to win. I was at Wembley in 1984, when I was a thirteen year old boy to see Everton beat Watford and it meant everything to me, my Dad and my football club. I guess it meant a huge amount to Wigan Athletic fans last season, but when I went to the Chelsea-Everton final in 2009, the F.A Cup was merely a consolation prize to Chelsea.

Back in 1984, I asked my Mum to record all the pre-match programmes on BBC and my Nan to record all the pre-match programmes on ITV! The pre-match build up on terrestrial TV started in mid-morning. The cameras followed the teams from their hotels on to the team bus and then through to Wembley. Nowadays, I'm not even sure if it is on terrestrial TV and if it is, it certainly doesn't have the same build up. It doesn't even kick off at 3p.m on a Saturday afternoon now. It has been moved to 5 p.m. I think to an extent the eyes of the world may still be on the F.A Cup Final, the sad thing is, the eyes of the English fans are no longer transfixed. I want to check out for myself how much passion is left.

Why start this now then, at 3.30a.m on a Saturday morning? I guess it is because of the title of the book, 'Another Saturday & Sweet F.A'. The title was there originally to represent the F.A Cup (for the non-footballing fans amongst you, the F.A stands for 'Football Association'). The F.A in my title potentially has a double meaning though of 'Fanny Adams' (or a triple meaning, which I will allow you to guess as it includes a profanity). Tonight, however, as I ended up watching a re-run of 'The Million Pound Drop' at two o'clock in the morning, starved of sleep through concerns about an emptying bank account. It was these latter meanings that sprang to mind.

As I write, in my opinion, there are direct comparables between myself and the F.A Cup. We are both seemingly past our best (not completely knackered yet but definitely showing signs of age), we are both in the doldrums and we are both, in the course of the next twelve months, hoping to change the way others think of us. Part of me already thinks this is a vain pursuit of happiness. Our glory days are behind us now and maybe we should accept that. Another part of me though, wants to keep chasing that 'golden dream', just in case we can prove the doubters wrong. I have no idea where this book will lead me, which villages, towns and cities I will end up visiting or whether my finances will improve enough to last out on this personal journey, but the positive side of me is looking forward to finding out. The negative side of me worries that footballing and personal misery lies ahead and by next May, things will be even shittier than they are now.

Friday 5th July 2013 – 11:30 a.m – The Magic Begins

The F.A Cup has begun! No games have been played but the draws for the Extra Preliminary Round, the Preliminary Round and the 1st Qualifying Round have all been made simultaneously and posted on the F.A Cup website this morning. My intention was always to start with the nearest game to where I live (in a village called Euxton, two miles from Chorley), but little did I know that even in the Extra Preliminary Round of the F.A Cup there are 370 sides, so 185 fixtures, with all games to be played on Saturday 17th August. I scanned through the long list (which appears, sensibly, to be done on a regional basis), looking for Euxton Villa, but they are seemingly not a big enough side to qualify and then looked for Chorley, who are too big a side and only come into it in the 1st Qualifying Round, playing FC United of Manchester. Thus already, before a ball has been kicked, I am on to Plan B.

I wanted to find a side that means something to me. My eyes were drawn to the name of West Didsbury & Chorlton. Back in the late 1980's/early 1990's, I did an Economics degree at Manchester Polytechnic and spent the first year living in Halls of Residence in West Didsbury and then the second and third years living in an end terrace house behind the Woolworths in Chorlton-cum-Hardy (ex Everton and Manchester City Manager, Joe Royle's father, Joe Senior, described it as the worst house he had been in since the war!). They were drawn against a team called Abbey Hey, who I hadn't heard of, but presumed (rightly) that they had to be reasonably local. A quick check revealed they were from Gorton, Manchester. To add to my interest, further checks revealed the winners would play Burscough (pronounced Burs – co), a side I played twenty something games for in the mid-1990s. Call it fate, call it good fortune, but whatever it was, this was a pretty obvious starting point. To add to the feeling of fate, this would be West

Didsbury & Chorlton's first ever game in the F.A Cup, in a history spanning over one hundred years.

Thus, as it stands, the F.A Cup draw that I will be followingis :-

West Didsbury & Chorlton or Abbey Hey or Burscough versus Alsager Town or Atherton Colleries or Radcliffe Borough.

The first game is 17th August, the second is 31st August and the third 14th September, with potentially a replay or two thrown in the mix for good measure. My wife, Alison, is a midwife at Preston hospital and two of the three games will be played whilst she is working. I have two sons, Brad and Joel, who are thirteen and eleven respectively, but although they like football, I cannot see them jumping up and down at the prospect of going to these early rounds. This is going to be a challenge for numerous reasons. Throw into the mix the fact that we have one car, a five year old Vauxhall Corsa, between us. This is going to take a charm offensive, some strong logistical planning and perhaps a Lottery win to get me through all fourteen rounds that lie ahead!

Wednesday 7th August 2013

I am hoping this journey becomes cheerier than it has started. The first game hasn't even kicked off yet and the three words that spring to mind to summarise how things stand in my personal life are fear, failure and guilt. Pre-banking crisis, I was a well respected, experienced Business Development Manager with a long history in financial services for both banks and building societies. Now, I am a former Business Development Manager who called time on a career for the sake of both my sanity and pride and I'm now trying to scratch a living in self-employment via writing and whatever financial services work I can get my hands on. The dream of becoming a successful writer still appears a distance away. The dream had partially succeeded when my first book, 'Forever Is Over' was greeted with moderate success, but my second book (or e-book so far as no paperback has been released) launched last week and initial signs are that it will be a flop. I currently have £80 to my name with a massive mortgage, lots of unsecured debt and no real Plan B in life to match the footballing one I devised. I feel like I have let my wife, Alison, down and my children down too. To exacerbate my feelings of guilt, it was my Mum and Dad's 45th Wedding Anniversary today and I completely forgot. A footballing analogy of my life currently would be that I am Portsmouth Football Club, who only a few years ago were riding high in the Premier League, appearing in two F.A Cup Finals and now find themselves skint, looking back on former glories, whilst languishing in Division Two.

As well as being financially out of shape, I am physically out of shape too. I am a tall man, just under 6 feet 3 inches tall, but that is not a good enough excuse for weighing in at a portly 16 stone 1 pound at this moment in time. Alison has decided we should both start a diet from today and given it is mainly me that needs to lose weight, I am not in a position to disagree. My goal is to be 13 stone 13 pounds by next year's F.A Cup Final and to be back to a 36 inch waist instead of 38 inch, as most of my trousers are 36 inch and I can't get into them. I have one pair of jeans and one pair of trousers that actually fit me. We are going to have weekly weigh ins every Wednesday, which seems a good day to do it, as you have enough time to diet if you lapse at the weekend. I am not going on Weight Watchers or any other prescriptive diet though. I just intend to be more careful with what I eat. I cat too much chocolate, drink too much beer and don't exercise which is a recipe for man boobs if ever there was one. Alison only weighs about ten stone so her physical shape just requires a minor tone up, whilst mine really does need overhauling.

With the plan for the diet in place, I need to now devise some sort of plan to resolve the financial crisis. As things stand, even the petrol cost and entrance fee to the Extra Preliminary Round, a week on Saturday, is going to be difficult to find.

Mixed emotions currently. First of all, let me tell you about an excellent day yesterday. The day wasn't good for my diet, but sometimes when things aren't going great, it is good to have a few beers and a curry (especially when you don't have to pay for them!).

Alison's Auntie Joy is married to Dereck (Del), a massive Pompey (Portsmouth) fan. When they moved from the South Coast to North Wales about twelve years ago, he kept his season ticket on, for a season or two, but nowadays he just goes down for a few games a season but tries to get to as many local Pompey away games as he can too. Dereck and his youngest son, Ben, who is in his early twenties, were intending to head across from their home in Rhos on Sea to watch Pompey yesterday at Accrington Stanley. Alison and I are good friends with Joy and Del, so he asked me if I fancied coming along. I originally said 'Yes' but this week, as I watched my money disappear out my bank account quicker than it would in a Nick Leeson investment bond, I began to question whether I could afford to go. My eldest son, Brad, was due to play cricket and Alison was due to be working, so if I did go, I would need to take my eleven year old youngest son, Joel with me. Surprisingly, Joel was really up for going, probably more to do with spending time with Del and in particular his cousin, Ben, than about the football itself.

At Accrington Stanley, it is only £1 for Under 12s, so when I told Del that I wouldn't be able to go, I asked if they could still take Joel with them, as he had been looking forward to it. Thankfully, Del said if they could stop the night here and I'd drive him and Ben up to Accrington from Chorley, allowing them both to have a drink, then they would either pay for my ticket or all the drinks and our planned evening curry, so I only had £15 to find. Even £15 is a big outlay right now but as it is years since I last went to Pompey with Del, I decided I would go. I'm delighted I did.

There is nothing better than watching your own football team. I love watching any football, but when you have an allegiance and passion towards one particular team, the whole game takes on a totally different meaning. I am an Evertonian. If I had the money, I would go and watch Everton home and away. Money doesn't allow for such luxuries though and if I can get to four or five Everton games this season with Brad, who is also a Blue, then I will be delighted. It is about a £75 day out to take Brad to Goodison these days and as I have to scramble around to afford a £15 trip, the £75 trips won't be happening until I have a financial boost. Anyway, although Pompey isn't my team, I could empathise with Ben and Del's excitement, so wasn't overly surprised when they turned up at our house at 9.30 a.m rather than the 10.30 a.m time we had agreed!

Portsmouth's slide from Premiership to Division 2 is well documented and economically for the club, it has almost led to its financial ruin. They are now owned by the fans that have put their hands in their pockets to prevent the club's demise, but for the average fan there is something quite charming about going to the likes of Accrington Stanley rather than the likes of Chelsea and Manchester United. You still get to see your team, you still get to go the pub, the football will certainly not be of the same quality but it probably works out about £30 a game cheaper on average and I'm sure sometimes it turns out to be more fun. I guess it is a bit like dating a supermodel a few years ago and now going out with a homely, girl next door type. You may look back with fondness on those supermodel days, but in reality, on a day to day basis, the supermodel was costing you a fortune and even then she was difficult to please. Your mates may have been jealous but now with your average looking girlfriend, you find yourself more relaxed, have more fun and feel more appreciated and contented. You aren't looking over your shoulder all the time worrying when the high life is all going to fall apart or if the person you love is going to bugger off with someone richer.

For me, standing on the terraces at Accrington brought back memories of standing on the terraces watching Everton at home and (sometimes) away as a teenager. Everton are likely to stay in the world of millionaires, but if the Accrington Stanley – Portsmouth experience is anything to go by, life in the lower reaches is just as much fun.

As intended, I drove to Accrington and we arrived before 10.30 am at a pub called 'The Crown' which had been mentioned on the Pompey supporters website as a welcoming pub for away fans that was a stone's throw from the ground. I parked over the road from the pub and walked across and even at that time, the pub was overflowing with Portsmouth fans with dozens outside.

There are a fair few rough diamonds amongst the Pompey fans, no more so than Johnny Anthony Portsmouth Football Club Westwood, a die hard fan and a minor celebrity in the footballing world who walked into 'The Crown' thirty seconds after us, to adulation in some quarters. Most English football fans would know who Johnny is, but if you don't, key in his name on Google images and he will be there, looking like a malfunctioned version of Slash from Guns N Roses. He has dozens of Portsmouth tattoos, blue dreadlocks and tends to watch each match in shorts and without a top. Amazingly, Ben informed me, in his working life, Johnny runs a family book shop! We only saw him briefly in the pub, but later, when we stood on the terraces, Johnny and his mates arrived behind with their bugle and drums and proceeded to play throughout the ninety minutes.

The pub experience was an eye opener for Joel, my eleven year old son, but perhaps an eye opener he could have done without. Pompey fans are no different to many other gatherings of supporters, but there seemed to be a competition to see who could cram the 'c' word into a sentence the most. Its use was obligatory in several fans sentences, but there was one bloke, who was about fifty, whose c##tometer must have registered about half a dozen every sentence.

There was a scattering of Accrington fans in the pub and they were looking bemused as they were being told their manager, James Beattie, was a 'Scummer'. A 'Scummer' as far as Pompey fans are concerned is someone who has a link to Southampton Football Club, Portsmouth's bitter rivals. Beattie is a former Southampton player, which makes him a 'Scummer'. As far as I could hear, this fact wasn't being explained, Pompey fans just expected the Accrington Stanley fans to be aware of this South Coast trivia, but their bemused looks suggested that they did not appear to be. A Pompey victory, they were being told, would be much sweeter today as it would mean getting one over on a 'Scummer'. Overall though, the mood in the pub, despite the bad language (which I probably noticed more than normal because I had an eleven year old with me) was jovial and there wasn't a hint of trouble.

When we left 'The Crown', there were a dozen downward steps out the back that led through to the outside of Accrington's Crown Ground. I suspect there is a reason the pub and the ground are 'crown' related but also suspect it isn't because Her Majesty Queen Elizabeth regularly has a gin and tonic in the pub or a singalong with the 'Accrington Stanley Ultras' in the home end. Away fans are housed in an uncovered area called the 'Coppice Terrace', but thankfully, although it was a cloudy day, rain never really threatened. It is pretty hilly in East Lancashire so a visit in August is probably a lot more pleasant than a visit in the depths of winter.

The entrance fee was £15 for adults and £1 for Under 12s. Joel is a big lad for eleven, but the old dear at the turnstile didn't ask for ID, she just took me at my word, which I was thankful for, as we had no ID with us. Maybe if you are eighteen you carry it, but not eleven. Had we been asked, we would have been reliant on Joel remembering his own date of birth, which would have been likely but not guaranteed after a couple of glasses of coke as he tends to go a bit hyper on sugar and had sneaked an extra one in whilst Del was at the bar.

Anyway, we all got in no problem, Del and Ben took our early arrival as an opportunity to get another quick beer in and Joel and I took the opportunity to have a quick wee. Accrington had prepared themselves for an away end full of supporters who liked a drink so had put in extra portakabin toilets.

Once in the ground, we were stood behind a goal. Our vantage point was a few rows back so we looked down diagonally to our right to see the near goal which Portsmouth were warming up in. Of just over 2000 fans in attendance, Portsmouth had brought a thousand, a fantastic effort for a midday kick off for a televised match about five hours drive away from home. Portsmouth is a decent sized city, but it's not Liverpool, London, Birmingham or Manchester so for that many people to make a ten hour round trip for a game televised on Sky, shows the loyal band of supporter they attract. Add into the mix the fact that they had also lost their first two games in Division Two, it is pretty incredible.

I have been to watch Pompey many times before with Del. I have seen them away at Bolton, Bradford, Tranmere and Everton (although at Goodison, Del came in the Gwladys Street End rather than me sitting with the Pompey fans) and I've been to Fratton Park about half a dozen times, including one memorable occasion when they beat Barnsley to preserve their Championship status during the Graham Rix brief managerial era. I have never been clustered together with so many of the hard core fanatics though as I was at Accrington Stanley. Johnny Anthony Portsmouth Football Club with his bugle and drummer playing pals.

As an Evertonian, I have no hatred for the Accrington Stanley manager, former Southampton and Everton striker, James Beattie. His spell at Everton was a little disappointing as he didn't really suit Everton's style of play at that time but he gave it his best shot and came across as a decent bloke. For the Pompey diehards though, he will always be considered an 'ex-Scummer' so he became the pantomime villain for the day and was subjected to a tirade of abuse from them. Beattie took it on the chin, even smiling to himself on occasion. The old Pompey favourite, "If Beattie can play for England, so can I!" was re-sung with as much passion as ever!

Singing songs is something Portsmouth fans do very well. They have a vast array of them and during a ninety minute match there aren't too many moments when they aren't singing. Amongst the favourites are, "Play up Pompey, Pompey play up!" (an easy one to remember), "We're fu****g brilliant!" (equally easy), "You are my Portsmouth, my only Portsmouth, you make me happy, when skies are grey" (Everton used to sing this a bit replacing the word Portsmouth with Everton so I can identify with this one), "And we're Porstmouth City, Portsmouth City FC, we're by far the greatest team, the world has ever seen" (another song shared with Everton which was ironic for Portsmouth to sing on many levels including the fact that they aren't called Portsmouth City and the fact that their greatest team in the world status must be challenged by the fact that they are playing a Division Two game at Accrington Stanley!) and finally some song called "You're Only A Poor Little Scummer" (which involved lines about hitting the Scummer with a brick). Nevertheless, despite the hostility towards James Beattie and 'Scummers' in general, the vast majority of the banter was amusing. The most amusing chants were reserved for their captain, the Dutch centre half, Johnny Hertl, who had been sent off the week before, for elbowing, so was watching from the sidelines. "Johnny Hertl, Ninja Turtle" and "He Hits Who He Wants, He Hits Who He Wants, Johnny Hertl, He Hits Who

He Wants" were both sung at their sidelined skipper (which don't sound hilarious on paper, I guess you had to be there).

All things considered, I don't think I've ever been to such an inconsequential game where the atmosphere from those surrounding me was that intense. My eldest son, Brad, who is thirteen now, but could not go because he was playing men's cricket, would have absolutely loved it!

The game itself was a stereotypical game of two halves. This one had two very different halves, not because one team dominated the first half and the other the second half, but because the first half was incredibly dull (other than the singing) and the second half was incident packed. At half time it was 0-0, at full time 2-2. Accrington Stanley took the lead with a curling, dipping shot from Peter Murphy which looped over the despairing Portsmouth keeper, Phil "Phil Mitchell" Smith. Obviously, the Pompey fans have christened him with the name 'Phil Mitchell' because he bears a passing resemblance to the Eastenders character of the same name, which reminds me of two further Pompey songs, "There's Only One Phil Mitchell" and "Where's Your Brother Gone?" As a former goalkeeper myself, I would have been disappointed to let that one in, as he got a weak hand to a ball that went right over his head when a strong hand would have pushed it over the bar.

Portsmouth then dominated for the rest of the game. David Connolly, a seasoned pro who has played for the likes of Leicester City and West Ham United and represented Republic of Ireland, looked like the class act on the pitch and equalised from a knock down from the big, strong centre forward, Patrick Agyemang and then scored his second from the penalty spot when Agyemang had been brought down. Accrington Stanley came back to equalise when Murphy popped up again on the back post to tap in an equaliser, leaving Pompey to rue their missed chances.

Another thing that amused me during the game was that even Pompey, a side who have a devoted bunch of fans who have been put through the mill by the poor handling of their football club by a succession of owners, still had their very own stereotypical moaning git fan! Amongst a thousand loyal, overly optimistic, diehard fans, there is always one who loves nothing more than a good moan. To be fair to Portsmouth, Everton, my team, have a higher proportion of them. When I used to go in the Paddock at Goodison, there were several moaners, one in particular comes to mind, who liked to call his own players "a shower of shit" about a dozen times a game. Anyway, Pompey's moaning man spent the entire ninety minutes berating his team's players, manager and fellow supporters. This man who has probably never even played for his local park team, let alone professionally and has no coaching badges of any description, has become the self-appointed fountain of all footballing knowledge.

When his fellow supporters sang,

"We're f***ing brilliant!"

Moaning man sang,

"You're f***ing stupid!"

When they sang a song about a game that resulted in the "Scummers" being relegated, he was very quick to point out that they were now a "very useful Premier League side, whilst our lot are a crap Division Two team!"

Ten seconds before Pompey scored, he announced Pompey were "never going to score" and after dominating eighty minutes of a ninety minute match he reflected, "I knew we would be bad, I just didn't realise we were going to be this bad!"

This is the type of man, who would win £7 million on the Lotto and moan about the fact that the payout was £8 million the week before. The grass on the other side is always greener, whilst on his side the grass has been dug out and been replaced by Portsmouth's sewerage works. For want of a better description, he was just a miserable sod. Why go to the game if you resent everything about it so much? I remember my grandfather taking me to Liverpool (my family are half Evertonians, half Liverpudlians) regularly in the 1970s and early 1980s when they were often Champions of Europe and there was a woman behind who screeched out her resentment towards Alan Kennedy, every Saturday. This is a man who scored two match winning goals in European Cup finals and has an array of top flight medals. There was also a bloke who went to every Everton home game in our mid to late 1980's golden era, who would moan how crap we were on every train trip home. If Everton were crap, I hate to think how bad every other team were, as we won two League titles, a European Cup Winners Cup and an F.A Cup in that "crap" period. I've never understood it, but some people like to go to football for no other reason than to have a good moan.

Overall, though, I thoroughly enjoyed being part of the Pompey brigade for the afternoon. Ben and Del are great blokes and their love of Pompey was infectious and I too came away feeling slightly aggrieved that their club weren't returning to the South coast with all three points.

It was also a great warm-up for the F.A Cup journey that I am about to embark on, as I was following a team other than my own (Everton) and it gave me insight into some of the similarities and differences from one band of football supporters to another. Can't wait until the F.A Cup starts now and wonder which individuals I will get to know over the next nine months, who are complete strangers to me now.

Friday 16th August 2013

My financial woes continue. My book sales are nowhere near where they need to be for me to take this up as a career and my "back-up plan" career in financial services isn't working out too well either. Without boring you with a vast amount of detail, changes in self-invested personal pension regulations and EU life cover regulations has limited opportunities for me in an introductory role, so I have had to start looking for other jobs that provide a regular income. Today, I have applied for a job doing three nights a week in Asda and also another one doing three days a week as a postman. I will keep you up to date you on the progress of both.

Tomorrow, the F.A Cup Extra Preliminary Round takes place and my journey from the start to the finish of the 2013-14 F.A Cup gets under way. I'm off to West Didsbury & Chorlton AFC versus Abbey Hey. It is a historic day for West Didsbury & Chorlton as they have never played in the F.A Cup before, having been promoted to the North West Counties Premier Division last season. Apparently they needed to come in the Top Four of the 1st Division to qualify and only a great finish to the season saw them guarantee an F.A Cup place with them ultimately finishing third. They are not a new team either, they have existed for 105 years, although I believe Chorlton was only recently added to the team name as that is where they now play. Abbey Hey were also promoted last season, finishing one place above West Didsbury in second, so it should be a tight game.

When I was checking out West Didsbury's website earlier, I noticed there was a post about a bloke called Alan Oliver who is also going to follow every round through to the Final. There are about one hundred and eighty five ties taking place tomorrow and I wonder how many of them have people going who intend to follow every round? I suspect not all that many, so it is quite a co-incidence that of the one hundred or so people going to West Didsbury tomorrow, there are two intending on taking the same path to the final. Alan is doing this footballing journey to raise money for The Christie hospital in Manchester, a specialist cancer hospital. His mother-in-law, Pat, had died of cancer aged 61 and he is raising money in Pat's memory. Alan has his own website and blog called 'The Casual Hopper' (www.thecasualhopper.co.uk) about his visits to various football grounds. He has been to all 92 League grounds and about 250 non-league ones too.

I sent Alan an email message earlier, saying that I intended to follow the same route to Wembley as him and that I would be happy to donate some money from every sale of this book to The Christie too. I am currently sitting in the car by the field where my eldest son, Brad, is doing footy training, so I'm not sure if Alan has replied, but even if it is not tomorrow, I am sure Alan and I will cross paths at some point during the next fourteen rounds of football. If he needs me to carry a Christie's bucket, I would be more than happy to do so.

Logistically, I have been saved from problems for tomorrow's game by my Mum and Dad. Alison, my wife, has been asked to do an extra midwifery shift at the hospital tomorrow, which means she would need to leave here at 1:30.p.m and get back about 10.30.p.m. With us having little money and one car between us, I was working out times for getting Alison to and from work and how I would get our sons, Brad aged thirteen and Joel aged eleven to feel enthusiastic about an Extra Preliminary Round F.A Cup tie when as a rule, Premier League football seems to be all that appeals to them when it comes to spectating. Thankfully, Mum and Dad stepped in. Earlier in the week, I had mentioned to my Mum on the phone that I was going to every round of the F.A Cup and would Dad fancy coming to the first one. Mum rang just before I brought Brad out to football training to say that my Dad does fancy going to the game, so he will drive over here with my Mum and he will then drive the two of us over to Chorlton.

My Mum will stay at ours to keep an eye on the children. This also means Alison can take the car to work without us having to ferry her across. Perfect!

Saturday 17th August 2013

Really looking forward to the football today. Even before the first ball has been kicked, events have transpired to make me think this is going to be a fantastic experience. Last night, I mentioned on Twitter that I was trying to go to every round of the F.A Cup and an old footballing friend, Richard Knowles, contacted me to say that in the 2009-10 season, him and his brother, Robbie (who I played footy with for a few seasons in the Ormskirk Sunday League for a team called Metropolitan) tried to go to every game in aid of Cancer Research. Their journey was well publicised and they raised over £4000 including £20 donated by the great Preston North End and England legend, Sir Tom Finney. They never quite made it all the way to the Final as they had ticketing and fundraising issues at the Semi-Final stage once the competition arrived at Wembley. They had started at Runcorn Linnets as their Dad, Graham, had played for Runcorn. I said to Richard that I would mention his name to my Dad to see if he remembered him, as sadly Graham died in 1985, when Richard and Robbie were children.

When my Dad phoned this morning to see what time I wanted him here, I asked him if he remembered an ex-goalkeeper called Graham Knowles. It turns out that my Dad knew him pretty well. One of my Dad's best mates, Wally Bennett, who played in both Skelmersdale United's F.A Amateur Cup Finals in 1967 and 1971, played in the same side as Graham at Skem in the mid-1960s. My Mum and Dad, Richard and Robbie's Mum and Dad and also Wally and his wife Rita went out for a few drinks together on several occasions. My Dad said he had called in at Graham's cottage in Aughton many times. Small world! Pity I didn't know this when I used to play in the same team as Robbie, as I am sure he would have enjoyed hearing a few of my Dad's old footballing tales about his Dad.

As well as mentioning the F.A Cup journey on Twitter, I also mentioned it on Facebook. A Facebook friend of mine, Louise Craddock, who I know from my days as a mortgage rep in Manchester, sent a message back to say that her sister's boyfriend, Josh Harrison, plays for Abbey Hey. I'll keep an eye out for him and see how he plays.

The final positive to come out of this morning is that Alan Oliver has been in touch and added me as a Facebook friend. In his message to me, Alan says that he has already raised £250 for 'The Christie', which is a great start. He seems from his Facebook profile to be a similar age to me and shares a love of music, with similar tastes to me too, such as Arctic Monkeys and James, so all bodes well that we should get along fine over the course of this F.A.Cup journey.

This really was like the old days. Throughout my childhood many, many Saturday afternoons were spent with my Dad driving me to a non-League football match. It wasn't always non-League, sometimes it was lower league games, fairly often it was Everton, but hundreds of my childhood weekends were spent watching football with my Dad, then listening to Sports Report on the way home. I loved having the opportunity to do it again, it felt like going back in time.

I am 42 now, my Dad is 69. There can't be many 69 year old men who have looked after themselves as well as my Dad. He hasn't touched a drop of alcohol for over forty years (he never particularly liked it, vomited easily and had migraines the morning after, so decided it wasn't worth the hassle) and diets if he puts a pound on. I have the middle aged spread and the male pregnancy figure, my Dad does not. He carries no excess baggage. This does not mean he is a healthy man though. He has bad knees, a bad back and has had heart problems through his sixties. He has atrial flutter, atrial fibrillation and had a stent put in about six or seven years ago. I don't live each day worrying about his mortality, but at the same time, I enjoy every moment I get to spend with him (and my Mum) as I know time is precious.

My Dad has more of an F.A pedigree than I have by a huge distance. I played in the last sixteen of the F.A Vase for Burscough one season but my Dad made it all the way to Wembley as a player. He played in the F.A Amateur Cup Final in 1967 for Skelmersdale United against Enfield Town in front of a massive 78 000 crowd. Skem drew 0-0 (having missed a last minute penalty) and lost the replay at Maine Road (in front of 55 000) 3-0. They were managed by a guy called Roy Rees, but they were also coached by Liverpool legend, Ian St John, who was still playing for Liverpool at that time. My two Godfathers are Wally Bennett, who as mentioned previously, played at Wembley twice for 'Skem' and Joe Royle, who played there a number of times not only for his clubs but for England too and famously managed Everton to a 1995 F.A Cup victory over Manchester United. It would be safe to say I have an F.A Cup pedigree despite not really making the most of it myself.

As far as my Dad's footballing career goes, after the Final he broke his leg twice, the first time led to Skem organising a testimonial game for him which was played in by 22 professionals and refereed by England World Cup winner, Nobby Stiles. I was once at a corporate function at Old Trafford and reminded Nobby Stiles of this (he said it was a 'wonderful story as he had forgotten all about it'!) which was the one and only time I have had a conversation with a World Cup winner. He even waved at me in the Old Trafford car park as his son, Sean, was driving him home. I am sure no other World Cup winner will ever wave to me again.

My Dad subsequently left Skem for Marine, finishing his career there, latterly playing under the management of Roly Howard who would make the Guinness Book of Records for being the longest serving manager of a football team at a competitive level. Once my Dad finished playing, he took his coaching badges and ended up coaching schoolboys and the 'A' and 'B' teams at Everton, helping the careers of many young footballers who went on to be top professionals. Off the top of my head these included, Gary Stevens, Kevin Richardson, Kevin Ratcliffe, Peter Davenport, Ian Bishop, Mark Ward, Steve McMahon, Andy Mutch and Shaun Teale. Whilst there, he became friendly with a lot of the other coaching staff including Colin Harvey, a legendary former Everton player, coach and manager (known to Evertonians as 'The

White Pele') and Ray Hall, who went on to become Youth Development Officer at Everton for many years, both of whom also played a part in the rise to stardom of a certain Wayne Rooney.

I am very much a believer of 'The Butterfly Effect' whereby everything we do impacts on the next thing and so on and so forth. I often think that if that penalty had gone in for Skem, back in that F.A Amateur Cup Final in 1967, the lives of my Mum and Dad would have mapped out very differently. My Dad may never have broken his leg, he would never have had that testimonial and in all likelihood, I would never have been born. The same logic, it could be said, applied on my Mum's side. My maternal grandfather, Ernest Russell McGrae, met my Nan in the pub near her house soon after returning from a prisoner of war camp. Perhaps if Adolf Hitler had not ordered his troops into the Sudetenland, I would not have come into being. The same could be said for every event, but the Second World War and the F.A Amateur Cup Final are two of the more significant ones!

Back to matters in hand (I will get a touch of the Ronnie Corbetts and go off at a tangent from time to time, but hopefully you will get used to it), our drive to 'The Recreation Ground', West Didsbury's ground, should only be just over half an hour from our house in Euxton (pronounced 'Exton') but with not untypical traffic problems on the M60 caused by the police closing the turn off to the Trafford Centre (Manchester's huge indoor shopping centre), we left home at one and crawled through to West Didsbury arriving after half past two.

The entrance to 'The Recreation Ground' is tiny, as you drive along the road you feel like you have reached a dead end, but there is a small sign welcoming you to the ground which offers re-assurance that a three point turn is unnecessary. It is barely wide enough to squeeze a car through though, so I have no idea where away teams who arrive by coach disembark.

On the road leading up to 'The Recreation Ground' are the pubs 'The Horse & Jockey' and the 'Bowling Green', home to many a drunken evening in my student years. Looking around, the area has become a lot more cosmopolitan than it was in the very early 1990's. Back then it was just a run down suburban town, but it seems to be a trendy place to live now.

The Recreation Ground itself is a modern looking ground with standing areas either side of the pitch, but a few seats and a modern building that houses the changing room and a pleasant cafeteria/ refreshment area are behind the far goal from the entrance. Dad and I nipped in for a pre-match coffee and as we came out, I noticed Alan and Jordan Oliver standing outside in their blue Christie's T-shirts, so I pointed them out to my Dad and I went across to do the introductions.

In my years of Sales training, I have been told it takes about six seconds for your brain to make an initial judgement on a person. In those initial six seconds, I decided I'd get along fine with Alan and Jordan. Perhaps this book will detail a horror story further along the line, but I don't think so. They seemed happy, warm hearted people who were excited by the F.A Cup journey they were about to set out upon. Alan is a small, stocky, bald headed man in his early fifties with a strong Mancunian accent. There is something that hints that he may have been a bit of a lad in his day. I can imagine him enjoying a few boozy nights on the tiles in his prime, but most of us have got up to a bit of mischief in our younger days and it is obvious immediately that he has a close bond with his daughter. Jordan appears quieter than her talkative Dad, but has a confidence and maturity that belies her eighteen years. I introduce them to my Dad too and as we are heading around from the clubhouse to the halfway line, my Dad asks Jordan her name again. She tells him.

"Jordan? Like Jordan Henderson?" he asks.

I smile at this. My Dad doesn't watch much TV. He enjoys his sport and his wildlife programmes, but not a lot else. He probably hasn't a clue who the former glamour model and now ubiquitous fly-on-the-wall TV character, Jordan, is, so can only associate the name to a Liverpool footballer.

On our way to the halfway line, Alan and Jordan are stopped by Ken Haigh from the Press Association. I presume 'The Christie' have put Ken in touch with Alan to try to raise the profile of his fundraising for their hospital. Ken is a Scottish gentleman who is a similar age to my Dad and like my Dad has tales of football matches from a bygone age. As previously mentioned, Dad played in the F.A Amateur Cup Final in 1967, whilst in 1968 Ken was at Wembley as a journalist for the F.A Amateur Cup Final between Leytonstone and Chesham United. With common ground, Ken and my Dad chatted away like old friends so I took the opportunity to get to know Alan and Jordan. As well as being a football fanatic, a Manchester City fan who has been to all ninety two League grounds and hundreds of non-League ones to boot, Alan is a keen music fan. Echo & The Bunnymen are his favourites and although I don't know much about them, other than the fact that they are from Liverpool, their singer was Ian McCulloch and 'Echo' was the name of their drum machine, we had a good chat about some other mutual favourites such as Nirvana, James, Arctic Monkeys and Elbow.

Jordan, Alan's daughter, is also interesting to talk to. She has just done her 'A' levels and is off to Staffordshire University in October. She is intending on living at home and is going to get the train to University every day for lectures. Jordan's ultimate ambition is to work for the FBI.

"If you shoot for the stars," Alan explains, "you may not hit one, but you may hit something interesting on the way back down."

I can't remember what the Degree course is that Jordan is doing, but presumably it will be something like Psychology and Criminology, if such a course exists!

We watch the game with interest but admittedly not with rapt attention. West Didsbury have got off to a stuttering start to their League campaign in the North West Counties Premier Division whilst Abbey Hey have started brightly, but despite some attractive football from Abbey Hey in patches, it is the West Didsbury & Chorlton side that look more threatening. West Didsbury have a very fast centre forward called Tre Baldwin Willis, who was causing panic in the Abbey Hey defensive ranks, with the keeper having to sweep up several times after he had outpaced the Abbey Hey defence. Baldwin Willis did slot a well taken goal away before half time, carving his name into West Didsbury history as their first F.A Cup goalscorer and West Didsbury were almost two up when a twenty five yard strike hit the base of the keeper's right hand post just before half-time.

It was a windy day and the breeze had been blowing directly into the Abbey Hey keeper's face for the whole of the first half, so when the ref blew the half time whistle, with the wind picking up and the rain starting to fall with the score at one-nil, we headed for a drink thinking it was anybody's game. Bovril is often my hot drink of choice at football, but if I'm not watching a match, I don't touch the stuff. I can honestly say I have had thousands of Bovril's over the years, but without exception, they have been drunk at a football match.

I was expecting big things from Abbey Hey in the second half. I had not been able to establish whether Josh Harrison, my Facebook friend's sister's boyfriend was playing as there were no team sheets, but him and his team mates had probably had a rousing talk from their manager about playing with the wind on their backs and it being important to start well. It was West Didsbury who started well though, with an Anthony Potts bullet header early in the second half putting the home side two up and ruining Abbey Hey's best laid plans. Abbey Hey didn't really threaten to get back into the game after that. Their left back, who was one of their better players, tested the West Didsbury keeper with a free kick, but West Didsbury were still creating the majority of the chances. When the final whistle blew, 2-0 to West Didsbury seemed like a fair result. Unless there was another side playing F.A Cup football for the first time today (and winning), West Didsbury had suddenly become, all be it temporarily, the only side ever who had not lost a game in the F.A Cup!

So that's the first game over. A thoroughly enjoyable afternoon that set us back £8 for admission (£5 for me, £3 for my Dad with him being an OAP) and a total of £4 spent between us on tea, coffee and Bovril! Just writing my Dad is an old age pensioner seems strange as this is a man who coached my junior football teams, beat me at tennis on 90% of occasions, did (and still does) an active job as a painter and decorator and did everything at running pace whether it was walking the dog (which for him was running the dog) or going (sprinting) up the stairs. Twenty years seem to have flashed past in an instant and all of a sudden my Dad is an old man and I am not exactly a youngster myself.

My Dad and I say our farewells to Ken Haigh and also to Alan and Jordan Oliver with handshakes and smiles, with me confirming to the Olivers that I will meet them back there in a fortnight for the West Didsbury v Burscough game. My Dad is non-committal as he is going over to Poland for a week as Paul Bennett, the son of Dad's close friend and ex-Skem United and Marine team mate, Wally, is getting married over there. Wally has two sons, Paul and Neil. A few years ago, Neil married a Polish lady and asked his older brother to be Best Man for the wedding over in Poland. Paul took his duties seriously and wanted to learn to speak some Polish, for his Best Man's speech, so enrolled on a Polish language course. The tutor of the course obviously caught Paul's eye as he started dating her and is now marrying her. I suspect Dad will be back to 'The Recreation Ground' with me in a fortnight but does not like confirming and then crying off.

Our journey home was free from any major traffic incidents and we listen to Sports Report on Five Live, with the old music bringing back a flood of happy memories. My team, Everton, have started the Roberto Martinez managerial era with a 2-2 draw at Norwich City, with Seamus Coleman and Ross Barkley scoring. Everton are currently trying to cling on to two of their star players, England left back, Leighton Baines and Belgian international, Marouane Fellaini, as former manager, David Moyes tries to tempt them across to Manchester United with him. I don't hold out much hope of us keeping them, with Leighton Baines, in particular, being a massive loss. I predict that both Martinez and Moyes will struggle this season to emulate the success of their predecessors. Martinez will be forced to re-shape his squad as departures look certain in the transfer window and Sir Alex Ferguson chose the perfect time to leave Old Trafford, as his squad is ageing and lacks a real quality central midfielder. As I can't afford to attend Goodison regularly, because of my financial plight, I will follow Everton's progress mainly from a distance, but I predict Everton will finish 9th and Manchester United 3rd this season. I would love for our F.A Cup journey to link up with Everton in the 3rd Round and then follow them through to the Final, but there are seven more rounds to go before Everton even enter the picture, so the most I can hope for at this stage, is a good Cup run from West Didsbury's next opponents, my former club, Burscough.

Of the other Premiership clubs that played today, the greatest sense of frustration was coming from Arsenal fans after their comprehensive 3-1 defeat at home to Aston Villa. Many Arsenal fans are suggesting another silverware free season lies ahead and are venting their fury that Arsene Wenger, their manager and their board of directors are sitting on their transfer funds when they should have been out and spent it. Arsenal have still to qualify for the Champions League proper and it is being suggested that if they fail to do so and string together some more poor results, it may be time for one of the greatest managers in their history to depart.

FINAL SCORE :- West Didsbury & Chorlton 2 Abbey Hey 0
Scorers :- Baldwin-Willis & Potts.
Our 'Speccies':- Calvin Wade, Richard Wade, Alan Oliver, Jordan Oliver, Ken Haigh.

- I've put Alan and Jordan in 'our team' as it seems we will be heading through to the F.A Cup Final together. I am not expecting Ken to be going through the rounds with us, but as he spent the ninety minutes with us, he deserves a place on the list.

Sunday 18th August 2013

Last night, I received messages from Jordan and Alan Oliver via Facebook to say that Alan was going to be on Radio5Live talking about our F.A Cup journey. Alan thought it was going to be on at 8pm, but it transpired that it was recorded at 8pm, but was only transmitted on the Non-League show that airs from 5.30am to 6am this morning. Thankfully for me, FiveLive allow you to listen back to earlier programmes so that is what I did. Alan was interviewed by a lady called Helen Barker and managed in his brief time on air to explain his pseudonym, 'The Casual Hopper' and that his F.A Cup journey was in aid of The Christie. I've already noticed one or two kindhearted listeners have been on to his Justgiving link and donated.

Monday 19th August 2013

This weekend's football has been a welcome distraction from my financial plight. I had been optimistically hoping that the launch of my second book, 'Kiss My Name' would be fantastic and sales would go through the roof, but that was no more than a pipe dream and despite excellent initial reviews, sales remain no more than steady. The financial services side of things has fared little better, with several of the pension and life cover policies that I introduced to the advisers, facing delays and cancellations. Currently lots of money is going out and little is coming in. At this rate, with commissions I am due continuing to be postponed like football matches in the midst of a big freeze, I have no idea how we are going to pay the mortgage this month, let alone all the other bills. Unsympathetic credit card companies will be ringing for their pound of flesh (rather than to check on my wellbeing) with demands that cannot be met. After over twenty years of perfect credit, financial commitments are collapsing and without a wholesale change to my approach, I can only see things getting worse. I need a new job, a job that pays a set wage and I need it fast. Time to start looking.

My Footballing Career (Part One)

With West Didsbury & Chorlton playing Burscough in the next round, I thought, at this point, it would be appropriate for me to write a Chapter about my footballing career. A journey that briefly stopped at Burscough. It won't be a long Chapter!

I knew at an early age that I wasn't going to follow in my father's footballing footsteps. I remember going to Marine (his final side) before I even started school, remember kicking the ball around in our garden and my grandparents garden too, but it was only when I started to play out in the road with the other kids, with a plastic ball and grids for goalposts, that I came to realise I wasn't much good. Most of the time from aged five to nine, I played with the boy next door, David Prescott, his next door neighbour, Andrew Wilkinson and a lad from the next road, David Lockett. I could perhaps attempt to use the excuse that I was the youngest, the two Davids were eighteen months older than me and Andrew Wilkinson twelve months, but truth be told amongst a bunch of average footballers, I was the worst.

In life generally, I am a mixture of dogged resilience and a quitter. I tend to be doggedly determined at things I have signs of natural ability at and a quitter at things I show little initial ability in. Thus, windsurfing, golf, Spanish, dieting and Art are some of the many things in life I only tried for a short time before giving up! Probably to my father's great disappointment, I gave up any ambitions of playing out of goal before I reached a double figure age. I am six feet three inches tall, had a decent turn of pace when I was young and was pretty fearless, so I probably would have made a reasonable centre back if I had kept at it, but I was a stubborn little sod and had realised I was better at catching than kicking so fancied the idea of being a goalkeeper.

David Prescott and Andrew Wilkinson both moved away due to their fathers starting jobs elsewhere (to Ilkley and Lichfield respectively), so I found new football mad friends from school to play with, namely Neil Addison and Kit Loughlin. Neil's Dad, Ken, was Head of Promotions at Liverpool Football Club and Kit's Dad, Frank, was a photographer at the Daily Post and Liverpool Echo, which meant that one was often up in the television gantry at Anfield (Ken) whilst the other (Frank) was often pitchside at either Anfield or Goodison Park. Neil was a big Liverpudlian, Kit, like me, a big Evertonian. We all played football for Aughton St Michaels 40th Ormskirk (Tuesday) Pack Cubs, where I started my goalkeeping career at the age of around eight and once we became too old for cubs, Neil, Kit and I founded our own football club, Park End, with the able assistance of our fathers, in particular mine who ran it.

My Park End career lasted two seasons. Thankfully for me, as a goalkeeper, Park End weren't much good, so I had plenty to do. Despite us being a team from Aughton, a village near Ormskirk, we couldn't get the Parish Council to give us a pitch to play on, so our home pitch was in Town Lane, Southport about eight miles away. This was 1982 and back then, every team had to have changing rooms. The changing rooms at Town Lane were extremely dilapidated though, as Sefton Borough Council had their eye on the land to build a new hospital on, so were not going to be wasting money repairing any damage, so any rooms that had the plasterboard kicked out of it (which was pretty much every one), were just left to decay. The changing rooms were awful, the pitches were average but thanks to Ken Addison's Liverpool Football Club connections, our kit was fantastic, as he managed to get us the Dundee home kit (not just the tops either, tops, shorts and socks, which was a novelty back then) courtesy of Coffer Sports.

In Park End's second season, the likes of Kit Loughlin and several others were too old to play, so an average, improving team became hopeless, as the older boys were replaced by school friends with abilities ranging from poor to hopeless. On the plus side, we found a spare pitch in Ormskirk, on a council estate called Scott Estate, but the reason it was spare was because the changing rooms were a damp, open doored portakabin and the pitch was sloping and had one goalmouth that remained two inches under water from September to March. Kids weren't as pampered as they are today, so the games were only postponed if it was icy or snowing, so I had to play one half of every game in an area that resembled a paddy field. As we were crap, I was normally soaked from head to toe in water and mud but this never stopped me leaping around my area with real gusto, as I have mentioned, if I thought I was good at something, I have always been resilient. My Sondico goalkeeping gloves acted like a pair of sponges but I loved those games and was earning myself a reputation as a good keeper, so was selected for the Craven Minor League Representative side.

The biggest flaw to my game was the very reason I went in goal in the first place, I couldn't kick the ball. My Dad, as manager, thought the best way to remedy this flaw was to persevere whilst I wanted to avoid the thing I wasn't good at, so often when we had a goal kick, I would try to persuade one of our centre backs to take it, whilst my Dad would be screaming at me from the touchline for me to kick it myself. In one game against Rufford Colts, a friend of mine from school, Phil Aldridge, who was aware of this deficiency, parked himself at the edge of the penalty box and helped himself to four goals from my duff goal kicks!

Overall, despite my kicking, I was still attracting the attention of some better sides, so the following couple of seasons I went to play for my local village side, Town Green, who had a reputation for challenging for League Titles. I played two seasons there and won the League both times. We were managed by a guy called Terry Sergeant, who I thought was a great guy and despite me being a quiet lad amongst a bunch of outgoing kids, he knew I had an inner confidence when I stood between the posts. Towards the middle of the second season, when I was fourteen, the local Everton scout, Arthur Stevens, asked me to go down to Bellfield,

Everton's training ground, for trials. My Dad took me for a few sessions over Christmas and February half-term but the big, important period was Easter when I was going to go for the full two weeks.

The fact that my Dad knew all the coaches at Everton ended up being my downfall. For a reason I don't know and my Dad doesn't recall, I went to Bellfield that Easter a day earlier than the other fourteen year old kids who were on trial. The likes of Colin Harvey and Terry Daracott, both former Everton players and now coaches took me under their wing. At fourteen, I didn't really know what to say to adults I didn't know well,so must have come across as being painfully shy, but they tried to involve me in training routines with the YTS lads and I even took part in a session with Neville Southall, Everton's Welsh international goalkeeper, in the morning, although my role was largely collecting the balls that went over his bar! After the session with 'Big Nev', Colin Harvey invited me over to play a game of head tennis, with him, the Everton manager, Howard Kendall and Terry Daracott. Head tennis involves using your feet and heading ability to get the ball over the net, but with my non-existent footballing skills, this was always going to be difficult. Terry Daracott was in a pair with me and we had to play against two League Championship winning players, both of whom had played in Everton's most famous midfield of all time, alongside the World Cup Winner, Alan Ball. Poor Terry didn't stand a chance but the game went even worse than Terry could have thought.

We must have lost nearly every point in head tennis. I tried to keep out the way near the net but Terry was getting fed up of doing all the work, so ended up telling me to go to the back for a while. On one point, the ball bounced up invitingly to me and Terry shouted, "Boot it, Calvin, boot it!"

I ran up to welly it as hard as I could, got a great connection on it so it flew off at a hundred miles an hour, but unfortunately not in entirely the right direction. Terry was standing at the corner of the net and had turned to watch me kick it, but it came at him so fast he didn't have time to move. It hit him square in the testicles and he collapsed winded on to the floor! Terry did not mix his words given he was dealing with a sheepish fourteen year old. He called me every name under the sun! Colin and Howard thought it was hilarious.

"Take no notice of him," Colin re-assured me, "he should have been quicker and moved out the way!"

After Terry recovered, he told me to go off and get myself some lunch from the canteen. I sat with Simon Morrissey, youngest son of former Everton and Liverpool player, Johnny Morrissey. Johnny Morrisey Junior, Simon's brother was also in the canteen, as was Ian Marshall, who went on to play for Oldham Athletic, Leicester City and Ipswich Town and Neill Rimmer, who I knew from Town Green. Neill was about three years older than me, had played for England schoolboys and subsequently played over two hundred games for Wigan Athletic. There was also a lad called 'Brookesy' who ended up playing over in Italy for a spell. They were discussing some Vietnamese lad, Diepp Van Lee, who Everton had agreed to take on trial. I was up there for about ten minutes when Terry came up to say Howard Kendall wanted the YTS lads to give the first team a game for an hour, as they were heading out to Munich later that afternoon for a vital European Cup Winners Cup Semi-Final First Leg game against the mighty Bayern Munich. I was pretty much left in there on my own, as everyone wanted a game, but within two minutes, one of the lads came back up,

"You're a keeper, aren't you?"

"Yes."

"Grab your gloves, then, we haven't got one, we need you to play."

Everton went on to win the League title in 1985 and not only that, they won the European Cup Winners Cup too. They drew 0-0 away at Bayern Munich and then clawed back a 1-0 deficit in the Second Leg to go on to win 3-1 in a famous night at Goodison Park. Howard Kendall said the fans in the Gwladys Street sucked the ball in to the net that night. Before they did all that though, the Everton first team had to beat nine YTS lads, Terry Daracott who filled in at centre half and a fourteen year old petrified keeper who was playing against his idols. I had regularly been to watch Everton since the age of six, several seasons having a season ticket in the '500' Club with my grandfather and now I was playing against the best Everton side I had ever seen. Well, most of them anyway. Jim Arnold played in goal instead of Neville Southall. I guess 'Big Nev' knew it was unlikely that he would be tested.

The game was only thirty minutes each way and it wasn't played at more than half pace because the Everton team wanted just a gentle run around. Against a team of sixteen to eighteen year olds they could basically play keep ball and that's what they did. We looked like we were going to get away with a 0-0 draw, without me being really tested, then with one minute to go, a perfect through ball found Kevin Richardson with only me to beat. Kevin Richardson was already an F.A Cup winner, he went on to win League titles at Everton and Arsenal and was in the running to become the only player in history to win League titles at three different clubs when he was at Aston Villa (I think they eventually finished Runners Up). This was my moment, my chance to be a hero. I charged out, narrowing the angle perfectly and set myself ready to make a glorious save. What I didn't do perfectly, an error made by many teenage girls with far harsher consequences, I didn't keep my legs close enough together. My legs were more than wide enough to fit a size 5 football through, especially for someone as talented as Kevin

Richardson. He didn't have to strike the ball hard, he just gently passed it through my legs and into the back of the net and we lost 1-0. Not a great start to my Everton career! In the space of a couple of hours, I had hit Terry Daracott in the knackers and given away a sloppy, deciding goal to prevent my side getting an honourable draw against a team that became Everton's most successful ever. I thought my day couldn't get any worse, but it did!

After a brief return to the canteen, whilst the first team players and coaches were getting themselves ready for their departure to Munich, it was left to Terry Daracott to run things for the YTS lads and myself. He decided it was time for some shooting practice so I was told to go in goal. It was a simple drill often repeated, whereby the players line up, pass the ball to the coach (in this case Terry) and he lays it back off for them to shoot at goal. I was keen to make up for my mistake against the first team and to show them all that I wasn't a bad keeper. It was immediately noticeable to me that 16 to 18 year old lads had a lot more power in their shots than 13 and 14 year olds, so I was on my toes to react quickly. I was faring pretty well, gaining in confidence, when the lad called 'Brookesy' hammered a shot in low to my left. I dived full length and parried the ball away, but immediately felt the impact on my hand and wrist. I grimaced as the pain shot up my arm, but oblivious to my pain, Terry was laying more balls off for the shots to continue. After a couple of minutes, he must have noticed that I was trying to save everything with one hand and was avoiding diving, so came over to see what the matter was. Realising I was in pain, he sent me over to see John Clinkard who was the Everton physiotherapist at the time, for him to check me out.

Back in 1985, John Clinkard was a minor celebrity at Goodison. The fans used to call him 'Magnum PI' because he looked like Tom Selleck and had the matching bushy brown moustache. Like the players, 'Magnum' was off to Munich and probably just nipped out on to the training pitches for a quick chat with someone, so gave the distinct impression he could not really be bothered with a minor injury sustained by a fourteen year old. He gave my hand and wrist a quick once over and told me it was just a knock.

"Am I alright to carry on training?" I asked.

"I don't see why not!" John replied before heading inside.

Perhaps if I had been more dramatic John would have taken my knock more seriously but I was trying to be brave and not show anyone how much pain I was in. I carried on, but continued just using one arm and Terry realised I wasn't making much effort so called the session to an end and brought out two tiny goals and we played a two touch game with no goalkeepers and unsurprisingly, I didn't get a touch, as players like Ian Marshall and Neill Rimmer had far too much ability for me, even without my distracting injury!

After that, the first day of the Easter holidays was over, we got changed, me using one hand to dress myself and headed home. I took the bus and train back with Neill Rimmer. Neill was an Ormskirk lad too and when his career was going from strength to strength with England schoolboys, his manager at Town Green, Jack Warner, on a few occasions, used to ask me to go down to the park with the two of them, so they could get Neill to practice his finishing. When we got to Orrell Park train station, we ran into my friend Kit Loughlin's grandad, Frank Senior. Old Frank was a big Evertonian who had a season ticket with Kit in the Lower Bullens and had perhaps been up to Goodison to get tickets for a Cup game (perhaps even the 2nd Leg against Bayern Munich). He sometimes used to get off the train at Orrell Park, rather than the typical Kirkdale stop, as he struggled getting up and down the stairs at Kirkdale. He had been the lollipop man at Neill's primary school, Christ Church, Aughton, so we all had a good chat at the station and sat together on the train. Old Frank was one of the loveliest old men you could possibly meet and I knew him well enough to show him my left wrist, which had now ballooned to three times its normal size.

"You need to get up to Ormskirk hospital, Calvin," he diagnosed and sure enough when I got home, my Mum took one look at it and said exactly the same.

Once my Dad arrived home from work, he took me over and an X-ray revealed it was broken. A cast and sling were put on and my Easter at Everton was over before the other lads my age had even arrived. My Dad was far from impressed with John Clinkard and said he would be having words with him once he arrived back from Munich, but my Dad was not one to rant and rave and whether or not John Clinkard had diagnosed it, it would have still been broken.

The night Everton beat Bayern Munich 3-1 at Goodison, to clinch a place in the European Cup Winners Final in Rotterdam against Rapid Vienna, I watched my Town Green team mates beat Ormskirk West End 7-0 at Southport's Haig Avenue ground. I missed two finals at Southport because of my wrist and have never played there since. I did go back to Everton in May, but to be a professional footballer you have to have a certain hunger, which I just didn't have. I was shy and lacking in confidence and being thrust into a group of strangers just made me feel introverted, so I had no desire to go. I think ultimately I rejected them rather than the other way around, but I wasn't good enough anyway, especially once picking up a back pass was outlawed, so I would never have made it. The highlight of my return in May was being the first person to shake Peter Reid's hand when he returned to Bellfield with the PFA Player of The Year trophy one evening. Peter was absolutely fantastic that season, forming a wonderful central midfield partnership with Paul Bracewell. He actually came fourth in the World Soccer Player of the Year behind Platini, Elkjaer and Maradona! The year after he was instrumental in England's positive change of fortunes in the 1986 World Cup in Mexico, despite being remembered by many for not being able to catch Maradona as he went off on his famous run for his magnificent second goal, in the Argentina-England 'Hand of God' Quarter Final.

After Everton, I went to a couple of trial days at Oldham Athletic, but didn't do anything that encouraged them to sign me on. On one of those days, my Dad also took over a talented lad who was a couple of years younger than me called Trevor Sinclair, who ended up signing for Blackpool rather than Oldham. Trevor went on to have a brilliant footballing career, playing for England twelve times, including during the 2002 World Cup in Japan.

After Oldham, my Mum told my Dad that I should be concentrating on my studies rather than football and I didn't really object. I continued to play socially though. At sixteen, I started playing open age football for the first time for a team in the Ormskirk Sunday League called Ruffwood Old Boys (a school in Kirkby). They were managed by a bloke called Colin 'Shady' Turner, who was better known as the official photographer at Aintree racecourse for many years. Most of the team, other than my old mate Kit Loughlin who asked me to go down there, were five to ten years older than me and could handle themselves. Several of them worked at Ashworth Hospital (known locally at the time as 'Moss Side'), a mental hospital that Ian Brady, the Moors Murderer was, and still is, in. If any opposition sides decided to give me the occasional elbow at a corner or discreetly knocked me over when I came to collect a cross, they soon found ten fierce Ruffwood Old Boys coming after them. I normally just watched from the ground as the mayhem ensued around me. My Dad believed if I could have sorted out my ground kicking, I may have had a decent lower League or higher level non-League career, but it's too late now. In 1989, I went to Manchester Polytechnic, had three brilliant years there, leaving with a 2:2 Honours Degree in Economics in 1992.

In June 1992, I moved back in full time with my Mum, Dad and sister, Lisa and started playing for a Sunday League team from Greasby, Wirral called Dingwall. Initially they weren't all that good, but over the four seasons I was there, we improved year after year and won several Cups and League titles. I was very confident playing at that level and was selected to play for the League Representative side. Most of the lads at Dingwall were in our early to mid-twenties and we enjoyed a drink or ten as well as a game of football. Several of them could have played semi-professional football easily but chose not to and their manager, during the successful spell, Will Watt was the best motivational manager that I ever had. As most of the lads were from a more affluent part of Wirral, one Birkenhead side branded us all "fannies and solicitors", but we still managed to beat them season after season.

During that time, I knew I was wasting my reasonable talent if I didn't try and make it in a semi-professional side, so having returned from a four month back packing trip around the world in September 1994, I indicated to my Dad that I wanted to give it a go. My Dad arranged for me to go down to Southport, a Vauxhall Conference side, but they had an experienced keeper there called John McKenna, who I didn't feel I was going to compete with, so told my Dad after a couple of weeks, that I wanted to try Burscough instead. Burscough were in the North West Counties league at the time, a few Leagues below Southport and my Dad felt I should be aiming higher.

As it transpired, my timing was perfect. Burscough had got off to a mediocre start to the season and their keeper, Paul Blasbery had made a few errors. Russ Perkins, the Burscough manager, had decided to sign a new keeper, Steve Johnson, a Tarleton lad who had been playing at Darwen, which prompted Paul Blasbery to leave. Steve Johnson had played in a qualifying round of the F.A Vase for Darwen, so although I didn't get in the team straight away, when it came to the F.A Vase, Russ had no choice but to play me. We then set off on a great run in the F.A Vase, whilst not playing too well in the League, which eventually led to me getting League games in too. The team was a mixture of youth and ageing top level semi-pros who had lost a yard of pace, so had dropped down a few Leagues, players like John Brady, who played for several top non-League sides like Altrincham, who he had helped to win the Conference title in 1991 and Mick Fagan, son of Joe Fagan, the legendary former Liverpool coach and manager. Amongst the youngsters was a lad called Hugh McAuley, son of the Liverpool coach of the same name. Hughie Junior went on to play professionally for Cheltenham. Just before I left Burscough, a young lad started training with them, called Lee Trundle. Lee went on to play professionally and still has a cult status amongst Swansea City fans.

The best game I ever had for Burscough was in the F.A Vase away at Arnold Town. Arnold were a strong Nottinghamshire side, who were winning their League and were favourites to lift the trophy. They played some really good football but I was in one of those confident moods that made me feel like it would have to be a really good effort to get past me. We eventually won 3-2 after being second best for long periods of the game and I made a full length save, up to my left, from a bullet header, which remains lodged in my brain as the best save I ever made. In the next Round we beat Brandon Town 2-0 at home in front of a decent crowd for Burscough, before losing 4-2 at Cammell Lairds in the last sixteen, which was a massive disappointment. Cammell Lairds were two Leagues below Burscough at the time, but despite looking the better side in the first half and leading 1-0 at half time, we just didn't seem to come out for the second half and were comprehensively beaten. From my own perspective, I had a few of my Sunday League side come down to watch, so was thankful I was one of the few that didn't play badly. After that, I was in and out the side for the rest of the season, but became first choice by the end of it and Steve Johnson left, but after a 4-0 win at Rossendale United on the last day of the season, we finished about eighth in the North West Counties and Russ Perkins was sacked. I never played a full League game for Burscough again. John Davison, another ex-Altrincham player who at that time was the most capped England semi-professional footballer in the history of the side, took over as Manager, with a lad called Peter King (who tragically died in his late 40s) as his playing assistant. John brought Paul Blasbery back and he was automatically first choice goalkeeper and to be fair to 'Blas', he played very well and stayed at Burscough for a few seasons.

I did 'play' three further games for Burscough which were all eventful. At the end of the 1995 season, Joe Royle led Everton to an F.A Cup victory (Everton have not won a trophy since unless you include the Charity Shield that they won a few months later!) with a 1-0 victory over Manchester United. My Dad and I went that day and although we had been to Wembley to watch them win the F.A Cup in 1984 against Watford and lose to Liverpool twice in 1986 and post-Hillsborough in 1989, the fact that Everton, our club, were now managed by a family friend made it even more special. My Dad is not one for hugs. I could count on one hand the amount of times I ever remember getting a hug from my Dad. He is more a firm hand shake type of guy. I am sure when I was a little boy he would hug me, but he is pretty conservative and I think male hugs are out of his comfort zone. In fact, I only remember twice receiving a hug from him. The first, was when I was about twelve. Our house in Aughton backed on to the school field of Town Green primary and me and my mates, especially Kit Loughlin and Neil Addison, would often climb over the fence to play on there. Regularly the caretaker, Mr.Johnson would come and chase us off, as we used to wear down the grass in the goalmouths, but on this occasion I am recalling, we had had a game and my Dad was working on something at the back of the garden.

For whatever reason, the normal gap in the fence was blocked, so my Dad was lifting us over, but we temporarily had to stand on the fence that divided our garden and next doors. When I was at my highest point, about seven feet up, my Dad lost his grip on me and I fell backwards on to the school field, landing on my back and taking the wind out of me. My Dad must have thought I had broken my back and he jumped over there, gave me a hug and kissed the side of my head, with relief. The only other time I remember him hugging me, was with delight when Paul Rideout scored the winner in that 1995 F.A Cup Final!

In July 1995, one of Burscough's first home friendlies of the season was against an 'Everton XI'. It was pretty much an Everton second string XI, but included John Ebbrell, Vinny Samways and Stuart Barlow, all of whom had played regular football at the top level. With Paul Blasbery back as first choice, I was on the bench. With it being a second string side Everton put out, they were taken by a reserve team coach rather than Joe Royle, but Joe turned up and after about ten minutes went into the away dugout. He obviously knew that I had been playing at Burscough, but would not have been up to speed with my demotion, so after two minutes of being in the dugout, he stuck his head across into the home dugout and said,
"Oh, there you are Callie! Why aren't you playing?"

Most of the Burscough players were either mad Evertonians or Liverpudlians and due to my quiet nature, were unaware that I knew Joe, so were taken aback that he had singled me out and enquired about me being dropped. My Dad later joked that if he had been any sort of friend, Joe would have signed me for Everton, put me on a five year contract at £3000 a week and let me languish in the "A"team! Anyway, that day, Burscough were totally outclassed by Everton, with Vinny Samways, a player that never really fitted the combative midfield mould that Joe Royle liked, scoring an absolute stunner from twenty five yards. With ten minutes to go and

Everton leading 6-0, John Davison told me I was going on. When you are losing 6-0, there isn't really much pressure to perform, but there were probably 700 or 800 down to watch, so I was keen not to make a fool of myself (ten years after the Kevin Richardson nutmeg)!

I savoured those ten minutes in goal that sunny, summer's day. The month before I had started working as a Graduate Trainee for Yorkshire Building Society in Wallasey and they were open 9am-1pm on a Saturday morning and although the District Manager, was an amiable Manchester City fan, Howard Slack, who was to become a great friend, I knew the rest of the staff would resent it if I tried to dodge my share of Saturday shifts. Thus, I also knew my semi-professional football career was probably fading away, at the ripe old age of 24 and opportunities to play against Everton were not going to be coming around again very often.

Everton were strolling at 6-0 so I wasn't put under a huge amount of pressure, but I wanted to be. Sometimes, as a goalkeeper, if the match has already been won or lost, you just wanted to be peppered with shots to save in the last few minutes. John Ebbrell put a headed chance straight at me when it was easier to score and then Stuart Barlow was put through with only me to beat. It was like the Kevin Richardson incident all over again. It was an opportunity for redemption. I rushed out to narrow my angles and made sure my legs were close enough together not to fit a football through. I had watched Stuart Barlow many times at Goodison Park, he was lightning quick, but did not have the composure of a great finisher. He could have probably ran past me and slotted the ball into an empty net, or lobbed me whilst I was rushing out, but he chose to drill the ball hard and low to my right and I stuck my long right leg out, as far as it could reach and diverted it for a corner. It was an unorthodox save, using my feet rather than my hands, but it had served Arsenal and Tottenham goalkeeper, Pat Jennings well, during his career and ultimately my job was to stop the ball going in. The corner was cleared and the full-time whistle went soon after. I was delighted, I had just kept a clean sheet against the F.A

Cup holders! OK, none of that side at Burscough had actually played at Wembley and I hadn't

played for ninety minutes just ten, but an aura of pride swept over me!

I only played twice more in 1995-96 for Burscough. One game was in a friendly against

Southport which we lost 5-0 with former Nottingham Forest and Manchester United player, Peter

Davenport scoring a hat trick. We were completely battered that Tuesday night, as John Davison

played a half-strength team. I performed heroics for 89 minutes to keep it down to four-nil. I was

never the fittest of keepers though, a liking for beer had seen to that, I sometimes even got cramp

in training and in the final minute, a cross found the head of Davenport who looped his header

over me and towards the goal. I started to backtrack from my six yard line to my goal but I was

weary from my earlier efforts. My legs just buckled under me. I fell over them, landing in a heap

on the floor, as the ball sailed into an empty net. My heroics were now forgotten and my comical

tripping up would be the only thing people remembered, such is the life of a goalkeeper! I wasn't

that bothered though, as by then, I had told John Davison I would not be continuing to warm the

bench up, as I could earn a tidy sum by working Saturdays. I shook Peter Davenport's hand

heartily at the final whistle and reminded him that my Dad, Richie, used to take him for training

at Bellfield when he was a fourteen and fifteen year old lad.

"Richie Wade! Bloody hell, that's a blast from the past," he said, as we began a decent chat

about his schoolboy days.

After that I played one more minute for Burscough. The lads had a really good season and

had reached the North West Counties League Cup Final. Paul Blasbery had played in every

game, but John Davison knew that only a goalkeeper who had represented the club in the League

could play in the Final. Thus, he needed me to come on in the final League game of the season, in case 'Blas' was struck down with a bug on the day of the Final. The Burscough players had more than half an eye on the final and lost the game 3-0, but John still left it until the last minute to bring me on. There was no fairytale ending for me. Blas remained fit and well and they won the final at Gigg Lane. I didn't play another semi-professional game again, but I did play at Burscough again and did play with and against professional footballers again, but will save those stories for another day. This Chapter has turned out much longer than I thought. I certainly didn't have a long, successful footballing career, but at least I had a few stories to tell!

Budweiser F.A Cup Preliminary Round – Saturday 31st August 2013

West Didsbury & Chorlton AFC v Burscough

Attendance – 136

After casting doubt on his appearance at this game, I spoke to my Mum and Dad after them spending a great few days in Poland and my Dad was keen to come along again. I doubt very much he will come to every Round, especially once the tickets become more expensive, because, as a former Scout, he is used to getting into football grounds free of charge! The concessionary prices have softened the blow, but if we end up having to pay £60 at Arsenal or Chelsea and my Dad is asked to pay at least half of that, I don't think he will be keen on going. I suspect he will make most, if not all, the non-League games though. For now, today was a fiver for me and £3 for my Dad, so all was good!

Burscough were always going to test West Didsbury & Chorlton to the limit. Burscough are in the Evo Stik First Division North and a division above West Didsbury. Both teams had got off to poor League starts, but if West Didsbury were struggling in the league below Burscough, we expected Burscough to have too much experience and class for their opposition.

Alison wasn't working this time around but Dad volunteered to drive again. We left at one o'clock but with no traffic hold ups this time, we were there well before two, despite making a wrong turn when almost there. We had not brought the route guide, confident in our ability to remember the way but we failed at the final hurdle, so had to stop a local for directions. It was a bright, sunny afternoon and we headed into the bar to find Jordan and Alan, who give the impression they like to be everywhere as early as they can, to stretch the event out and savour the experience. I wasn't surprised to find them in the bar area, sat down enjoying a hot drink with two extra supporters in tow, Phil Cooper and Steve Mulligan. Phil is from Bedfordshire and an Arsenal fan, Steve a FC United of Manchester supporter who had become disillusioned with the Glayzer situation at Manchester United. He was one of the few thousand who chose not to go to the game wearing anti-Glayzer clothing but instead to start following a newly created side. A bit like the Portsmouth situation in that their existence now is solely due to the fans of the club, but starting from scratch rather than having to endure an annual slide.

My Dad and I grabbed a drink and went to sit with them, but after a few minutes, I spotted the officials from Burscough and went over to speak to their President, Rod Cottam. When I was at Burscough, I'm not exactly sure what Rod's title was, but for me he was the man in the dugout with the bucket and sponge and the man who brought the supply of chewing gum. In the first few months of the 1995-96 season when my backside regularly had splinters from sitting on the bench, Rod was the man I sat next to. He was always up for a laugh and although I had my doubts whether he would remember much about me, I headed across to say hello. My doubts were misplaced.

"Bloody hell, Cal, what are you doing here?" Rod said, shaking my hand.

I explained the F.A Cup journey we were setting out on and Rod surprised me with his recollection of my time at Burscough, remembering the F.A Vase defeat at Cammell Lairds, my time as a goalkeeping substitute with 'Blas' as first choice and even remembering that friendly with Everton.

"How is your Uncle Joe?" he asked.

He isn't my Uncle (he's my Godfather, but as kids we may have called them Uncle Joe & Auntie Janet, as that's what we used to do with Mum and Dad's friends) but it was impressive that Rod still remembered so much about me, given I was only at Burscough for two seasons, almost twenty years ago. They will have had hundreds and hundreds of players coming and going since, so I was really pleased to know someone remembered me!

My Dad also wandered over as he had spotted one of the Burscough officials was a guy who regularly took Verdi Godwin to games. Verdi was a former footballer who played centre forward for Blackburn Rovers, Manchester City and Stoke City, amongst others, just after the Second World War, but my Dad knew him well because he became a football scout. It was Verdi that had taken Alan Mansley, one of the Skelmersdale 1967 F.A Amateur Cup team to Blackpool and more significantly, he also told Bill Shankly to sign Steve Heighway for Liverpool from Skelmersdale, three years later. Verdi is 87 now and not in great health but up until a couple of years previously, had been keen to get to as many games as he could.

Verdi had been a lifeguard at Southport beach with Tony Waiters, a goalkeeper who played over 250 games for Blackpool in the 1950s and 1960s and also played five games for England, at a time when Alf Ramsey was looking for a reserve keeper to Gordon Banks. Verdi and Tony had become great friends and my Dad said that he and my Mum often used to go to the Red Lion pub in Mawdesley on a Saturday night and Tony and Verdi would often be there, with Verdi always playing the spoons! I can't imagine there are too many professional footballers out in pubs these days on a Saturday night, keeping the locals entertained with their musical spoon act! My Dad knew Tony Waiters well too, and when Dad had his testimonial, Tony played in goal for one of the two sides. After retiring from playing, he went on to become the Football Association's North West Regional coach. From there, he ended up managing England's youth side, then Plymouth Argyle, then Vancouver Whitecaps before leading Canada to the 1986 World Cup. I have no recollection as a 15 year old, of my Dad pointing to the TV and telling me Canada's manager played in his testimonial, but then a whole host of professionals, including internationals and a World Cup winner, played, refereed and ran the line in his testimonial and I only found this out when I was a teenager and discovered the Testimonial programme in my Mum and Dad's loft. My Dad isn't one to brag!

As we were heading out to the same vantage point on the terrace, as the previous game, Derek Goulding, the Burscough manager, came over and had a chat with my Dad. Derek was a schoolboy at Everton and although a decent centre back, he was not quite up to making it at Everton, but my Dad recommended him to Altrincham, and Derek went on to have a good semi-professional career. My Dad told Derek that we had been to the previous round and to watch out for the pace of the West Didsbury centre forward. Derek said he'd watched them in midweek and was playing a lad at the back, who normally played in midfield, to deal with him.

Soon after, the game was under way. As a kid, I remember spotting a German film called 'The Goalkeeper's Fear Of The Penalty', but this ex-goalkeeper's fear for our F.A Cup journey, was a fear of the replay. With not having a lot of money (or realistically, barely any money), the replay would be a financial hazard I could do without. I mentioned to Alan and my Dad after a few minutes, that the replay was due to be on Tuesday night.

"This won't be a draw," my Dad commented.

Without needing to elaborate, I knew what my Dad meant. Burscough were going to win. They were in a higher league and although West Didsbury tried to play good football, there was an evident gulf in quality. Tre Baldwin Willis, who had terrorised the Abbey Hey defence a couple of weeks earlier, had become a chaser of lost causes and was already, minutes into the game, growing frustrated with the lack of supply and was starting to drop deeper, in search of a touch.

Burscough had a pacy forward themselves, called Liam Caddick, who seemed very quick and tricky, but if you played the ball in the air to him, he would do anything within his power to avoid heading it! Anyway, after about half an hour, another Burscough striker, Jordan Williams, latched on to a poor back pass, ran through and cooly slotted the ball into the bottom corner. To use a footballing cliché, it was no more than the visitors deserved and it remained 1-0 at half-time. We headed inside for a drink and Jordan Oliver and her Dad, Alan headed around the ground with their Christie's buckets to do some fundraising.

Despite the scoreline only being one-nil, we could see no way back for West Didsbury & Chorlton unless Burscough self-destructed. This did not happen. The second half progressed along similar lines to the first, with Burscough dominating proceedings and West Didsbury & Chorlton trying very hard to keep them at bay. Alan pointed out that the West Didsbury keeper was very vocal, perhaps unnecessarily so and this started a touchline debate about the merits of the mouthy keeper. A goalkeeper has a great vantage point on the game and can be useful to his defenders, telling them where there is an unmarked opposition player, for example, but often now, goalkeepers talk because they like to hear the sound of their own voice.

In this case, shouting things like, "Come on lads, we need to pass better than this!" and "Let's keeping working hard, Whites," were not going to be the nuggets of wisdom that would lead to his team suddenly passing brilliantly and working harder and ultimately going on to win the game.

West Didsbury & Chorlton did all they could to keep the game competitive, but with about twenty minutes to go, Paul Williams rose to head home from a great corner, by substitute Phil Clarke. Burscough then made it 3-0 with about eight minutes left, with Clarke again being the provider, sending a ball between the two West Didsbury centre backs for Mark Beesley to chase on to and then expertly slot in to the back of the net. West Didsbury & Chorlton's possible record as the only unbeaten team in F.A Cup history was coming to an end!

In the last few minutes, West Didsbury & Chorlton pushed forward looking for a consolation goal but it wasn't to be. I had been impressed with the Burscough keeper, Tim Horn, who was very good with his feet and swept up any over hit passes. The final whistle blew and West Didsbury's first adventure in the F.A Cup was over. It is a great little set up, well worth a visit. The ground has a good refreshment area for pre-match, post-match and half time entertainment and on both occasions we were given a warm and friendly welcome. Alan and Jordan also mentioned, before we headed home, that they had raised another £50 for 'The Christie' with their bucket collection.

The next round is, as I hoped it would be, a return to Victoria Park, Burscough. They will be playing the winners of Radcliffe Borough and Atherton Colleries. I have no preference. I am just hoping the victory is a catalyst for much improved performances by Burscough. Their previous four games this season had been two draws and two defeats, so perhaps they would now go on to better things. An excellent Cup run, that would take them through a few rounds, taking us along with them on the adventure, would be a bonus!

We once again said our goodbyes to Alan and Jordan and bade farewell to Phil and Steve. Phil, in particular, seemed to enjoy the non-League experience, so hopefully they may both pop up again at later rounds. With the next round being a stone's throw away from my home town of Ormskirk, I am going to do what I can to bring a few extra supporters along myself.

FINAL SCORE : West Didsbury & Chorlton 0 Burscough 3

Scorers :- J.Williams, P.Williams, Beesley.

Our 'Speccies:- Calvin Wade, Richard Wade, Alan Oliver, Jordan Oliver, Phil Cooper, Steve Mulligan.

Monday 9th September 2013

My Personal Fortune (or Lack Thereof)!

When I moan a bit about not having much money as part of this diary, I appreciate it is relative. I have a centrally heated house with hot water, gas and electricity and do not go hungry on any given day. We have a car, our children have their own bedrooms and televisions within them that have been bought during more prosperous times. We are all healthy. We have a happy marriage. We are lucky.

The moan is just related to a concern. The concern being that my wife, Alison's income alone is not enough to pay a relatively large mortgage, the council tax, the gas, the electricity, the water bills, the food for four people, the credit cards, the car loan, the social life which for me consists of a non-league football match every two weeks and for Alison consists of an occasional meet up with friends in a coffee bar. My second book just hasn't taken off and my financial services business development role is not paying me much at all either. I don't need to earn huge fortunes, I just need to earn enough to ensure we have enough money to pay for all the essentials and to provide for our children. It is time for Plan B. I just don't quite know how Plan B will manifest itself!

Over the last ten days, I have applied for three jobs. The first one, was as a postman for Royal Mail. The second was doing nights at Asda in Chorley and the third was via an old friend from my Yorkshire Building Society days, Chris Ayres, as he works in Scotland for a company that sells car warranties amongst other things to second hand car dealers. Chris seems to enjoy it and I asked if there was anything going in the North West. It transpires that there is, so he has recommended me to his boss.

I have already been rejected by the Royal Mail. I did an on-line test and the batteries on the mouse were running down, so I got timed out of a lot of questions! The ASDA job application seems to be progressing well. A couple of years ago, I was hosting events on corporate tables at Manchester United but last week, I found myself competing with 17 year olds for part time night work, doing exercises that involved making houses out of spaghetti and marshmallows. I can't harp back to what financial and job luxuries I have had in the past though, as right now, financially, I don't have much. The ASDA job would be useful if the other job with the car warranty company does not happen. I have a second interview at ASDA tonight at 6:30pm with a guy called Darren and I am waiting for a call from Chris Ayres boss in the next twenty four hours.

With regards to the objective of getting to every round of the F.A Cup, a regular salary would obviously make a huge difference. It is not expensive currently, as it is regional and the admission prices are cheap, but even in the later qualifying rounds we could be watching Conference sides in the North East for example, so both petrol costs and admission will not be as cheap. Factor in replays and it starts becoming an expensive hobby and those prices will only escalate as we get nearer the Final. Both with the jobs and with the F.A Cup draw, I need 'Lady Luck' to be on my side.

Tuesday 10th September 2013

I have an additional job at ASDA! It is not a new job to replace an old one, as a temporary job at ASDA won't give me enough money to live on, plus it is only temporary during a refurbishment to the store, but at least it is going to be extra money that I could really do with. I am on a training course for two days this week and then they are looking for me to start on nights this weekend, working Saturday to Tuesday nights. The potential negative aspect of this, is that if I am on nights next Tuesday, I would miss any replay between Burscough and Radcliffe Borough, which, in my mind, would mean that I have failed in my task to go to every game between the Extra Preliminary Round and F.A Cup Final.

Burscough are playing Radcliffe Borough because Radcliffe defeated Atherton Colleries in their Preliminary Round replay. Radcliffe won 2-1 but it wasn't without drama. Radcliffe's keeper had been sent off in a League game and it transpired that they didn't get the registration of their reserve keeper submitted in time for him to qualify for the Preliminary Round replay, so Radcliffe's centre forward had to go in goal! They went 1-0 down too, but recovered to win 2-1. Like Burscough, they have started the season poorly and are languishing in the bottom three of the Evo Stick First Division North, so it is likely to be a tight encounter. If it does go to a replay, I may have to drive over to Radcliffe and arrive for my shift in ASDA a little late!

With regards to the car warranty job, I have spoken to Rob Davies, the Sales Manager and I have to go down to Cheltenham later this month for an interview with Rob and the boss, Mike. The more I think about it, the more I want that job, so I hope things go well. Not only would it be a full-time job with a regular monthly wage, it would also provide a second car! That would be very useful indeed.

Friday 13th September 2013

I am now a fully trained up staff member at ASDA. In my eighteen years within financial services, I didn't expect to be returning to the retail trade that I started out in, after graduating from Manchester Polytechnic, but life does have a tendency to surprise you. Yesterday, during the second day of training, I noticed the Burscough FC President, Rod Cottam and his wife, arrived at the store to do their weekly shop which allowed my mind to drift onto F.A Cup matters for a minute or two.

I have been in touch with Burscough FC this week and they are putting an interview with me in the match day programme. It is about my writing, including this book about my F.A Cup adventures and also about my brief time at Burscough. They have also kindly given me a guest pass for the day, which given my lack of money, I was very grateful for. If I ever stumble upon better times, I will make sure those who have looked after me in my tougher times are suitably rewarded. I have friends who have distanced themselves from me since I have been skint and others who have gone out their way to help, so if the good times do return, it has been a useful barometer of true friendships.

Whilst mentioning friendships, I have tried via Facebook, to get some old friends along to the game tomorrow. Burscough is only a couple of miles from my hometown of Ormskirk and a lot of friends still live there, so I tried to drum up a bit of interest. Half a dozen old friends said they would go but now it is coming to the crunch, one or two are starting to drop out. As it stands, a total of four friends and work colleagues are due to turn up. One, Peter Abel, I don't think I have seen for twenty five years, so I will be using his Facebook photos to help identify him!

There was also some good news as the issue of a replay is no longer a concern. I am doing a couple of day shifts at ASDA next week, before the nights start the week after. The people on the course, Darren, my line manager and the trainers who work there, all seem very nice, so I am hoping it will be a relatively pleasant short-term experience. If I have a full-time job there, by the time the F.A Cup Final comes around next May, it either means I love it or alternatively it means that no-one else would have me!

Budsweiser F.A Cup 1st Round Qualifying - Saturday 14th September 2013

Burscough v Radcliffe Borough

Attendance – 144

It is several years since I have been to Victoria Park, Burscough, but very little about the place has changed. For many years, Victoria Park has been threatened with being consigned to history and memory, as it has seemed likely the ground would be sold and a new stadium built on the land behind it, but after a season sharing Skelmersdale United's ground, Burscough have returned to their natural home, where my footballing career peaked! I guess having a footballing career that peaked at Burscough, is like being a mountain climber whose career peaked when he climbed Ilkley Moor, but there are millions of footballers who never even made it that high.

As you enter Victoria Park, through an antiquated turnstile that has been there for many years, you find yourselves behind one goal, with the main stand to the left which is only small. There are probably about 150 seats in the stand and the players changing rooms are underneath it. There is also covered terracing on the opposite site of the pitch, with further covered terracing behind the far goal. To the right of the entrance, by the corner flag, is Barrons Bar. The back windows of Barrons Bar back onto the ground and I am unsure if you can watch the match free by going into Barrons and watching the game through the window. You probably can but you aren't exactly breathing life into non-league football if you are that devious.

As my Dad had driven to the first two games, I opted to drive to this one. Burscough is only twenty minutes drive from our house in Euxton, but I drove on past Burscough, to my Mum and Dad's in Aughton. I had lunch with them and my youngest lad, Joel. After lunch, we left Joel there with my Mum (at his request) and my Dad and I headed over to Burscough. It has been a sunny late summer's day with a cool breeze, but good weather for football watching.

We arrived in the ground at 2:15pm, the time we had arranged to meet up with Alan, Jordan and Phil, who were getting the train from Manchester and also the four friends of mine that I was hoping would also show their faces. We couldn't see any obvious signs of any of them being there yet, so decided to go and get ourselves a pre-match Bovril. I don't think I have ever been in the canteen area at Burscough before, as I have spent more time there involved as one of the playing staff, although one of my playing colleagues from those days, Neil 'Jockey' Hanson must have found his way in there more often than me, as he married one of the canteen ladies. It is the polar opposite of the shiny, new refreshment area at West Didsbury, as it is an old fashioned building that is only accessible through a back door that involves you manoeuvring past half-bricks and other discarded debris! All the canteen ladies are very friendly and cheerful and as we sat down at a table to enjoy our drinks, my first invited guest, Peter Abel entered.

When I was about twelve, my Dad had noticed I had a good eye for tennis and tried to get myself and my sister, Lisa, who also looked competent, into Aughton Tennis Club. Aughton, where I moved to from Maghull when I was four, is a village a couple of miles from Ormskirk. There are affluent areas within it and it is often deemed a 'posh place' by people from Merseyside. During the 1980's, there were plenty of people in Aughton Tennis Club, who were from wealthy backgrounds and they tried to run Aughton as though it was the Northern equivalent of Wimbledon. There were grass courts, members had to play in all white and you could only join after a long period on the waiting list, followed by an interview by the committee. Ormskirk Tennis Club, on the other hand, just allowed you to pay your membership monies and join, so that is what we did. It was at Ormskirk Tennis Club that I met Peter Abel.

Peter didn't go to my school, Ormskirk Grammar, he went to the neighbouring school, Cross Hall High, nor was he my age, when I was twelve, he must have been about fifteen, but

Peter and his mate, a lad called Andrew Moss, were very friendly and would always have a knock around with us or have a chat with us in the clubhouse. There was always some good football banter too, as Peter was a keen Liverpudlian whilst I was a mad Evertonian. My sister and I only stayed at Ormskirk for a couple of summers, because after that we were finally accepted into Aughton, but as an older child, I used to run into Peter in Ormskirk from time to time and his Dad turned out to be the 'gas man' who serviced my Mum and Dad's boiler. We lost touch but stumbled across each other on Facebook and old friendships and football rivalries were rekindled.

As an interesting footnote to the tennis story, when I joined Aughton Tennis Club there were some very strong junior tennis players. The two strongest were the Cowan brothers, Andrew and Barry, the next strongest were the Gilpin brothers, James and his older brother, whose name I forget. Anyway, I was about the seventh best. I had a great forehand, but my backhand was weak and my serve was erratic. The junior team needed four players and they played doubles, so usually the Cowan's were the first pair and the Gilpin's the second pair. Sometimes though, if someone was unavailable, they looked around for another reasonable player to fill in. Andrew Cowan was my age, his brother Barry was three or four years younger, but Barry was the better tennis player and Andrew a keen golfer. Thus, if Andrew had a golf event on, I was sometimes asked to step in. As the Gilpin brothers were used to playing together, I had to play with Barry, who was easily the best player in the club. He must have hated playing with me as I was soon identified as the weak link and the opposition avoided Barry and aimed at me! We lost as many as we won, which to Barry, a very competitive young man, must have been maddening. Luckily for Barry, he probably never had to play with anyone as bad as me ever again, as he went on to play Davis Cup tennis for Britain, once took Pete Sampras to five sets at

Wimbledon and is now Sky Sports News tennis correspondent! Also at Aughton Tennis Club was a lad called Simon Jack, who I had played football with at Park End. He wasn't the greatest footballer or tennis player, but he certainly had something about him as he went to Oxford University, recently going on to present the business and economic news on BBC One's Breakfast News programme then transferring over to BBC Radio Four to do the same job. He is now married to the eldest daughter of the late John Barry, composer of the soundtracks to many James Bond films.

Peter Abel, who was at today's match never joined Aughton Tennis Club, never played Pete Sampras at Wimbledon or married the daughter of a famous father, as far as I know, but was also an intelligent bloke. He is now a Senior Lecturer at Lancashire University. He studied Genetics as a degree, which is what I think he now lectures in. He bought a cup of tea and sat down with us. Despite having not seen Peter for twenty five years and never having been a particularly close friend of his, the conversation flowed easily and comfortably. Football lovers always have that to fall back on if a conversation stalls and if I ever meet anyone new, I often ask them if they follow football, as a conversational safety net. The net wasn't needed with Peter though and after our drinks we went out to find the rest of our group. After bumping into Rod Cottam, Burscough's President, once again, we went to the far side of the stand and met up with Alan and Jordan Oliver. Once again Phil Cooper had decided to join them. He had not previously watched non-League football, but had been so impressed by the standard at West Didsbury, he had decided to come along once more.

We were also soon joined by Nick Boycott and his Dad, Tom. Nick was another childhood friend, who had been to my school, but was a few years younger than me. Much like the situation with Peter, we had never been close friends, but had a lot of mutual friends and many shared interests such as football and horse racing, so found ourselves sharing regular Facebook conversations. Nick is a season ticket holder at Liverpool, but they are away on Monday night (Everton were at home to Chelsea in a late kick off, surprisingly winning 1-0), so Nick decided to come along with his Dad who often goes to Victoria Park. We had swelled the crowd by at least eight!

The first half was hard fought but without goals or any real golden opportunities. Last year, Manchester City reached the F.A Cup Final and their total prize money had they not lost in the final to Wigan Athletic would have been £3 million. A drop in the ocean for the richest club in the world, perhaps not even enough to cover one week's wages. The winners today will receive £3000 to add to the £1925 winnings from the last round and opportunity for further riches in the following rounds. I would guess the Burscough wage bill would be less than £500 a week, so two wins in this competition can pay the wages for ten weeks, yet Man City could probably not pay a week's wages by winning it. Does this round mean more to these two clubs than the final meant to the owners of Manchester City? Probably.

The one thing that disappointed me from the first half was the petty squabbles that seemed to be going on amongst the Radcliffe Borough players. They had only picked up one point from their first five League games and seemed to have developed a blame culture. The right back pumped a channel ball along the touchline and then started swearing at one of the forwards for not tracking across. The forward swore back and then a midfielder joined in, saying the right back was right. Having worked in a subsidiary of a part-nationalised bank and witnessed everyone trying to blame everyone else for their collective failings, I know this type of environment does not improve performance. It just leads to poor morale and no-one really wanting to be there. Two things a team needs to get them out of the mire are a positive mental attitude and a sense of collective responsibility, Radcliffe Borough did not seem to have either. I'm not saying they looked like a bad team, they definitely didn't, it just seemed like they had a bad attitude.

We were cold at at half-time, largely because we had stupidly stood in the shade for the first half, so the Ormskirk contingent went for heated beverages, whilst Alan, Jordan and Phil went to get their bucket ready to do their collection for Christies hospital. We made the decision to go and stand on the other side of the pitch for the second half and when we reached the middle, by kick off, it felt about ten centigrade warmer than it had done in the first half. My Dad stood with Nick's Dad, Tom, as they were both from Liverpool and both of a similar age so lots of mutual connections had come out during the half-time break. I stood with Nick and Peter and listened to them optimistically evaluating their hopes for Liverpool's season. Alan, Jordan and Phil had gone to count the money they had collected at half-time and by the time they joined us, three goals had been scored! The only three goals of the game to boot!

Radcliffe took the lead early in the second half. Radcliffe surged forward in numbers on a counter attack with Matt Landregan slotting home. This seemed to shock Burscough and they played without rhythm for about ten minutes and it appeared that we would be following Radcliffe into the Second Qualifying Round. After the shock wore off though, Burscough re-established themselves as the better side and started to press forward with purpose. On about the hour mark, Burscough midfielder Darren Brookfield, one of the smaller players on the pitch and I guess a player not noted for his aerial ability, looped a header beyond the despairing Radcliffe keeper. The Radcliffe players bodies sagged visibly and Burscough were lifted. Burscough continued to push forward and minutes later Liam Caddick neatly brought down a through ball and then blasted his second touch into the back of the net. Only Alan, Jordan and Phil looked more gutted than the Radcliffe defence as they emerged from their coin count to discover they had missed three goals. On a positive note, just over £50 was again added to the Christies kitty.

After Burscough went ahead, they looked more likely than Radcliffe to score the fourth goal of the game and when Radcliffe did go forward Tim Horn, in goal for Burscough, looked like a keeper who was at the top of his game. Tom Boycott mentioned that he is a student and had recently represented the British University team in the World Championships in Russia. Along the way to the Final, they defeated a Russian side that included professionals who had played for the full Russian international side and their Under21s, in front of 10 000 Russian supporters (including the team manager, a certain Fabio Capello).

When the ninety minutes were up, with the game finishing 2-1, a voiced called out to me, "Calvin, Calvin!"

I saw a man with a thick brown beard approaching me. He looked like he was in his mid-30s. My brain immediately tried to register who he was but came back without an answer. "Hi Calvin, it's Matthew Nayler, Andrew's brother," he said with a jovial smile. I immediately felt a little embarrassed that I had failed to recognise him. There had been a clue as he was my fourth Facebook friend who had said he would come along! I think his Facebook profile picture even shows him with a beard, but my memories of Matthew were from secondary and primary school and back then, unless I am very much mistaken, he had no facial hair! I don't know where he had been standing for the duration of the game, but it is shame he hadn't found us earlier, as Matthew is a really nice lad.

Back in my primary and secondary school days, I had been friends with Matthew's brother, Andrew who was my age. In 1981, when Tottenham Hotspur played Manchester City in the F.A Cup Final, remembered mainly for the Argentinian Ricky Villa's mazy run and goal,

Andrew was the only boy in our year at primary school who wanted Spurs to win. His Mum and Dad were from down South and his Dad had passed on his love of Spurs to Andrew, who would proudly wear his Spurs top every time we played football on the school field. Matthew was about four or five years younger than us. When he started in first year infants, he was universally accepted as the cutest five year old that had ever attended the school. Thirty something years later, how things had changed!

I had been friendly with Andrew at school, he hung around in the same group of lads as me and got the train to and from school with me every day, but we had never been best mates. When he was fourteen or fifteen, he started getting in to Heavy Metal music and grew his curly hair long. Matthew told me he was now a teacher and to my surprise, and to some extent horror, he revealed that Andrew now supported Liverpool!

Andrew wasn't the sportiest of people. He had played for Park End, the junior team my Dad ran, but was not a regular the first season, only playing regularly when we were hopeless the following season. He was a reasonable cricketer and could swing the ball miles when he bowled, but as his interest in Heavy Metal grew, seemingly his interest in sport faded.

The relevance of Andrew Nayler's lack of sporting prowess dates back to a phone call, I had received in from my Dad, in August 2012. He called to say that he had been told that Andrew Nayler had died. It was a real shock. Although I hadn't seen Andrew for twenty years, he had played a big part in my childhood. I asked how he died and when my Dad said he had died whilst doing the swimming leg of the New York Iron Man triathlon, it seemed totally bizarre. I know some people get into sport in later life, but I had been in touch with Matthew for a few years on Facebook and he had never mentioned Andrew getting involved in extreme sporting activities. The penny then dropped.

"Hang on, Dad, which Andrew Nayler are we talking about here?" I asked.

"What do you mean? Do you know more than one Andrew Nayler?" Dad asked.

"Yes. Who told you that Andrew Nayler had died?"

"Robin Hyslop."

Robin Hyslop was a friend of my Dad's who used to be in Aughton Tennis Club. I regularly

played tennis with, and was good friends with, his son, James.

"Right, well the Andrew Nayler that has died, isn't the one you know."

At our primary school, there had been two Andrew Naylers, one my age and one a year

older, whose name was actually Andrew Naylor (with an 'o'). Andrew Naylor wasn't massively

sporty as a child either and although he didn't go to my Secondary school, I knew him from my

days at Aughton Tennis Club as him and his brother, Marcus, used to come down regularly. I can

still picture them now turning up on their bikes. Both Marcus and Andrew were really, really

great lads. I knew Andrew had moved to Hong Kong to join the police force and remember

making attempts to track him down over there, when I went to Hong Kong, as part of my

backpacking trip around the world in 1994.

In my thirties, I ran four marathons (and did a further one in Liverpool in my 40s). I was

pretty slow, generally running just under or over the five hour mark, but remember hearing that

Andrew Naylor had come in the Top100 in the London Marathon. I have checked this out since

and in 2009, he was an amazing 74th place and ran it in two hours 32 minutes. The previous year,

when I had run, I was barely past the half way point after two and a half hours. Andrew Naylor

was just the type of sporty, athletic man who would be doing a triathlon and Robin Hyslop would

have known him through the tennis club link. I was equally shocked and saddened to hear of

Andrew Naylor's death. I spoke to my sister that evening and she said she had been in Ormskirk town centre and a lot of people who only knew Andrew Nayler, were wrongly talking about his death. I sent a message on Facebook to Matthew telling him about the tragic death of the other Andrew and warning him that people were jumping to the wrong conclusion. I am glad I did this, as Matthew told his Mum and Dad and within days they had received a few bereavement cards in the post, from people saying they were desperately sorry to hear of his death.

Last month, I read on the internet that an inquest into Andrew Naylor's death had revealed that he died of a heart attack caused by a blocked artery. He had become a police superintendent in the Hong Kong police's counter terrorist unit, where he had served for twenty years and only a week before his death had won a leg of an endurance kayak race with a friend.He had been a superb athlete and reading the comments on the internet from friends, it appeared he was a much loved and respected family man.

Driving my Dad back from the Burscough game, he told me another story with Far Eastern links, that himself and Tom Boycott had been discussing during their second half chat. My Dad is from pretty much the middle of Liverpool. His Dad died when his Mum, Catherine, was only in her mid-thirties, by which time they had had nine children, four boys and five girls. My Dad's brother, John, drowned in the Leeds-Liverpool canal in the 1950s, but my Grandma had to bring eight children up single handedly. My Dad adored his mother, but laughs when he recalls the day of his eleven plus exam, as he remembers his Mum shouting after him as he left home,

"Don't you dare pass that exam, Richard!"

The reason for this was because my Grandma could not afford the Grammar school uniform. My Dad duly failed and went to Lambeth Road Secondary Modern in Kirkdale.

My Dad often tells a story of a teacher, Mr.Whitby who taught Music, Art and History. In his first year at Lambeth Road, my Dad and his class mates were going into Mr.Whitby's class and found a fifteen year old boy standing there with his 'Teddy Boy' haircut. The lad had been misbehaving in the playground and Mr.Whitby had caught him and asked him to report to his class. Before dealing with the 'Teddy Boy', Mr.Whitby was giving instructions to the eleven year olds in his class, telling them what work he wanted them to do. As he was doing this, the 'Teddy Boy' had stood behind Mr.Whitby, mimicking his actions. He thought he had gone unnoticed, but either the pupils smirks or the 'Teddy Boy' hairstyle bobbing around behind him had alerted Mr.Whitby to the boy's theatrics. Mr.Whitby swivelled round, punched the boy straight in the face, knocking him to the ground. He then pulled the lad back up by his collar and warned him that if he ever pulled a trick like that again, he would do far worse. Neither the lad nor any of the kids in my Dad's class ever messed around in Mr.Whitby's class again! Despite this, my Dad maintains to this day that he was a great teacher.

Co-incidentally, Tom Boycott had been to both primary school and Secondary School with my Dad's mate, Wally Bennett. After his schooldays, Tom himself had become a teacher. One of his first roles was teaching in inner city Liverpool. Lambeth Road had, by this time, been closed down, but it had amalgamated with three or four other schools and Tom Boycott found himself working at this newly amalgamated school alongside my Dad's old teacher, Eric Whitby.

Tom said he very much respected Eric Whitby. He related stories to Tom of his days in a Japanese prisoner of war camp during the Second World War. Eric Whitby said that the Japanese commanding officer who had been in charge of the camp had been a man of honour and had not treated the soldiers there brutally, like many other Japanese run prisoner of war camps. The Japanese had not signed the Geneva Convention and often treated their prisoners like they had dishonoured their countries, supplying very limited food and used the POWs as forced labour. This was not the case in Eric Whitby's camp. In fact, after the war, Eric Whitby had even traced the officer who had run his camp and met up with him in Singapore.

Tom also told my Dad a story that one day, after giving a cheeky pupil six of the best with his cane, the child had said to Mr.Whitby that he was going to go home and tell his Dad. "Go on then, lad," Mr.Whitby said, "run off and tell your Dad and when he comes back here with you, I'll give him fu##ing six of the best too!"

FINAL SCORE : Burscough 2 Radcliffe Borough 1

Scorers :- Burscough – Brookfield & Caddick.

Radcliffe Borough – Landregan.

Our 'Speccies':- Calvin Wade, Richard Wade, Alan Oliver, Jordan Oliver, Phil Cooper, Peter Abel, Nick Boycott, Tom Boycott, Matthew Nayler.

An exciting day lies ahead. Since before the Extra Preliminary Round, we have had a good idea where we would be going for the first three rounds of the F.A Cup as all three were drawn at the same time. We knew our destinations were going to be either West Didsbury & Chorlton, Abbey Hey, Burscough or a combination of the three. Today is different, we have a 50% chance of going back to Burscough and a 50% chance of travelling to anywhere in the Northern sector of the draw. For the sake of adventure, I hope we travel to somewhere new. There is still a possibility that Burscough could draw local rivals, Skelmersdale United, which would divide support between me and my Dad or they could even draw Chorley. If that happened I wouldn't even know who to support. Former Blackburn Rovers and Manchester City player, Gary Flitcroft is currently working wonders at Chorley and they had a great 1-0 win over FC United of Manchester on Saturday.

From Alan's perspective, he is hoping Burscough get Ashton United. Alan has a number of contacts there and it is always nice to have a personal interest, as I have found watching Burscough in the last two rounds. According to Alan, the draw is at 1pm, so I will be checking out the F.A website at lunchtime, excited to see where we are heading next.

12:47pm

Just had a text off Alan, not sure if the draw was posted early or Alan got the times wrong, but Burscough have been drawn against Workington away! Workington were actually a League side when I was first getting into football and remember them being up for re-election and being replaced in the Football League by Wimbledon. A little known fact about Workington is that Bill Shankly managed them in the mid-1950s. They are currently languishing in the bottom reaches of the Skrill Conference North, but as Burscough are in the lower reaches of the Evo-Stik First Division (two Leagues below), you would have to fancy Workington in this one.

When I worked for BM Solutions (part of Lloyds Bank), for a while I covered all the way up to the Scottish border and made the occasional visit up to Workington. I would say it is a good two hour drive from Chorley. You come off the M6 at Penrith, but then have to drive west for about 45 minutes. It is a beautifully scenic journey through though, past Bassenthwaite Lake, so I'll be quite happy to drive to this one. Hope I can get the car, as I would imagine trying to get there by bus or train would be a nightmare.

On the work front, I am doing two shifts at ASDA tomorrow and Wednesday, 9am to 5pm, then four nights next week, which will boost the meagre income I am currently getting from my books and the financial services development work. An even bigger positive, is that I have an interview down in Cheltenham on Thursday for the repping job for 'World of Warranty'. I am due to meet Mike Grindle, the MD and Rob Davies, the manager of the Sales team. Chris Ayres, a good friend who I worked with at Yorkshire Building Society for many years, is confident I will get the job, but I don't want to start taking things for granted before I get any confirmation. The pay isn't fantastic, less than half what I was getting at Lloyds Bank, but money isn't everything. At Lloyds I was earning more than I had ever been paid before, but towards the end I was desperate to leave.

The Lloyds situation was strange as I seemed to go from a well regarded, experienced staff member to someone the management didn't like, in the blink of an eye. One of the reasons appeared to be the fact I had written a book in my leisure time, which seemed to irk the management at BM Solutions, even though there was never any doubt that I worked long hours, gave my all and was well regarded by the mortgage brokers and financial advisers that I called on in my role as Business Development Manager.

One Friday night, when I was still working at ten o'clock, I sent out an email to colleagues about a work related matter and put in a "P.S" to say that the first Chapter of my book was now on my website if anyone wanted to check it out over the weekend. On the following Monday morning, one of the managers oversaw the email being read by one of her staff, reported it to the Sales Manager and on the Tuesday, I was hauled into an office by my manager, severely reprimanded and given a documented warning for publicising an external website.

My old bosses at Yorkshire Building Society, on the other hand, where I had left five years earlier, have always been hugely positive about the book and encouraged me to go over to their Head Office to publicise it, but unfortunately, some of the BM Solutions management could not have been more negative. The reaction to the book was just one of many unpleasant aspects of my last eighteen months at BM, and the job became a daily grind as I hated the way I was managed. Sometimes you were treated like you were worth a million dollars and other times like you had soiled your pants, despite not changing the way you worked. If you were being praised, you knew someone else in the team would be getting a hard time, as everything revolved around League tables, targets and bonuses.

League tables have their place but used incorrectly they are just a stick to beat you with. BM Solutions sales managers could not accept that they may actually have thirty sales staff all working hard and all doing an excellent job. If I was one or two of those managers, I would have struggled to sleep at night, because of the negative impact I had on some lovely people. I suspect those involved never lost a wink of sleep. Perhaps if I wasn't a sensitive soul, I could have endured the soul destroying vindictiveness of some of the sales management team, but I would rather change career and endure the financial strain than put up with a job where some of the management saw it as a badge of honour to treat their staff badly.

Once, all the Sales staff turned up to a Sales meeting with an Olympic theme to discover the management were putting them on four different tables based on how the managers felt they were performing. The tables were marked 'Gold', 'Silver', 'Bronze' and 'Dropped The Baton'. Rather than try to motivate the whole sales force, the ones who were struggling in the League tables were regularly belittled.

Ben Hunt-Davis, a Gold Medallist in the Men's Rowing Eight in the Sydney Olympics, was once a motivational speaker at one of our meetings and gave a great talk entitled, 'Will It Make The Boat Go Faster?' about what can be done in sport and in work, to make things turn out better. Ironically, at BM Solutions, there were too many sales managers who wanted to paddle their own canoes rather than work as a team.It was all a real shame as BM Solutions should have been a great company to work for. The products offered and service provided by the underwriters and mortgage processors were excellent, but, in my opinion, it became all about the Sales management staff exerting their power and boosting their own egos rather than trying to empower, facilitate and enable the staff in their team. Walking away from an excellent salary was a tough thing to do, but the positive impact it has had on my family life cannot be measured in monetary terms. Life is too short to be wasting time working for self-serving, unpleasant people when there are so many good people around. Despite the financial struggles that my family have had to deal with since my departure, I have never had a single second that I have wished I was back there. I hope the BM Solutions sales management staff treat their workforce with more respect and dignity than they ever used to, but suspect there are still staff that they make life unnecessarily difficult for.

Thursday 19th September 2013

Just arrived back from my interview in Cheltenham.Both Mike and Rob seemed like really good guys and it appears to be a good company to work for. Rob said he will ring me tomorrow, so keeping my fingers crossed that it will be good news!

Friday 20th September 2013

From 1st October, I will be back working as a full-time employee. Rob Davies rang to say I could start on Tuesday 1st and he would see if he could get my car to me the day before. It's a BMW One Series, so I won't have to take Alison to and from Preston Hospital any more on the days I need the car. I am still going to work my nights at ASDA next week and on the Sunday the week after and will see if they still want me to do the occasional weekend shift after that. I also intend to keep writing. Obviously, I am fairly progressed with our F.A Cup story, but I have an idea for a fictional book I would like to get out in 2014 too. Things will still be tight but hopefully the financial burden will ease over the next few months.

Alison has been incredibly supportive since I went self-employed in February 2012. She really pushed for me to leave BM Solutions, as she saw first hand how miserable the management were making me and the impact it had on our family. We have been married sixteen years now, but I had never had job issues before that, but when things were unpleasant, she was always there to help me through it. Thankfully, there are strong signs now that better times lie ahead and I can hopefully go to the rest of the F.A Cup games without wondering whether I will have enough money in the bank to pay for the tickets and the petrol money. I started this F.A Cup journey more in hope than expectation, but things have shaped up really positively and I am confident that this will be a challenge I can meet, wherever it takes me along the way.

There has been a bit of disappointing news on the eve of the 2nd Qualifying Round of the F.A Cup. Two of the four in our little group of spectators with a 100% record of attendance, after the first three games, cannot come along tomorrow. Jordan Oliver, Alan's daughter, had bought a ticket for the Miles Kane gig at the Manchester Academy tomorrow night, prior to the draw and as she isn't confident of getting back there in time for the gig, she has decided to give this round a miss. The second of our group to withdraw from this game is my Dad. In January this year,my Mum and Dad moved out of the house I grew up in as a child and moved into a bungalow, a mile or so down the road. My Dad has spent the last nine months trying to get it how he wants it, especially the garden. He asked one of his friends, Brian Toole to make a new side gate and he needs my Dad to help him lift and fit it. My Dad says he has put Brian off now for a couple of weeks and the only mutually convenient time they could fit it in, was tomorrow. I guess it was always my plan (and Alan Oliver's) to go to every round, so some of the others will have other commitments. It's a shame though, as it's been great going with my Dad to the games again, so I hope he continues to come to more games than he misses.

Alison isn't working tomorrow, so I have made arrangements to drive up to Workington in our Corsa, picking Alan and his mate, Phil Cooper, up at Buckshaw Parkway train station, just down the road from our house. Phil seems to be enjoying the journey too, so it's a shame he didn't go to the West Didsbury & Chorlton versus Abbey Hey game, as he has been to all rounds since. I asked my sons, Brad and Joel whether they fancied coming, but once again the magic of the F.A Cup has failed to sprinkle its wonders on them and they have opted out.

On the work front, I have done four nights at ASDA this week and have one more to do on Sunday night. It's a long time since I have done a job that involves me getting my hands dirty, so lugging boxes to and from the warehouse and stacking shelves through the night has been an education! I was mainly working with day staff who had volunteered to do some night work to help out during the store's refurbishment, so they were as knackered as me doing nights. They were a good bunch though. Darren, my line manager, was fine about me getting a new job and said he wasn't surprised, but he has agreed for me to stay on, on a seasonal basis, working there weekends, as and when he needs me. The extra money will be useful.

Budweiser F.A Cup 2nd Round Qualifying - Saturday 28th September 2013

Workington v Burscough

Attendance – 381

The weather today has been fantastic, really bright, sunny and warm. The football witnessed wasn't at all bad either with two fairly equal sides giving it a real go to try to earn their club £4500 and just as importantly a place in Monday's draw for the Third Qualifying Round.

I picked Alan and Phil up, as arranged, at 10:30 am. As is seemingly the norm, they arrived early and were waiting by the car park when I arrived. Having met Alan at three matches previously and Phil at two, I knew a bit about them, but it was good to spend a few hours in a car with them, as you obviously get to know a lot more. For starters, I didn't know Phil was a solicitor. He is originally from Bedfordshire, moving up North to study at Hull University, where he met a girl and moved to Manchester with her after his degree. The relationship with his former girlfriend is now long behind him, but his life in the North continues. I will find out his exact age, but I presume he is in his early to mid-30s.

Alan is the chattiest of the three of us and his passion for football knows no bounds. He is a superstitious man and believes he cursed Manchester City to a prolonged spell in the doldrums. Once he stayed away, the good times returned until he went to last year's F.A Cup Final and handed victory to Wigan Athletic in the process. He also says he shifted his bad luck on to Altrincham, as he followed them in the Conference for a season and they ended up being relegated! I might see if I can persuade him to start following Liverpool.

We didn't stop on the way up. It is a fantastic drive through the Lakes to Borough Park, Workington and it looked particularly spectacular on a beautiful early Autumnal day. Each time I go up to the Lakes, I always think we should go up more, but mine and Alison's lives seemed to be dictated to all year round by our kids sporting adventures. Both the boys play football on a Sunday in the winter and in the summer, Brad plays mens cricket on a Saturday and junior cricket during the week and sometimes on a Sunday, but having said all that, we could still go more than we do, given we can get to many parts of the Lakes within an hour's drive.

Phil was a good co-driver and he guided me in to Borough Park with only minor diversions. It only took us just over two hours to get there and we parked right outside the ground, so by quarter to one, we were looking to get in. As it was more than two hours before kick off, the only people there were club officials, so we entered via the players/officials entrance, paying our £12 admission fee to one of the Directors – a lot dearer than West Didsbury but still only about a third of the Premiership prices that are currently beyond me. Thankfully Phil and Alan also donated £20 to the cause for petrol.

The first thing we did once we were in, was do a lap of the ground. Alan had been here once before to watch Stalybridge Celtic, so we were amused to see a Stalybridge Celtic sticker on a turnstile by a corner flag, as Stalybridge had visited again only weeks before.

Borough Park is a former League ground, which has undoubtedly seen better days. There are about 400 seats on the far side of the ground and around 100 on the side that has the dressing rooms and clubhouse. Everywhere else is a mass of terracing which looks tired and strewn around the ground are signs of its more glorious past, such as the base of the old corner floodlights and rusting turnstiles that have been dismantled as they are no longer needed. The capacity is 3100 now, but back in 1958 there were 21000 to watch Workington take on Manchester United in the Third Round of the FA Cup. This famous game (which will forever remain as their record gate unless they are bought out by a Russian billionaire and move to a new ground) took place a month before the Munich air disaster that saw eight of the Manchester

United team lose their lives. Manchester United won the game 3-1 with a hat-trick from Dennis Viollet. Amongst their eleven that day was the legendary Duncan Edwards, a vastly experienced twenty one year old who was to die in Munich. My Dad ranks Duncan Edwards as the greatest player that he ever saw play with John Charles coming second.

Despite its dilapidated surroundings, the playing surface itself looked first class. The six yard boxes in each goal area seem slightly elevated to the rest of the area, especially at the end to the right of the main entrance, but other than that, it was a pitch fit for a footballer of any level. We were confident that the weather and the surface had provided the perfect ingredients for an excellent game and safe in this knowledge, we went inside to the clubhouse bar/snack area, for some lunch.

I've noticed a lot of footballing blogs talk about the quality of the pies, which isn't really my style, I'm more interested in people than pies (but just this once I'll mention the steak & kidney pie at Workington is a lot of crust and not much meat). I asked the girls serving at the canteen what sort of crowd they were expecting and they looked at me blankly, so I asked what crowd they normally had, blank looks again. I suspect they are there to do their own job and are not overly interested in what is happening on the pitch or how many spectators come to watch events unfold. Alan, Phil and I were hoping for around 400, by far our biggest FA Cup gate so far, but unlikely to hold the record for long. The gates had gone up marginally round by round, but were set to more than double today. It transpired later that there were 381, a decent enough gate and certainly a lot more than the Burscough players played in front of most weeks.

As I was tucking into my pie and slurping a bog standard weak footballing cup of tea, Phil was having a pint to ease his Friday night hangover. Alan, like my Dad, is a non-drinker, but his alcohol free life has been forced upon him through ill health. Apparently a few years earlier, he was four stone heavier and his blood pressure was through the roof and lifestyle changes needed to be made to ensure his continued existence. Thankfully, those changes were made and although he is still by no means skinny, he is a long way from fat now too.

With full stomachs and with Phil's brain probably having expanded slightly to aid that hungover feeling, we went in search of programmes and souvenirs. Both myself and Alan want a programme from every round, but Al wants a badge from every club too, so was keen to discover when the container that doubled up as the souvenir shop opened. We found the programme sellers and each bought one at a fairly pricey £2-50. Whilst chatting to those guys, an elderly gentleman with aided black hair and an uneasy walk came over to talk to us.We discovered his name was Brian Rothery and he was one of the Workington officials. He had helped run Workington in the past but returned the previous season after moving back from Lincolnshire and ending his involvement with Goole Town. The programme doesn't indicate he has any senior role at the club, but I think he has a commercial involvement. He kept us engaged for about quarter of an hour telling us several non-league stories about both his clubs.Lively characters like Brian must exist at every level of the football pyramid but when you go to non-League games you tend to find yourself speaking to them a lot more than you would at top flight level. There is definitely more of a feeling of community in the lower tiers.

Brian also mentioned that the souvenir shop didn't tend to open until ten or fifteen minutes before kick off, which suggested that Workington were missing a trick with regards to maximising fan spend. It could well be that they just don't have the staff to open the shop any earlier, but if it opened an hour before kick off, I am sure more money would be spent in there. Workington still managed to get Alan's souvenir money as he dashed in to get a Workington badge. Once Alan had bought it, we walked around to the far side of the pitch to watch the first half from there. The players emerged on to the pitch to the sound of the 'Z' cars theme tune which is also the music played at Everton's Goodison Park, making the place feel like a home from home.

As I mentioned after watching the Accrington v Pompey game, when it comes to football, there is nothing that quite matches watching your own team play. The second best thing though, is to watch a team that you have an allegiance to and it was great to see Burscough starting really positively and looking from the first few minutes that they could provide the first real shock in our FA Cup journey. Darren Brookfield fired a free kick just wide in the first couple of minutes and Burscough continued to press forward dangerously looking to open the scoring.

After twenty minutes though, a self-inflicted disaster struck. Tim Horn, the Burscough goalkeeper is excellent with his feet. He regularly drives his goal kicks from off the floor to twenty yards into the opposition half and deals competently with any balls played back to him. Unfortunately, this competence was a contributory factor in the opening goal. Tim was on the edge of his box and Liam Dodd, Burscough's centre back decided to play the ball back to him. Horn isn't the tallest of keepers, appearing to be under six feet tall and Dodd over hit his back pass from about fifty yards from goal and it sailed towards the Burscough goal at a height about six inches above Tim Horn's head. The keeper now had two choices, try to head it or put his hands up and catch it and risk receiving a red card. Horn opted for a header but although he kicks a ball like an outfield player, he looks as awkward in the air as their forward, Liam Caddick and his mis-timed jump meant he had landed by the time the ball went past his head. Agonisingly, the ball lost momentum after it passed the keeper and hit the ground about eighteen yards out and proceeded towards goal at a leisurely pace. Horn turned round and began an ambitious chase but then realised it was too little too late and watched helplessly as the ball trickled over the line. As a former goalkeeper myself, I think more of the blame should be directed towards Dodd than Horn, but who was to blame was immaterial, what was important was that Workington had taken an undeserved lead against the run of play.

Burscough went straight down the other end and Dodd was unfortunate not to atone for his error when he headed just wide, but Workington had gained a little confidence from their lead, coming into the game more and pressing Burscough quicker when they were in possession. The pressing of the Burscough defence led to another Workington goal. The Burscough left back was robbed of the ball towards the corner flag and the ball was pulled back to Workington forward, Ross Wilson, who smashed a shot into Tim Horn's top left hand corner. It was a brilliant finish but Burscough had been punished for failing to clear their lines. Workington were the better team for the rest of the half, but when the half-time whistle blew, 2-0 seemed a very harsh scoreline as Burscough had had the majority of the game, even though Workington's debutant, American keeper, Alex Wimmer had barely been tested.

Alan, Phil and I nipped back over to join the queue for a hot drink. We universally agreed that Burscough had been the better side and thought an early goal for Burscough would make it very interesting whilst one for Workington would kill it. The own goal was also universally blamed on the centre back, Dodd. The good thing about making an awful mistake in the early rounds of the F.A Cup is that it gets watched by 381 people and no-one else. If Dodd had made that mistake in the final, 80 000 would witness it live at Wembley, hundreds of millions on their televisions and subsequently millions more via the likes of You Tube. Even worse, it would be replayed for ever in subsequent years and he would probably have had to face tabloid headlines about Diddymen and tickling sticks.

The queue for tea was pretty long and service wasn't too spritely so by the time we emerged for the second half, it was just kicking off. We decided to stay on the nearside of the pitch and took up a vantage point right next to the Burscough officials. Some of them remembered Phil and Alan from Victoria Park and once again I was greeted warmly by Rod Cottam. He even offered me a stick of chewing gum, old habits obviously die hard!

Workington started the second half strongly and it is for this reason, I now have to do something in this book that I haven't done before, I have to mention the referee. Referees get a hard time, normally from one eyed, biased fans, who are quick to complain about injustices done to their team, but fail to spot the times that their team are fortunate. Most supporters can remember when a ref failed to give their side an obvious penalty or a linesman adjudged a subsequent goal to be offside, when it was "yards on", but when it's our team that gets that lucky offside or avoids that obvious penalty, we conveniently forget. Referrees have a thankless task. The refs who refereed the previous games in this book must have done very well, as they received no mention at all from me, so achieved the objective of officiating in a way that allowed spectators to focus on the players. Sadly, it must be said that the referee in this match had a stinker of a second half. Like goalkeepers, refs tend to be mentioned more for their errors than for their quiet efficiency. The problem the ref had, was that in the second forty five minutes he failed to give ANY major decisions.

The first major decision was during Workington's early dominance. Paul Williams tripped Conor Tinnion inside the box, for what looked like a certain penalty, but the ref waved played on. Had the penalty been given and converted , the game would have been out of Burscough's reach but this incident seemed to end Workington's purple patch and Burscough edged their way back into the game. Several half-chances came Burscough's way and Rod

Cottam said this was typical of their season so far, dominating possession but not finishing a high enough percentage of the chances they carved up. At long last, in the 72nd minute, Burscough managed to get the goal that their dominance merited. The super fast, super tricky Liam Caddick, who looks like he will score bags of goals at this level (but not in the air), finished clinically after a well worked one-two and 381 spectators looked at their watches to see how long Burscough had to grab an equaliser. With about twenty minutes left (including injury time), there was definitely time to take the tie back to Victoria Park for a Tuesday replay.

The last twenty minutes were incident packed. Initially, a huge penalty claim for handball was turned down by the referee, who failed to spot a hand in a crowded box. Jordan Williams hit the bar when he rifled a ferocious shot that shook the bar for an age and Liam Caddick missed a glorious back post chance when it appeared easier to score. The ref, a young lad who seemed out of his depth, also failed to punish a player from each side when they traded punches in the centre circle. Everyone has bad games and I hope it doesn't dent his confidence too much, but his failure to give anything, whenever there was a moment of controversy, provided one final sting in the tail for Burscough.

Liam Caddick was the most dangerous player on the pitch and as he danced his way speedily into the Workington box once more, he was met by a challenge from Dan Wordsworth that belonged on a DVD about football's hard men. Wordsworth flew in to Caddick with a tackle from side on which carried with it a mixture of determination and venom. He emerged from it with a lot of Liam Caddick and very little of the ball and as Caddick was left in a motionless heap on the penalty box floor, all eyes turned to the ref to watch him pointing towards the penalty spot....except he didn't. He didn't point to the spot, he didn't point to anything, he just waved play on. Burscough players, officials and supporters felt hugely aggrieved but it must be pointed out that if the ref had given the first Workington penalty, the circumstances would have been very different. I am not saying one bad decision deserves another, I am just saying the ref managed to go through the half without pleasing anyone. I hope he learns to be a little braver, as sometimes giving nothing is just as bad as whistling too much.

To add to Burscough manager, Derek Goulding's fury, the ref decided to ignore the three or four minutes of attention that Liam Caddick subsequently received from the physio and blew for full time after only a couple of minutes of injury time. Goulding stormed on to the pitch doing his best Sir Alex impression to question the ref's decisions, but it would not change anything. Burscough had performed admirably but they had lost and their FA Cup dreams were over for another season. Workington were fortunate winners, but if they perform like that again in the next round, they will find things very tough indeed.

Our drive back to Chorley was largely spent discussing the game and debating where we might go to next. Alan would like to go somewhere that he hasn't been before, as he is expecting there won't be many opportunities to do so. Once there are only League clubs left in the competition, there is no chance as he has been to every ground but there are clubs in the Midlands, Yorkshire and the North East still in, where Alan hasn't visited, so we are hoping for an unusual one. I have probably been to about thirty five League grounds and only a small percentage of the non-League grounds, so I could go through every round visiting a ground/stadium that is new to me until we hit the semis at Wembley.

I was hoping to get Alan and Phil back to Buckshaw Parkway in time for the seven o'clock train to Manchester, but I stayed in the slow lane during roadworks in the Lake District and didn't notice the slow lane diverted off the M6 and then, to make matters worse, was blinded by the low sun when looking for the slip road back on and ended up heading North for a junction rather than South! Those two mistakes added about twenty minutes to our journey, so they had to settle for the eight o'clock train instead. If Alan's daughter Jordan had been with us and had been rushing back to get to the Miles Kane concert, she might not have been too impressed but neither Phil nor Alan seemed in a desperate rush to get home so they took it in their stride.

So that's four rounds under our belts already. Today's game was probably the best and most incident packed of our journey so far, but I get the feeling things are only warming up. Roll on Monday and let's see where we are heading to next!

FINAL SCORE : Workington 2 Burscough 1

Scorers :- Workington –Own goal (Dodd), Wilson. Burscough - Caddick.

Our 'Speccies':- Calvin Wade, Alan Oliver, Phil Cooper.

<u>**Monday 30th September 2013**</u>

<u>11:45 a.m</u>

    I should be asleep now, as I worked my final night at ASDA last night, but my mind is pretty active so I can't sleep. My new company car (a BMW One Series) is being delivered this afternoon, which the boys are really excited about and I am looking forward to, as it will make our life so much easier. Almost as importantly, the F.A Cup Third Qualifying Draw is coming up at midday!

<u>12:10 p.m</u>

    Just been on the F.A website and we don't know exactly where we are going for the next round, but know it is in the North East as Workington have been drawn away to the winners of Guisborough Town and (the spectacularly named) Jarrow Roofing Boldon Community Association. The pair drew 3-3 at Jarrow on Saturday, thanks to a 96th minute Guisborough Town equaliser, which aggrieved Jarrow as there were only supposed to be four minutes of injury time! The replay will be on Wednesday at Guisborough. A quick internet check reveals Guisborough is pretty close to Middlesbrough and Jarrow Roofing Boldon is close to Sunderland. Further checks also revealed that whereas Workington are in the 6th Tier down of the footballing pyramid, Guisborough are in the 9th Tier and Jarrow the 10th ! These two are real footballing minnows and it will be a brilliant trip out to either. Both teams entered the F.A Cup at the Extra Preliminary Stage, so have done fantastically well to get this far. I am thinking it must be quite unlikely that Alan has been to both grounds, so have text him to check this out. It will be great for him if we go somewhere new.

<u>1:00 p.m</u>

Alan has just been on the phone, he hasn't been to either ground, so this is a right result for him. He is absolutely delighted. Both of us have a slight preference of going to Jarrow, as they are such a tiny club. There were only 87 there for the game on Saturday, so the financial boost the F.A Cup is providing to them is massive. Guisborough seem to attract crowds between one and two hundred, so it will be a big game for them too but not their biggest ever F.A Cup tie. Back in 1988, Guisborough made it all the way to the F.A Cup First Round Proper and were drawn at home to Bury. They moved the game to Middlesbrough's former home ground, Ayresome Park and the match was televised, but Bury emerged victorious winning 1-0. Guisborough also have some real F.A Vase history too, reaching the final in 1980 and playing Stamford at Wembley in front of 11 500 supporters, where they lost 2-0. The Semi-Final home leg had seen a massive crowd of 3 112 at the KGV. Even though they are three Leagues below Workington, I reckon if Guisborough get through, they will fancy their chances.

Guisborough Town it is! Guisborough beat Jarrow 3-1 tonight to earn a Third Qualifying Round home tie against Workington. I have already let Alan know that I will drive him, Phil and Jordan up there, as well as my Dad. The route guides on the internet seem to indicate it won't be much more than two and a half hours in the car, so I've said to Alan that I will pick them up at Buckshaw Parkway train station again. It would have been an interesting trip to Jarrow Roofing as their ground is in Boldon Colliery, but I'm really excited about heading over to Guisborough now. Having taken in Manchester, West Lancashire and Cumbria so far, it is great to be heading over to the North East.

Yesterday, my new boss, Rob Davies came out with me for the day. He seems like a great bloke and happily for me, he is football mad. He's a big Leicester City supporter, manages a team himself, is the son-in-law of former Leicester centre half, Malcolm Manley and his daughter is an Under 15 at Leicester City girls team and has also trained with the girls England squad. Rob said his father-in-law once marked Joe Royle in a game at Goodison and Joe scored a hat-trick!

I absolutely loved everything about today. The weather has turned in the last two weeks and the glorious sunshine that greeted us in Workington, has now been replaced by damp, drizzly weather, but that could not put a dampener on a terrific day out. This one had everything, a real non-league buzz, plenty of goals, pie and mushy peas, a television appearance and very nearly a six second interview for Alan on Radio5 Live!

Today saw the return of my Dad and Jordan Oliver, after their absence from the last round, but unfortunately Phil Cooper couldn't make this one due to work commitments. I think Alan and I will be hell bent on going to every game, including replays, but Phil, Jordan and my Dad will just come along when they can. I hope my Dad makes it to most of the games from now on, as the best aspect of this journey is spending time with him.

As arranged, I picked Alan and Jordan up at Buckshaw Parkway at 10:30a.m and once again they were waiting for me when I arrived. I decided I would go via the M65 and through Skipton, as we tend to do the M6 and across route when we go to the North East and I fancied a change. It probably wasn't the best idea in the world, as it was a bit trickier for my Dad to navigate and we missed one or two turnings, but still arrived at Guisborough by half one. The football club shares a relatively small car park with the leisure club next door, which is fine for this game, but I remember thinking that if they won a couple more games and drew the likes of Wolverhampton Wanderers in the First Round Proper, it would be bedlam!

As we made our way through the drizzle to the turnstiles, we noticed a camera crew with a young man armed with a microphone doing an introduction to the tie. We asked the guy on the turnstile what was going on and it turns out that FATV choose a game from every round to feature and Guisborough Town v Workington was their choice for the Third Qualifying Round. FATV don't follow a team through each round, they just pick what they feel will be a good game and this one has obviously fallen on their radar. With Guisborough Town in the Ebac Northern League Division One and Workington in the Skrill Conference North (three Leagues higher), perhaps they saw it as a potential giant killing.

The advantage for our little group of spectators of watching a team from the ninth tier of English football is price. Alan, Jordan, my Dad and myself entered the ground for a grand total of £21 (£6 for adults, £3 for OAPs – Alan paid for me and my Dad which I suggested rather than give me petrol money). A very comprehensive programme with bags of information and limited advertising was available for only £1.50.

Alan isn't backwards in coming forwards generally and his quest to raise as much money as possible for 'The Christie' hospital was given a new sales opportunity when the cameraman and presenter from FATV followed us into Guisborough's King George V ground. Alan related the story to them about us having been to everyone round so far (this being the fifth qualifying round including the two preliminaries) and the young bloke presenting thought it was well worth a five minute interview. Four and a half of those minutes were Alan answering questions but one question was directed at me.

"So", the interview said, pushing his fluffy microphone in my direction, "what has been the highlight so far?"

With hindsight, I should have said getting an opportunity to spend Saturday afternoons at the football with my Dad again, but in the spur of the moment, I wasn't thinking clearly. The 45 yard

Burscough own goal flashed into my brain but I didn't want to say that, as it was a 'lowlight' rather than a 'highlight'.

"Meeting me?" Alan said jokily, trying to prompt me out of the blank look that was probably written all over my face.

I then nervously rambled on for thirty seconds about everything being a highlight, mentioning everywhere we've been so far and telling him the winners of each game. I would not like to see my thirty seconds of fame played back, but suspect it will not make it any further than the cutting room floor. After concluding the interview, the FATV presenter told us it would be on the internet on Sunday or Monday, so I shall look forward to watching it, in the hope that I'm right about my part being deleted!

After a brief chat with a couple of friendly programme sellers, we were pointed in the direction of the social club. Guisborough Town were shrewdly milking the opportunity to make money, so had opened the bar from midday, so when we walked in there, it was chockablock. About two hundred fans of both clubs were in there, enjoying a friendly pie and pint, as Guisborough had brought in outside caterers to provide pie and mushy peas for £3. With driving, I avoided the pint, but enjoyed the pie and peas. Whilst eating, Alan spotted that Guisborough had given his fundraising campaign a mention in the programme and had included thecasualhopper.co.uk web address. With a bit of luck, it may encourage one or two kindhearted souls to contribute.

Half an hour before kick off, we ventured around to the far side of the ground. The KGV is a really pleasant looking ground, surrounded by large conifers. There is a real family feel to the place and it was encouraging to see a dozen young lads, none older than about nine, playing football behind one of the goals.

We took up a vantage point by the halfway line, but under cover to protect us from the drizzle that was continuing to fall. The pitch looked in good condition, but not surprisingly a little heavy, given the amount of rain that had fallen in the previous week. This, I deduced, may play into Workington's hands, as their players were likely to have superior levels of fitness, with playing at a higher level. About ten yards from us, there was a cluster of Workington fans, who seemed keen to make their presence felt. One of them placed his Workington flag over the Guisborough Town flag at the back of the stand, which we felt was a little intimidatory, but thankfully most of their behaviour was good natured. These Workington supporters also provided us with our very first chants of this year's F.A Cup! Not sure where they had all been when Workington had been at home, but perhaps they were scattered around the ground and their unification had got them all singing.

As expected, when the game kicked off, Guisborough Town really went at Workington and dominated the early exchanges. Guisborough have two lively young forwards, Mikey Roberts and Danny Johnson, who had already scored 31 goals between them in the 17 games Guisborough Town had previously played this season and it was no surprise when they took the lead. A short corner routine saw a Michael Roberts header parried away by Workington's keeper, Alex Wimmer, but Tommy Marron followed up on the far post and despatched the ball neatly into the back of the net from close range.

Workington reacted well to going behind and began to dominate possession and push Guisborough, nicknamed The Priorymen, deep into their own half. A massive turning point in the game, though, was when Guisborough managed a rare break away and Lewis Wood struck a shot from over twenty yards that rattled Workington's crossbar. Perhaps at 2-0, Guisborough could have clung on for an hour, but at 1-0, Workington sensed they were going to outclass their opposition and looked especially dangerous from set pieces. The Guisborough Town keeper, Ben Escritt looked an excellent shot stopper, but was hesistant on set pieces and seemed rooted on his line after Workington forced corner after corner. The wind and rain probably did nothing to aid Escritt's confidence, but Workington picked up on the fact that he wasn't coming to collect anything and every corner was swung in closer and closer to goal. On the forty minute mark, Workington managed to convert their twelfth corner of the half, with Dan Wordsworth heading home from about four yards out. The half finished level at 1-1, but the chances of an upset seemed to be fading as the half went on. Unless Guisborough could find fourteen cans of Popeye's spinach in their dressing room at half-time, we concluded it was only going to get harder for them in the second half.

To no great surprise, the second half started as the first half had finished with Workington showing there was a reason why they were three Leagues higher. They were winning the midfield battle, winning everything in the air and Ben Escritt, the Guisborough keeper had to make a series of saves at the start of the half to keep his side in the game. Joe Jackson had seen several of his efforts saved by Escritt, but ten minutes into the second half, Escritt was unable to hold yet another Jackson effort and Anthony Wright followed up to give Workington a deserved lead. The Guisborough players looked shattered as they had worked valiantly to keep the match competitive, but the need to push forward in search of an equaliser, was, in all likelihood, going to provide space for Workington to exploit.

The fact that Joe Jackson had been presented with countless chances, triggered off a conversation between Alan and myself about music, as I am a big fan of Joe Jackson's namesake, the 1980's pop star who had had numerous Top10 hits including, 'Stepping Out', 'It's Different For Girls' and 'Is She Really Going Out With Him?' I had been to see him at

Manchester Apollo in 1990, but during that same year I missed out on seeing a concert that would have made millions of people (including Alan) incredibly envious.

Back in 1990, Manchester University had just opened a new venue called the Academy that attracted a lot of well known and rising musical stars. One evening, I was complaining to my student friends about the lack of decent bands at the Poly compared to the University. "Look at the rubbish we have on at the Poly," I moaned, "I mean look at the crap that are on this weekend, a bloke called Tad and a band called Nirvana! Who the hell are Nirvana?" Within twelve months, the album Nevermind was selling in its millions and the single 'Smells Like Teen Spirit' had become a worldwide phenomenon. Not my best bit of talent spotting that!

Halfway through the second half, it was all over with Jackson once again the provider. He cut in from the left wing, then passed to Danny Forrest who slotted the ball confidently into Escritt's far corner. This was the 15th goal we have seen on the F.A Cup trail, but before the end the 16th followed and it was probably the best. Scott Allison from the right back position sprayed a diagonal long ball, Beckham-like, in to the path of Conor Tinnion, who was surging forward at speed. Tinnion took the ball in his stride before lashing the ball past a weary Escritt and into the back of the net. The second half had been dominated by Workington, and their fans, who had endured a tough season so far, were in raptures.

With the result a formality, we headed towards the exit, with the intention of making a dash for the car when the final whistle blew. As we headed behind Alex Wimmer's Workington goal, Guisborough had a rare attack that was cleared for a corner. The ball fell a yard from me and I bowled it out to the corner flag. I am guessing this will be my one and only touch of the ball in this F.A Cup campaign!

Seconds later, the ref (who along with his assistants had performed admirably) blew for full time and ended a thoroughly enjoyable trip to Guisborough. Workington were deserved winners this time and would receive £7500 from the F.A for this victory, taking their F.A Cup prize money to £12 000. There would be very few Tier 9 sides left in the draw for the next round and although Guisborough Town gave their all, whoever Workington face in the next round will be an entirely different proposition.

On the journey home, we decided to go West from Scotch Corner and head down through the Lakes, which turned out to be a lot quicker. We had Radio5 Live on and Alan wanted to spread the word about his fundraising to the masses of supporters heading home from games all over the country. He managed to get through to a 'Five Live' researcher straight away and explained to him about his F.A Cup charity fundraising journey. The researcher said he would get Alan on air and would ring him back. Ten minutes before '606' finished, Alan's phone rang saying he could have six seconds on air, before putting him on hold.

"I think he said I could have six seconds," Alan said sounding confused.

"You'll have misheard him," I said, trying to reassure him, "he must have said sixty seconds, Al, six seconds is barely long enough to say hello."

A minute later a caller was introduced and rushed out a sentence before being cut off.

"Now we'll go to Line Two, hello Line Two...." said the Five Live presenter.

Silence. Six seconds of silence.

"Looks like we've lost Line Two, that would have been Alan on the M6," said the presenter.

Alan was gutted! His six seconds of fame had been stolen from him!

"Nobody bloody told me I was Line Two!" poor old Alan complained.

FINAL SCORE : Guisborough Town 1 Workington 4

Scorers :- Guisborough – Marron.

     Workington – Wordsworth, Wright, Forrest, Tinnion .

Our 'Speccies':- Calvin Wade, Alan Oliver, Richard Wade, Jordan Oliver

10:00a.m

One of the most exciting things about this F.A Cup journey is not knowing where you are heading next. Today, for the first time ever, the F.A Cup draw is being made live on a commercial radio station, TalkSport. With it being a sports radio station, I listen to TalkSport a lot and enjoy the Colin Murray show that the draw is being made during. Colin is a Northern Irish Liverpudlian, who has found his way on to TalkSport after a longish spell with BBC Radio and Television, during which time he presented Match of The Day Two. It is a relatively new show, sounds fresh and often gives me something to chuckle about as I am driving around.

The Fourth Qualifying Round draw is still regional, so once again we can avoid any trips to the South coast. This is the last round the draw is split North and South though, so after this one, we could be heading anywhere in the country. This is the round that the Skrill Conference Premier sides enter the draw, so the likes of Luton, Wrexham and Cambridge United could be a plum draw for a tiny club. Winners in the Fourth Qualifying round receive another £12 500 from the FA, but perhaps more importantly, they get a chance to play against the 2nd and 1st Division sides in the First Round Proper. Teams like Portsmouth, Sheffield United and Wolverhampton Wanderers enter at that stage and that is when the TV companies really take notice of the FA Cup and start televising games. If your team are lucky enough to be selected for a televised game in the First Round Proper, you receive a whopping £67 500 from the FA. This may not be a huge amount to Wolves but to a tiny non-League club, it could keep your club running for a season. To say there is plenty to play for is an understatement.

We are heading back to Workington! Workington were ball '28' out of '28' in the Northern draw (which was done first) and were drawn to play against Stourbridge who are flying high in the Calor League Premier. As far as I am aware, the Calor League Premier is the Southern equivalent of the Evo-Stik Premier, the League that Chorley and Skelmersdale United are in. This means Stourbridge are only one league below Workington and given they beat Curzon Ashton, a team flying high in Burscough's league, 3-0 on Saturday, I am going to stick my neck out and say we will be following Stourbridge into the first round.

Not sure whether I am pleased or disappointed with the draw. Having already been to Workington, from a personal perspective, I would have preferred a trip to somewhere new, so if it had been at Stourbridge that would have been ideal, but at least it gives my Dad and Jordan Oliver a chance to go to the ground that they missed out on.

An eight minute film of the Guisborough Town v Workington game has been posted on FATV. At the outset, when the presenter is doing his introduction, my Dad and I can be seen entering the turnstile and nosing back at the camera as if we are smuggling in a flare! Thankfully, my part of our subsequent interview didn't make the final cut (as expected) but Alan got his fifteen seconds of fame (more than the six Radio 5Live would have given him!), as they showed a brief part of his section with Jordan, my Dad and myself standing by his side. This was the most important section of the interview anyway, as it mentioned the fundraising for 'The Christie'. Hope it swells the pot as it seems to have gone a little quiet on that score recently.

Our phone doesn't ring very often at 7a.m and when it does, there is a general sense of foreboding. People don't tend to ring at 7a.m with good news, so as I headed to answer the phone this morning, bleary eyed, I worried about whose voice would greet me. The voice I heard and the greeting I heard weren't ideal.

"Don't panic, I'm just ringing to tell you that I am taking your Dad to the hospital, as he is having pains in his chest," were the first words out of my Mum's mouth.

My Dad doesn't have the best heart. He has angina, atrial flutter, atrial fibrillation and an enlarged aorta. Several years ago he had a stent put in and also had an operation to try to correct the atrial flutter, but it didn't seem to have worked. If he drank and smoked, he would probably not have reached 69 years old, but as I have previously mentioned, he takes great care with his diet and as a former competitive sportsman, he has always been in good physical condition. News of him being in poor health always scares me, not necessarily because I think he is going to drop down dead that minute, but because it is a reminder that every story has an end and we can never be quite sure how soon that end will come. My Mum and Dad have been there through every second of my existence and I cling to the hope that they will continue to be there for some time yet.

I speak to my Mum for a few minutes. She says my Dad has had a tightening across his chest for a number of days and as it hasn't gone, he thinks he should go over to Southport hospital to get it checked out. My Mum puts my Dad on the phone to me and he sounds calm, as always, but a little concerned that the pain remains. He was due to be playing Senior Golf today and didn't like the idea of taking a bad turn a couple of miles down the course, so thought he had best get himself checked out. He said on a scale of pain from one to ten, it is probably only a four, but sensibly doesn't want to take any chances.

My sister, Lisa, who still lives within a couple of miles of my Mum and Dad, has gone down to London, with her daughter, Olivia, and they don't want to worry her by letting her know, in case she rushes back, but just want me to be aware in case they need me to drive across at lunchtime to let the dog out. Having spoken to my Dad, I was still a little worried, but certainly more re-assured. I went to work as usual, but said to my Mum to phone me if she needed me.

This afternoon, I spoke to my Mum after she returned from the hospital leaving my Dad there for tests to be carried out. She said the initial diagnosis is that he may have unstable angina, but are going to keep him on a monitor and run some tests. As Dad is going to have to stay in overnight, I said to my Mum that I would drive over to their house and pick her up and take her in for visiting hour. My Mum isn't the most confident driver, so it will make it easier for her than me meeting her at the hospital.

We've been in to see him this evening and I must say on previous occasions I've visited him in hospital, he has looked a lot worse. He has a lot of colour in his face and said that a nurse mentioned it may just be a chest infection, so they have put him on antibiotics for that. With a bit of luck, he will be out of hospital tomorrow, with a chest infection being diagnosed and will be fit and well enough to come to Workington v Stourbridge with us on Saturday.

There are a million and one reasons why I would hate anything to happen to my Mum or Dad, the primary reasons being that I love them and want them to live long healthy lives, but another reason currently is that I want them to know I am back on my feet financially and everything is going well for me. Over the last three years, since the hassle began whilst I was at the bank, I have sometimes been stressed and irritated when I have spoken to them. My Mum has bore the brunt of this rather than my Dad and although things have improved greatly by starting the job repping, I would like to go through a period of stability with them knowing everything has been straightened out and I am back on an even keel. This target is certainly a step nearer now I have a steady job and I just need to work hard at it over the next few months and ensure they want to keep me on when my probationary period finishes.

After visiting time finished, I gave my Mum a lift home to Aughton, went in and had a coffee with her and then drove back to Chorley.Hopefully the news tomorrow will be positive and this was just a false alarm.

Good news! My Dad was discharged from hospital today. All the tests on his heart revealed there wasn't a new, previously undiagnosed problem and the current chest pains were very likely to be down to a chest infection. My Dad said the pain has eased further already with the antibiotics and he is hopeful that he will be coming with us to the game on Saturday.

We will definitely be having a new spectator with us on Saturday as Alison is working nights from Thursday to Sunday, so I will be bringing my youngest son, Joel, to the match. I don't think a day has gone by in the last five years when Joel and his older brother, Brad, have not found something to argue about, so if I left them alone in the house whilst Alison was sleeping, no doubt all hell would break loose and she would not get much sleep. Brad is capable of being quiet if I left him on his own, but Joel isn't, so he has to come along. He has already asked if he can bring a friend with him, which I have said is great, so he is going to ask a lad called Alex Santos to come.

On the basis that I will be driving my Dad (hopefully), Joel and a friend to Workington, I have had to get in touch with Alan and tell him that I can't give him a lift to this round and we will have to meet him there. Alan is fine about that and actually sounded pleased that we were adding a couple of extra spectators to the attendance. I explained to him that my Dad had been in hospital overnight and said he could sympathise as his Mum and Dad are in their late seventies now and are pretty frail, especially his Dad, who his Mum, Hilda, works very hard to look after. Alan said Phil Cooper is up for going back to Workington and Jordan is wanting to go too, so the three of them will get the train there and we will meet them in the bar.

If Workington surprise me and win on Saturday, I am hoping they are drawn away next round. We went to West Didsbury twice, after Saturday will have been to Workington twice and as long as we can get hold of the tickets, we will be going to Wembley twice, but I hope we don't visit any ground more than twice on the journey, as it's more exciting checking new places out. Having said that, we were warmly welcomed at Workington in September and I am sure we will be again on Saturday. The drive through to the ground is fantastic too, so there are definitely worse places that we may have to re-visit.

We have a few new spectators joining our little gang for the trip to the Workington-Stourbridge game tomorrow and they will add a bit of European flair to the experience. Alex, Joel's mate from school is coming with us, but earlier this evening, I had a phone call from his Portugese father, asking if he could come along too.

I've only met Alex once as him and Joel have just started at Parklands Secondary school last month, but he seems a livewire and a cheerful, outgoing child, so I am keeping my fingers crossed that his Dad is good company too. We are going to be with them for most of the day, so it won't be much fun if he isn't a decent bloke, but it adds a different dimension to the trip. I have said I will pick Alex and his Dad up from their home in Chorley at 10a.m and then we are coming back to our house to meet up with my Dad, who is leaving his car here. My Dad says his chest pains are still there, but are fading by the day, so he feels up to going.

I decided to quiz Joel a little about Alex's Dad,

"What's Alex's Dad like Joel?"

"He's nice, you'll like him."

"Is he about my age?"

Joel looked me up and down.

"How old are you again?"

"Forty two."

"Well, Alex has an older brother, so his Dad is probably about your age, but he looks much younger than you and he is a LOT cooler than you, too!"

So tomorrow Joel is heading to Workington with his mate's cool, Portugese Dad and his own very uncool one! I didn't take offence, I am not cool now, never have been and certainly never will be! The word 'cool' wasn't designed for me or for that matter, my Dad, but my two boys are both considered fairly cool. They must get it from their Mum.

I had a text off Alan this week to say that him, Jordan and Phil are getting a train to Workington from Manchester at half past six in the morning. They go up to Carlisle and then back down to Workington, arriving there at 9:25 a.m ! There were later trains, but they are saving thirty quid each by leaving that early.I've no idea what they are going to do for the five and a half hours between then and kick off, but I am sure they will keep themselves busy. Having met Alan a few times now, I know he isn't likely to sit around and do nothing. He is one of life's 'doers'. Pity there aren't more people in the world like him.

Today has been another excellent day at the football. Joel and I headed over to pick Alex

and Santos up at ten o'clock and to be fair to Joel, Santos is a lot cooler than me! He is a

personal trainer at the local David Lloyd's gym, so is in a lot better shape than me, wears modern

clothes and has his long, black hair in a bandana. I am sixteen stone, wear any jeans I can slip my

bulging waist into and any top that hides my moobs is fine with me. Alex is a very polite,

friendly eleven year old who is currently training with the Academy at Blackpool and his Dad is

a knowledgeable football fan, particularly at Champions League level and had been to

Manchester United against Real Sociedad in midweek. Santos predicts United will qualify from

their Group then get knocked out at the first knockout stage. He may well be right. I think the

English clubs are still some way short of the top German and Spanish sides. United themselves

are a long way short of their very best sides in the era that Giggs, Cantona, Scholes and

Kanchelskis were in their prime.

Having picked Alex and Santos up, we headed back to my house to meet my Dad. He

arrived soon after us, so we all jumped in my car and headed up to Workington. It was strange

going up there a second time on the F.A Cup trail with a completely different car load of people

than on my first trip there four weeks earlier.

Last time, when I travelled up with Alan and Phil, we just went directly to the ground, but

a journey of over two hours is virtually impossible with two eleven year old boys in the back of

the car and I don't think we had gone more than ten miles before Joel started asking when we

would be stopping for something to eat. I managed to keep going up the M6 to Penrith without stopping, but as soon as we came off the motorway, I said I would look for a place to eat and when we spotted a Little Chef, within a mile or two of the motorway, we all agreed it would be a good place to have lunch. There are not many Little Chef's left these days, after the company went into administration and the three that I remember most are all closed down.

My three favourite Little Chefs all have a different sentimental reason for a place in my memory banks. The first was between Ormskirk and Southport. I always had my childhood birthday parties at Burscough or Skelmersdale Sports Centres playing 5 a side football and afterwards my Dad and a volunteer extra driver would take all ten lads to the Little Chef on the road to Southport. Back then there wasn't the same emphasis on child safety in cars and I can recall cramming six or seven kids in a car on many occasions for football matches. I even seem to remember once the whole cub football team crammed into 'Arkcla' Peter Lloyd's car. For parties, there must have only been five kids in each car, which was a luxury. I remember all ten boys making sure we had a clean plate, as if you did, the waiter or waitress would give you a free lollipop.

The second Little Chef I remember was near Penwortham, Preston. Every year, in the late 1970s, my Mum and Dad would take my sister, Lisa and me on our annual pilgrimage to the Blackpool lights. Back in the 1970s, the lights were much more of a novelty to children than they are now and we used to count the days down to our trip. On the way there, we would always stop at the Little Chef in Penwortham. I remember one year, the staff made a mess of the bill and it cost my Dad £3-60 to feed the four of us!

The third Little Chef I remember fondly is a much more recent memory. From the mid-90s until about four years ago when the credit crunch kicked me in the wallet, several of my friends and I would go to the Cheltenham Festival of horse racing in March. We would head down at the crack of dawn on the Tuesday morning, like a bunch of excited children at Christmas, then come off the M5 at Junction 9, taking the back route towards Bishop's Cleeve (where my good friends Andrew & Sarah Moss live) and Prestbury Park. Within half a mile of the M5 junction, there is a Little Chef. All the lads would pile out the car, nip into the petrol station next door to buy a Racing Post and then settle down to a large English breakfast and a cup of tea. Every Cheltenham Tuesday we would dream of being millionaires, but more often than not we would return home with empty pockets but great memories. Sadly, that Cheltenham Little Chef, as well as the Preston one and the Ormskirk one are also now merely memories.

My Dad must have fond memories of the Little Chef too, as all three restaurant experiences I have just related, have involved my Dad being there with me. He wasn't an annual Cheltenham racegoer, but did come down a couple of times and really enjoyed the day out. As he settled down at the table in Penrith, he leaned back in his chair and contentedly said, "This is the life!"

I smiled. My Dad isn't known for over enthusing. If he goes to see a film, he will often describe it as a "B" Movie (in reference to the old days at the cinema when a second rate film was shown before the main event, I only experienced that once, when Tarka The Otter was shown before Digby, The Biggest Dog In The World). If he goes to see a show at the West End or eats at a new restaurant, he often just describes it as 'alright', so the 'This Is The Life!' comment was a real rarity and although it was slightly tongue in cheek, I knew deep down he meant it.

As a child from the middle of post-war Liverpool, my Dad could only have dreamed of eating out in a restaurant, even if it was just a Little Chef. My Dad was one of nine children, four boys and five girls and until his father died, when my Dad was eight, there were eleven of them sharing two bedrooms. My Dad said at one stage he shared a bed with his three brothers, but prior to that, him and his brother, James, would just sleep on the floor besides his Mum and Dad's bed. They had no hot water, no electricity and from 1952 onwards, no father, but he still looks back on the times he lived on the 'landings' in Brasenose Road, as happy times. They were happy times mixed with tragedy though, as three years after his Dad died, my Dad's brother John drowned in the canal when he was only seven.

My Dad's Dad was only forty two when he died. Henry Wade was a docker, a hard man and a drinker. When the film version of Frank McCourt's book, Angela's Ashes came out, telling the story of his impoverished upbringing, my Dad always used to say 'that wasn't much different to growing up on the landings in Liverpool'. He said as well as the two bedrooms, they just had a living area and an eight feet by eight feet multi-purpose room which housed the coal bunker, a toilet, a cold water tap and a cooking area. You can picture the chaos in there when his mother was trying to get food ready to feed eleven mouths.

The circumstances of my grandfather's death are unclear although his death certificate stated that he died of meningitis. He had had a series of operations on his back which my Dad has been told was because his father had been hit by a tank as he was helping unload it from a ship during the Second World War. Two different unrelated people told my Dad that his father was known as being one of very few dockers to be given an American pension. My Grandma always told my Dad that this story about the pension was not true, but my Dad says perhaps his father just didn't reveal this additional money to his Mum, as just like in Angela's Ashes, my grandfather would enjoy nothing more than spending any additional monies at the pub. Perhaps it was those childhood days that my Dad was thinking back to when he made his comment or maybe he was just thinking back to Monday night in hospital, but his look of satisfaction in that

Little Chef was like the look of the prisoners having a cold beer on the roof of Shawshank prison.

We left the Little Chef with a couple of free lollipops and continued on towards Workington. Alex had tried valiantly to leave his mobile phone on the table, but Santos grabbed it and waited to see how long Alex would take to realise he had left it behind. Give him his due, we hadn't left the car park before Alex realised it was missing, although I think this was largely down to him wanting to play a game on it, as soon as we were on the go again!

Having been to Workington's Borough Park only four weeks earlier, we found the ground easily this time. We arrived at about two o'clock and there were plenty of cars outside already, hinting at a decent gate. I was hoping for 600-800 so the official attendance of 519 was a little disappointing.

One of the 519 that attended the game was another football fan and blogger, Nigel Farnworth, who like ourselves, was hoping to go to every Round. His blog thegiantkillingadventure.blogspot.co.uk is absolutely first class and Nigel presents a very in depth analysis to each game. Being a true groundhopper, Alan had pointed out on the phone that Nigel had missed a replay, but he has been to every round. Knowing he would be going to all the same games as us from now on in, I followed Nigel on Twitter but as yet he has not followed back. He has replied to every Tweet I have ever sent him though. Funnily enough, Nigel is from Chorley, but now lives in Preston. He wanted to start at the ground nearest to the current holders, Wigan Athletic, so began at St Helens Town (co-incidentally I once played there when Burscough beat St Helens Town 5-0). The previous round had introduced him to Stourbridge and he had been down there to see them beat Curzon Ashton 3-0. Nigel seems to want to do his own thing rather than join up with fellow 'every rounders', which is fine, so we didn't arrange to meet up with him. It will be interesting to read his perspective on each game though.

On arrival, Santos went over to the Tesco supermarket across the roundabout from Borough Park whilst Alex, Joel, my Dad and I went straight in. Last time when I had been to see Workington against Burscough, it had been a glorious day, but this time the wind was picking up and the rain was starting to fall heavily. As an eleven year old, a bit of rain isn't too much of a hazard, so Joel and Alex went to stand behind the goal to collect stray balls for the Workington team, who were shooting in, whilst my Dad and I headed to the bar to meet up with Alan, Jordan and Phil.

My previous observation that Alan seems to like to be early for everything seems to have been spot on. They were in the ground early and had taken up seats near the bar entrance so they wouldn't miss us coming in. Jordan revealed that her Dad had dragged her out of bed at quarter to four, so she would be ready in plenty of time for the train! My Dad sat down with them whilst I kept nipping outside to keep an eye on Joel and Alex, whilst also waiting for Santos to return from Tesco, so I could point out where we were sitting. My Dad was enjoying some banter with Alan, Phil and Jordan about the trip to Guisborough. They all seemed to be reminiscing like old friends, so it is strange to think before mid-August, we didn't know each other.

Santos soon returned with a Tesco bag containing a variety of drinks. Joel and Alex had beaten him to us though and were slurping their way through two J2Os by the time Santos came into the bar. I introduced Santos to Alan, Phil and Jordan and being a lover of football, got on well with them straight away. Alan was pleased that we had added a European wing to our supporters group! Santos and his wife had moved over to the UK when they were in their early twenties, when his wife was pregnant with their first son.

Alan related the tale to Santos, my Dad and me about what they had been up to since arriving at Workington station at twenty five past nine. They had initially gone in search of a traditional cafe (if you met Alan or even if you checked out his photos on his blog, you would immediately appreciate he is not a Latte and croissant type of bloke) and stumbled across the headquarters of the Cumbrian FA. After a quick stop for a photo outside there, they found a cafe called Katies where they had full English breakfasts all round, before Phil requested that they nipped in to a pub so he could have a quick pint to tackle his hangover. Phil's Saturday morning hangovers are becoming part of the routine and I think he needs to plan his weekends better, so his hangovers are on the Sunday! They turned their noses up at a Wetherspoons, deeming it 'not a proper pub' and found themselves in the Railway Working Mens Club near the rugby club. They played a few games of pool and ran into a bloke who was mates with 'The Smid' , another groundhopper who founded an association called the '100 Grounds Football Club' which Alan is member number 187! After a couple of pints, Phil was feeling better, so they said their goodbyes, received some money for the Christies appeal from kindhearted locals and headed to Borough Park.

Ten minutes before kick off, we headed to the seats at the far side of the ground. As we walked around, the rain had become stronger and the wind was really gusty now, blowing straight into the face of the Stourbridge keeper. The sides stayed where they were after the toss up and I knew the first half would be crucial because if Stourbridge could get to half-time level, the likelihood would be that they would end up winning, with the wind on their backs in the second half. As we took our seats in the stand, I told Phil that I fully expected a Stourbridge win. Phil agreed predicting a 3-1 scoreline.

The Workington fans were in welcoming mood, initially presuming we were Stourbridge fans but still keen to have a chat when they heard we were on the F.A Cup trail. As we had entered the ground, I had been chatting to one middle aged gentleman who told me that Darren Edmondson, the Workington manager, was starting to get a bit of stick from disgruntled, perplexed fans. After a good performance to win convincingly at Guisborough, they had managed to take a point in the Skrill Conference North off top of the table, Hednesford, drawing 2-2 at home last week, but then Edmondson had made wholesale changes to the side for the midweek trip to Harrogate and Workington had ended up getting trounced 3-0. Another interesting fact I gleaned from that conversation was that the Workington player/Assistant Manager, Gavin Skelton, was the brother of former Blue Peter presenter, Helen Skelton. Helen has done great work for Sports Relief, kayaking more than 2000 miles along the Amazon river in 2010 and completing a five hundred mile trek to the South Pole last year. Workington could probably do with utilising her as a motivational speaker.

Gavin Skelton, himself, managed to bag himself a minor celebrity status back in 2006 when he played for Gretna. For the first time in their history, Gretna made it all the way to the Scottish Cup Final and performed magnificently at Hampden, drawing 1-1 with Heart of Midlothian. The game was eventually decided by penalties and who missed the decisive spot kick for Gretna? Gavin Skelton. He went on to play for Kilmarnock, Hamilton and Barrow, before joining Workington.

In the stand at Workington, there was an elderly gentleman sitting alone in the row in front of us and he struck up a conversation with us. He had an old wooden rattle with him, that used to be ten a penny back in the 1950s but had generally died out of supporters armoury. He had a Southern accent but Workingon must have become his adopted team, as it was obvious from our conversation that he had attended every home game this season and many previous seasons too. He was a man of trivia and riddles. When commenting on the weather, he said, "Locals say, if you can't see Skiddaw from Workington, it means it is going to rain soon and if you can see Skiddaw from Workington, that also means it is going to rain soon! It is always going to rain soon in Workington!"

Not all the old man's trivia was jovial though. He pointed out the new Northside Bridge that we had come across to get to Borough Park from the town centre. This bridge, he explained, had been built to replace the previous Northside Bridge that had collapsed during the floods of 2009, tragically killing policeman, Bill Barker. PC Barker was directing motorists off the bridge when the force of the floodwater caused it to collapse, sweeping him in to the River Derwent. He was 44 years old, had been a policeman for twenty five years, was happily married and the father of four children.

As the players came out on to the pitch he fired a couple of quiz questions at us. The first one was a sporting one:-

"Which footballer has played in the Premiership, managed in the Premiership, played for England and played against England?"

None of us knew, but frustratingly it turned out to be ex-Everton player, Dave Watson, who took over as caretaker manager of Everton after Joe Royle's resignation and also played against England for a Hong Kong Select XI in a pre-tournament warm-up game, prior to Euro '96.

The second one was standard trivia:-

"Can any of you speak for a minute, without hesitating, without repeating a single word and without saying a single word with the letter 'A' in?"

We all agreed that we couldn't.

"I can," said the old Workington supporter, "One, two, three, four, five....fifty eight, fifty nine, sixty!"

Once the game kicked off, we were all immediately impressed by Stourbridge. Workington started in a lively fashion but the Stourbridge centre backs, in particular their number three, Will Richards, seemed to be dealing with high balls exceptionally well. Stourbridge also had two lively forwards, Ryan Rowe and Luke Benbow who were causing problems for the Workington defence. It came as no surprise when Stourbridge took the lead after ten minutes, with Jamie Oliver heading home after a right wing corner. Alan immediately started thinking of headlines for his blog after a goal by the man who shared his surname. 'Keeping it in the family, as Jamie Oliver cooks up a winner' was what he came up with should the score remain 1-0. Chances continued at both ends though, which hinted that a one goal game was very unlikely.

Just before half-time there was a controversial incident that completely changed the shape of the game. On our F.A Cup journey, all the referees seem to have gone under the radar, except at Borough Park, Workington. Dan Wordsworth, the Workington defender lunged into a tackle just outside his own box in an attempt to tackle the busy Luke Benbow. It was a one footed tackle that perhaps connected with part of the ball, as well as the leg of Benbow, but the Stourbridge players took offence to the ferocity of the tackle and a melee ensued as Benbow nursed his leg. Twenty years ago, it would definitely not have been deemed anything more than a yellow card offence, but the referee deemed it reckless and brandished the red card at Wordsworth. Workington had battled hard but had already looked second best with the wind in their favour and having eleven of their men on the pitch, so playing against the wind second half with only ten men almost certainly condemned them to defeat.

When the half-time whistle blew, the sending off was the main talking point. We all agreed it was harsh, but Alan felt it was belated justice for Workington's fortunate refereeing decisions against Burscough two rounds earlier. All of us felt a little disappointed though, as Stourbridge had been the better side anyway and we felt the second half could become a procession.

To be fair, Workington came out for the second half with the wind blowing even fiercer than it had done in the first half and the rain coming down much harder, but they gave it a real go. The first fifteen minutes of the second half were relatively even and on the hour mark, David Lynch put a ball through to Joe Jackson, who advanced menacingly on goal. Jackson probably hesitated a fraction too long though and Stourbridge keeper, Dean Coleman raced off his line and smothered the ball before Jackson could shoot on goal.

This turned out to be a costly opportunity wasted, as for the next twenty minutes Stourbridge totally dominated. Luke Benbow is an interesting character, as when the ball is nowhere near him, his body language indicates that he would rather be anywhere else in the world than on a football pitch, but when the ball nears him, he suddenly comes to life and is fast, energetic and dangerous. He terrorised the Workington defence but spent half the time looking like he was desperate to be taken off. Benbow had been the victim of some tough tackles though, including the one that earned Wordsworth a sending off, so perhaps he deserves a lot of credit for playing on beyond the pain barrier.

Two minutes after Jackson's missed chance, Stourbridge scored a second. It was another headed goal, this time from the mightily impressive Will Richards. With twelve minutes left, Benbow was rewarded for not being substituted as he latched on to a through ball, rounded Workington's American keeper, Wimmer and stroked the ball into an empty net to make it three-nil. A large portion of the travelling Stourbridge support had gathered on the uncovered terrace behind the goal and they were delirious as this wrapped things up and would ensure Stourbridge would be in the hat for the First Round draw for the third time in five years. A victory would also earn them £12 500 from the FA and take their total earnings from the competition so far to a healthy £27 500. A lucrative draw in the First Round could even earn them £67 500 if it is televised live on BT Sport or ITV.

Workington's ten men soldiered on. We had watched them for three games and they had always been determined if sometimes lacking a touch of real class. With eighty six minutes on the clock, Workington scored a consolation goal that they thoroughly deserved when Phil McLuckie finished brilliantly with a rising shot from a Ross Wilson cross.

Stourbridge spurned one or two further half chances before the final whistle but when ref David Richardson blew for full-time there was no doubting Stourbridge had been comfortable and deserved winners. They looked a stronger side than Workington and I imagine they would probably have triumphed even without the sending off. Workington were left to concentrate on moving up the table in the Skrill Conference North whilst the Stourbridge players acknowledged their jubilant officials and supporters who could now dream of a massive First Round tie.

Our journey of a few hundred metres to the car was a tough one in driving rain, but the journey home afterwards was straight forward. Joel and Alex were again keen to stop, but we only made a brief stop at Killington Lake so they could use the toilets. Santos had loved the scenery on our journey up to Workington and mentioned on the way home that he must make more effort to go to the Lake District more frequently. I felt the same way. We have the luxury of living within an hour's car drive from one of the most beautiful places in Great Britain but only tend to go there once or twice a year. With Workington now out the F.A Cup, I doubt very much we will be journeying there again on our F.A Cup trail. We may pass through it on the way to Carlisle or the North East, but for now, the Midlands home of Stourbridge is a 50% likelihood for the First Round Proper.

FINAL SCORE : Workington 1 Stourbridge 3

Scorers :- Workington – McLuckie. Stourbridge – Oliver, Richards, Benbow.

Our 'Speccies':- Calvin Wade, Alan Oliver, Richard Wade, Jordan Oliver, Phil Cooper, Joel Wade, Alex (Joel's friend) and his Dad, Santos.

The draw for the F.A Cup First Round Proper takes place on ITV this afternoon. The Football Association stop mollycoddling us at this stage and rather than guarantee us a ground to visit in the Northern half of England, we can now go anywhere. With Alison's Uncle Dereck's support of Portsmouth, I half think that would be a good one, but having thoroughly enjoyed the non-League element of the F.A Cup so far, my ideal preference is for us to go to Stourbridge. Alan has been to all 92 League grounds, so this will be his last chance to visit a new ground on the F.A Cup trail.

Stourbridge may well be hoping for a trip to somewhere like Sheffield United or for local interest Wolverhampton Wanderers, to benefit from some massive gate receipts and the TV revenue, but they have only been to the Second Round once in their history, so a home draw against a Conference side, for example, would give them a chance of going to the Second Round and then, if they won that one, the holy grail of the Third Round would arrive. Most Conference sides are professional, so Stourbridge are one of the few semi-professional sides left in now, so it would really be witnessing history and the magic of the F.A Cup if they could somehow manage to get to the Third Round. Another important factor is how much a win would mean to Stourbridge. A First Round win nets them £18 000 from the F.A, this is massive for a small club whilst for the likes of Wolves, it would probably not pay their striker, Kevin Doyle, for a week! That's my cards on the table then. A home draw for Stourbridge against another non-League side would be perfect.

Alan, Phil and Jordan did not have as comfortable a journey home from Workington last night as we did. They had to walk across to Workington train station in the monsoonal like rain and then get a train from there to Barrow before getting a train down to Manchester. Alan said the driving wind was ramming the rain against the windows and shaking the train about a fair bit, as they headed Southwards along the coast but that wasn't their only problem. Cable thieves also caused a delay to their journey and they weren't back in Manchester until quarter to eleven.

From now on, I am hoping most rounds I will be able to give the Olivers and Phil a lift. My thirteen year old, eldest son Brad is already hinting he may want to get involved once the bigger teams come in which would mean there would be six of us (me, my Dad, Brad, Alan, Jordan and Phil) which would be too many for the car but I am not sure I will agree to Brad coming anyway. He has been happy to miss all the non-League stuff but once the big boys enter, he is suddenly showing an interest. Not sure that is in the spirit of the journey. Alan has been to every round and if I can give him a lift to most, then it will save him a fair few quid. It will also save me a fair few quid if Brad stays at home, so unless my finances improve, he may not get too many opportunities to come along. If he decides to do the same F.A Cup journey in twenty years time, hopefully I will play my Dad's role then and join him.

2:30 p.m

My wish was granted, we are heading to Stourbridge in the First Round Proper. With replays still to come, there were 87 possible destinations, but it was still a 50% likelihood that Stourbridge would be given a home tie and we would head there. That is how it transpired. Funnily enough, they have been draw against another team in their own division, Biggleswade. I immediately text Alan the fountain of all non-League knowledge asking where Biggleswade is and he immediately replied that it is in either Hertfordshire or Bedfordshire. Biggleswade is actually the neighbouring village to where Phil Cooper is from and his parents still live there! He'll be hoping they get through and get a big team at home in the Second Round. They were promoted last season, so the two teams haven't played each other before, but it will be a massive game for both. They will both have been slightly disappointed that they didn't draw a big League side, guaranteeing them a bonus of TV revenue, but from our perspective it means we will definitely have a non-League side to follow in the Second Round. Stourbridge's War Memorial Athletic ground will be the fifth different ground on this journey and the fourth new one for me, so I'm delighted. It will also be Alan's second new ground which is superb as he didn't expect to go anywhere new at all!

Having reached the First Round Proper, selected games are now televised. I am not sure whether BT Sport or ITV will want to show this game as it isn't a David versus Goliath contest, but if they do, it could be moved away from a Saturday 3pm kick off. In all likelihood, that won't happen though and we will be heading down to Stourbridge in the West Midlands on Saturday 9th November to see which Calor League side goes into the Second Round. They are both in the seventh tier of English football, so could well be the last representative at that level or below in Round Two.

As expected, the Stourbridge v Biggleswade game is going to be a 3pm Saturday kick off as it hasn't been selected as a televised game. The one thing that has caught us a little unprepared is that Stourbridge have announced that the game is going to be all ticket and that tickets are going to be available to Stourbridge season ticket holders and members first. This wouldn't overly concern me if each season ticket holder and member wasn't allowed to purchase four tickets each. Stourbridge look like they tend to get 400-500 for their home games, so may have 400 season ticket holders and members. If they all buy three or four tickets, that is the home end full! I know it is unlikely, but I am not able to gauge from Chorley exactly how high a temperature the FA Cup fever is hitting in Stourbridge. Also, if there are 500 tickets left after the season ticket and members have had their quota, we aren't going to be front of the queue in Stourbridge either, so I took pre-emptive action and sent e-mails to Stourbridge Football Club's board of directors. I was expecting a fight for tickets in the later rounds but wasn't quite expecting it in the First Round Proper!

My e-mails basically explained our situation. We are a band of five football fans from the North West intent on going to every round of the F.A Cup, following the winners from each round on to the next round. Stourbridge are our winners and we would love to come to the game, could we have five tickets please.

The beauty of non-League football is that the clubs are generally run by about a dozen well meaning people and it is not hard to make contact with the people running the show. Tonight I have had a reply from Andy Pountney, Stourbridge's Chairman, saying that he does not think it will be a problem to get us five tickets, but he will have to wait a few days to confirm. He sent a subsequent e-mail asking whether it is four adult tickets and an OAP ticket, which I confirmed that it would be. I do have a tendency to worry about the worst case scenario, but in my mind, that is just a way of acting quickly to avoid problems. That cub scout moto of "Be Prepared" has generally served me well.

Earlier this evening, Alan posted something on Facebook about appearing live, with Jordan, on North Manchester radio, on a drivetime show hosted by Caz Matthews. Despite it being aired earlier, I went to the North Manchester FM website and listened to a play back of it. North Manchester FM is one of many independent radio stations that has cropped up in recent years and is run by volunteers. I have no idea what listening figures Caz Matthews gets, but there will definitely be a fan base and all publicity Alan can get for his campaign to raise money for 'The Christie' is a good thing. He was given a good half hour by Caz Matthews and both Al and Jordan came across very well on air.

Alan would be the first to admit that he isn't the cleverest bloke in the world. His blog has more than enough spelling mistakes to make his school English teachers cringe or turn in their graves (depending on whether they are still with us) but he has an encyclopaedic knowledge of his ground hopping exploits and an enthusiastic manner that goes up several notches when talking about his footballing travels. This was evident throughout their half hour chat. I hope a few people heard it who will decide to go on to his blog and chuck a few quid into the pot. Alan is making a fine effort to raise cash and it would be great if 'The Christie' (and cancer sufferers) reaped the rewards. Caz Matthews kept referring to him as Alan Holiver (instead of Oliver), so I must remember to call him that next time I speak to him!

I have had further communication from Stourbridge today, this time from their Vice President, Steve Hyde. Steve said that he would guarantee that we will get a minimum of two tickets and he should be able to confirm a further three in a few days time when he knows how many the season ticket holders, members and Stourbridge junior sides want. The junior sides are a further addition to the logistics, but in my e-mail I had pointed out that Alan and I had been to every round so far and were intending on going to every round to come, so at the very least, Steve has acted to preserve that. I spoke to Alan today (managing to remember to call him 'Holiver') and he seems pretty chilled out about it and convinced we will get all five. I am pretty sure he will be proved correct.

During my conversation with Alan, he confirmed it is unlikely Jordan will be coming to this one. Jordan has been tremendously supportive of her Dad but with starting at Uni and having some close friends at home, she has other things going on in her life too. Phil Cooper is definitely going to be coming though. The fact that Stourbridge's opposition are Biggleswade must have been an extra incentive for him to come. My Dad is also a definite, which means we are, in effect, trying to get an extra ticket.

The reason I am still intent on getting five tickets, despite Jordan not coming, is because I like the idea of introducing new personalities to the journey and Jordan's absence means I can see if I can bring another football fan along. My initial thoughts are to ask Dereck, my wife Alison's Uncle, who I went to see Accrington Stanley v Pompey with earlier in the season. Dereck and Joy are over at ours on the Saturday night, so I am sure if he came along to the footy during the day he would really enjoy it. 'Del' is another bubbly character too, so I am sure he would get on well with all the lads.

I don't believe there is any truth in the saying, "good things happen to good people," as I have seen a lot of unpleasant, arrogant idiots do well in life and a lot of good people struggling. You can work hard to try to increase your chances of achieving your life goals, but ultimately there are times when luck plays a part, both good and bad. I don't know Alan Oliver well enough to know whether he is a great person or not, but from what I can make out, he is a decent man and is doing a very honourable thing in raising money for The Christie Hospital. Six years ago, his mother-in-law, Pat, died of cancer aged 61, so Alan wanted to do every round of the F.A Cup in her memory, raising as much as he could for The Christie along the way. Today, I have spoken to Alan and he has been at the hospital with his Mum, Hilda, as she has had a collapsed lung and tests are being carried out to see whether she has cancer. Alan believes the signs are not good and once again is preparing for the worst, this time, for his own mother.

I am no expert on cancer. In 2002, I lost my Nan, who had been like a second mother to me, to cancer when she was 76. This was not a huge tragedy, she had lived a full life and lived to a respectable (although not wonderful) age. The tragedy was seeing how the cancer took hold in her final few weeks. Alan's Mum is a similar age to my Nan and he is hoping that if she does have cancer, it does not stretch out her suffering. He says she is too good a woman for that. I am hoping his fears are unfounded and her illness is treatable, but if the news does turn out to be the worst possible, it is an unfortunate reminder of why fundraising for the Christie is so important. Cancer can strike any race, any sex, any age and if anything can be done to assist the treatment of those suffering, then that can only be a positive thing.

Alan has a steely determination to come to the game on Saturday. He has said if his Mum takes a turn for the worse, then he may have to weigh the whole situation up, but as things stand, with his Mum being well cared for, he fully intends to come with us to Stourbridge on Saturday. He now has more drive than ever to raise money for the Christie.

I have again volunteered to drive to the game. I am going to pick my Dad up around Ashton-in-Makerfield (he is going to leave his car there) and then pick Alan and Phil up from Warrington Bank Quay train station at around eleven o'clock. Steve Hyde, Stourbridge's Vice President, has now confirmed that we can have all five tickets, but who the fifth member of our gang will be, I do not know. Dereck, Alison's Uncle, is working during the day on Saturday, so he can't make it and up until now a posting I made on Facebook has failed to draw any interest. It would be a shame if no-one used the ticket as it is only £10 and from all accounts it appears it is going to be a sell out. There are still a few days for a fan of football to come forward, so fingers crossed it will get used.

We now have a fifth member of the group for our trip down to Stourbridge and it is rather an unexpected addition. Brad plays football for the Chorley District team and they train on a Wednesday night, so whilst I was in the car waiting to pick him up, I phoned and texted a few friends, but didn't receive a single positive response. When we came back to the house though, there was a message waiting for me on Facebook from a gentleman called Keith Brian asking if the ticket was still going for Saturday, as he would like to come along.

When I did my roles as 'Business Development Manager' at Lloyds Bank (BM Solutions) and Yorkshire Building Society, I used to call at Keith's company, Rivington Mortgages in Horwich. I wouldn't say we were ever particularly close, there were other companies who gave us more business and brokers I saw a lot more, but over a period of about ten years, I got to know Keith pretty well and he always struck me as a decent guy. Once the Facebook phenomenon gathered momentum, I noticed Keith and I had some mutual friends, so I added him to my Facebook friends. Having become 'cyber friends', I have actually got to know Keith a lot better. He has several passions in his life including his family, music, his two particular favourites appear to be Barry Manilow and Genesis (an odd mix!), plane spotting, amateur dramatics, which he does with his wife Jacqui and Liverpool Football Club. What I have also discovered and benefitted from, is that he is a very altruistic man and is keen to support anyone who he feels is doing something a little different. Thus, when I released my first book, 'Forever Is Over', Keith not only bought it for himself, but also bought it for friends, plugged it consistently on Facebook and would do whatever he could do to help me along. If there were more people like Keith around, I would definitely not be scratching a living now, I would be a lot further along the road to success. I like to think of myself as someone who tries to help others, so I appreciate everything Keith has done, especially considering some people who know me ten times as well as Keith does, would not want to spend a second helping me along. Some people are thoughtful and helpful, others are not, that's the way of the world, I am old enough and ugly enough to understand that, but it does make you value the good guys more. How he will take to my Dad, Alan and Phil (and vice versa), I am not too sure, as I think Keith can come across as quite a serious soul at times, but I don't foresee there being any major problems. All of them have had working roles that involve them dealing with the public, so I am sure they will get along fine.

Sadly, the news on Alan's Mum Hilda is not good. She does have cancer and it is terminal. Apparently, Hilda has been caring for Alan's Dad Stan, who has become increasingly muddled in old age, so Hilda has tried not to reveal the extent of her own health problems, but is not surprised by the diagnosis. Alan seems to be trying to be as pragmatic as possible about the situation, but you can tell from speaking to him that he dotes on his parents and I am sure when the time comes, Hilda's death will hit him hard. He is an only child too, so I am guessing he will need to sort out care for his Dad. Old age can be very cruel, but the alternative can be crueller still. Healthy moments should never be taken for granted and inconsequential issues should never be dwelt upon. If nothing else, the last few years have taught me to move away from anything in life that makes you unhappy and make as much effort as possible to find time to do the things you enjoy. As is often stated, dying wishes don't often include a desire to have worked more.

Friday 8th November 2013

The excitement is building for tomorrow's trip to Stourbridge. I spoke to Keith yesterday and he has volunteered to drive down. He suggested that Phil and Alan go to Horwich Parkway to meet him, then he will come to Euxton to get me and finally, we are meeting my Dad in Wrightington, before heading down to Stourbridge. On Twitter, I have started following quite a few Glassboys fans (Stourbridge) and Waders fans (Biggleswade) and the sense of anticipation is huge. This is the biggest game in Biggleswade's FA Cup history and they are desperate to do well. Having missed out on a lucrative tie this round, the incentive of getting a League side next time around is a massive one and the £18 000 the winners receive from the FA is not to be sniffed at either. Some Biggleswade fans on Twitter were saying they were going to bed early as they knew they would hardly be able to sleep tonight!

A little bit of added spice was added to the fixture when Biggleswade took offence to the reasons Stourbridge gave for making the game an all ticket one. They said one of the reasons for making it all ticket was because it would be make it easier to administer the distribution in the Second Round should they be drawn against a League side at home. Chris Nunn, the Biggleswade Town manager, felt this was Stourbridge making assumptions that they would progress and tweeted his displeasure, sarcastically questioning whether Biggleswade should even bother turning up! I am sure his team talk will be geared around this.

When I decided back in the summer that I wanted to go to every round of the F.A Cup, today's game and venue was the type of scenario I imagined. Lots of supporters packed in to a tight little ground on a cold winter's afternoon and plenty of goals. Our trip to Guisborough was fantastic but today's journey reminded me of the trips I made as a teenager to the likes of Rochdale and Macclesfield to see F.A Cup 1st Round games. For the armchair fans, the magic of the F.A Cup begins in the Third Round, but once the word 'Proper' replaces the word 'Qualifying', there is a real sense of something special. Today was certainly no exception.

Keith arrived to pick me up in his red Jaguar just before eleven o'clock, with Alan and Phil already on board. Keith is inquisitive by nature and was asking a lot of questions about our journey and also about my Dad's footballing career. It transpired that although Keith has watched a lot of football in the higher echelons, he was a non-League "virgin", so did not really know what to expect. His knowledge of players, matches and the F.A Cup are very detailed at top flight level, but this is all new to him, so there was a real contrast between Keith and Alan, who is like Raymond Babbitt, (Dustin Hoffman's character in Rain Man) when it comes to non-League football.

When we pick my Dad up in Wrightington, Alan gets in the back of the car with myself and Phil and allows my Dad to sit in the front. I am glad it is a big car because the front row of a rugby team would not be carrying much more weight between them than Phil, Alan and me, so it was still a bit of a squash!

Our journey down to Stourbridge was a pleasant one, with everyone chatting about the game and about football in general. Alan has taken on a role at Oldham Boro' to try to help keep them afloat and relates a story of them recently only having had three 'paying' supporters to a game. Keith asks my Dad about playing at Wembley and how it came about and interestingly my Dad said a lot of it was down to luck. Skelmersdale United brought in about seven new players for the 1966-67 season and they immediately gelled both on and off the pitch. Normally sides take time to get to know each other, but my Dad said that side hit the ground running. They only stayed together for a season because after that several of them signed for League clubs, but almost fifty years on, several of them still meet up, as a group, a few times each year.

Alan was very candid about the situation with his Mum, Hilda. With being terminally ill, the objective is now to make her as comfortable as possible. Alan has been visiting her every day, but Hilda was happy for him to come to the football with us, so Alan rang her on his mobile to see how she was doing. He took some comfort from hearing that she had had some cereal and was continuing to be well looked after.

Keith had complained that his new satellite navigation system did not appear to be working properly and when we got on to the M5, I was immediately concerned that it was telling him to come off at Junction 8. Having lived in Gloucester, I normally took Junction 11 for Gloucester and Junction 9 for my friend's house in Bishop's Cleeve, so knew Junction 8 was about fifty miles in the wrong direction! There is a natural inclination these days though to trust computer technology more than the human brain, so Keith was keen to see where it was taking us, perhaps thinking we may spot a junction marked for Stourbridge along the way. I am starting to be known as a bit of a panic merchant by Alan, so he seemed unperturbed as I became more flustered, but after three junctions of heading southwards along the M5, I asked Phil if he could get a route planner up on his phone and check where we should be coming off. The problem was compounded by Phil not being able to get a signal at first, but when he eventually managed to get one, he saw that we should have come off at Junction 3 and had already passed Junction 4. We came off at the next junction and doubled back, with plenty of time to spare, but I've no idea where that SatNav wanted to take us. You see pictures of cars in rivers because of satellite navigation systems and although I doubt it would have dumped us in the River Severn, we may have struggled to make kick off if we had been totally reliant on that contraption!

Having lost all trust in Keith's satellite navigation, Phil used his route planner to guide Keith to the ground. We had probably only gone fifteen minutes too far along the M5, so it only added half an hour to our trip and we were still at the War Memorial Athletic Ground with plenty of time to spare, arriving at around two o'clock. Steve Hyde had advised us to go under the arch to collect our tickets and when we approached the steward, he said,

"You are 'The Casual Hopper', I presume?" which Alan was chuffed to bits with, as he said it made him feel like James Bond.

The steward pointed us in the direction of Steve Hyde who gave me the tickets and pointed us towards the correct entrance to the ground ('back out the arch, turn right and the entrance is on the right').

Before we headed into the ground, I distributed our tickets.

"Calvin, mine hasn't got a seat number on. How do we know where we will be sitting?" a confused Keith asked.

"We won't be sitting, Keith. It's standing room only, I'm afraid!"

The War Memorial Athletic Ground is one of the strangest football grounds that I have been in, because, in effect, it is situated within the outfield of Stourbridge Cricket Club. The majority of the football pitch is inside the boundary rope. The cricket pavilion is on one side of the cricket pitch and three sides of a football stadium are on the other. I later discovered that Stourbridge generally have to play their first game of the season at an alternative pitch, as it clashes with the cricket season and obviously both the cricket and football teams cannot play there at the same time, although I produced a vivid mental image of this happening, with the men in white chasing on to the football pitch to retrieve their ball and throwing it back to the wicket keeper, with the ball whistling past a centre back jumping for a header.

As the football pitch is on the cricket pitch, there are only three sides to the football pitch, which means that Stourbridge would be unable to rise above Tier 6 in the footballing pyramid as their ground would not pass the necessary requirements. As they are currently in Tier 7, they can still be promoted, but there can be no grand plans to achieve League status unless Stourbridge move elsewhere.

Once we were in the ground, there were not a lot of places we could go. Understandably, the social club within the ground had been restricted to season ticket holders and members, so we had to head to a refreshment stand for a pie and a cup of tea and then headed around to the side of the pitch to choose a terrace to stand on. The stand that runs along the side of the pitch at Stourbridge is pretty dated, with a couple of hundred seats in the middle and terracing either side, but it is all covered so keeps the rain off. We chose to stand on the side of the ground where the Biggleswade players were warming up, but were still amongst the Stourbridge fans as only one section behind the Biggleswade goal was for away supporters.

At every ground we have been to so far, we have got chatting to the locals and Stourbridge was no exception. I struck up a conversation with John, a grey haired, bright blue eyed, cheerful gentleman in his fifties, who turned out to be a Wolves fan, but a regular at the

War Memorial Athletic ground too. Whenever I have met any Wolves fans over forty, they always pull a face like they have been sucking a lemon when I say I live in Chorley. This is not a reflection on Chorley as a town, it is a reflection of a dark time in Wolves history back in 1986 when Chorley defeated them 3-0 in an FA Cup 1st Round second replay at Bolton Wanderers old ground, Burnden Park. Back then, you could have as many replays in the F.A Cup as needed, which could have padded out an F.A Cup trail like ours somewhat! At least nowadays, if the tie hasn't been settled by a replay, then it is extra time and penalties (and no replays at all in the Semi Final and Final).

I talked to John for quite a while and it transpires he is quite heavily involved at Stourbridge. His wife is a teacher at Ridgewood High School and through her school, Stourbridge Football Club have created an unlikely alliance with Sintet Football Club in The Gambia. The school had been working with communities in the West African country for six years and John and his wife encouraged Stourbridge FC to get involved which they did, raising money for Sintet FC, a non-League side in The Gambia, which paid for their team kit initially and then assisted with the running of the club. They also asked Stourbridge fans to donate old football tops which were taken over to The Gambia, whilst children from another local school donated their old primary school uniforms, so the children in Sintet village could have a uniform. The whole thing sounds like a brilliant initiative and perhaps a decent F.A Cup run may allow Stourbridge Football Club to increase what already sounds like a very positive involvement.

At five to three both teams re-appeared on the pitch, having disappeared a few minutes earlier, for their team talks. As it is Remembrance Sunday tomorrow, a two minute silence was perfectly observed. I asked John why the ground is called the War Memorial Athletic ground, when there does not appear to be a war memorial there and John isn't sure, but thinks the whole area is known as a War Memorial. I have subsequently had a look at internet records for Amblecote, the part of Stourbridge where the ground is, and it appears that sixty two local men that were killed in the Great War and a further seventeen that were killed in the Second World War have their names inscribed on 'The Lych Gate War Memorial' at the Holy Trinity Church in Amblecote, perhaps this is the reason that the ground has been given its name.

I also discovered from reading up on the area that Worcestershire Cricket Club have played sixty one first class matches on the ground and two ICC trophy matches were also played there in 1979 and 1986, the former between Bermuda and Papua New Guinea and the latter between Argentina and East Africa!

The game kicked off at 3pm, our seventh consecutive Saturday afternoon game and with Biggleswade Town being the furthest team from home so far, a seventh straight game that avoids a draw would be great. Stourbridge started brightly once again and I immediately observed that the Biggleswade Town goalkeeper, Ian Brown, looked like he was carrying a groin injury. I don't know what it is about this FA Cup journey, but there appears to be a footballer at every turn that shares his name with a celebrity, Joe Jackson at Workington, Jamie Oliver from Stourbridge and now Biggleswade have contributed the singer from The Stone Rones. I'll keep an eye out for Frank Sinatra, Mick Jagger and Harry Styles in later rounds.

Stourbridge were rewarded for their early dominance in the 11th minute, when Ryan Rowe managed to get on the end of a Drew Canavan cross and head home from close range. John informs me that Ryan Rowe has now scored ten goals this season, the other two coming in just two games! He scored four in the away game at Redditch United and five in the away game at Chippenham Town. The latter game made some national tabloid headlines because of what happened to the unfortunate Chippenham Town manager, Steve Winter. As his 40th birthday was approaching, Winter's wife decided to book him a surprise trip to Egypt, but understanding it was in the midst of the football season, she contacted the club and asked for their permission to whisk him away for a wonderful holiday. Permission was granted, but whilst he was enjoying the hot weather and the pyramids, Stourbridge were trouncing Chippenham 9-0. Subsequently, the Chairman phoned Winter in Egypt, told him the result and let him know that there had been a board meeting following the defeat and he had been sacked! Happy 40th Steve!

Biggleswade seemed to liven up as soon as Stourbridge scored. The pre-match nerves which appeared to have lingered on after kick off, were suddenly forgotten about and Biggleswade began to play with some real purpose. This was rewarded within a couple of minutes, as Lee Allinson crossed to Evan Key who planted a firm header past Dean Coleman in the Stourbridge goal. The Biggleswade Town fans, who were down the other end of the pitch, went crazy but their excitement was proved to be shortlived, as by the 16th minute, Ryan Rowe once again showed his goals come in clusters by striking a right footed shot beyond Ian Brown and his injured groin to put Stourbridge back ahead.

2-1 after sixteen minutes and we were all thinking this could become a cricket score. Phil, Alan, my Dad and I had a quick discussion about the highest scoring non-League game we had witnessed and the best we could come up with was Altrincham's 7-4 defeat of Nuneaton Borough that my Dad and I had attended, back in 1985. After sixteen minutes, we were hoping Stourbridge-Biggleswade Town could set a new personal best.

Once you begin to anticipate a monumental event, it tends to put the kibosh on it and that was the end of the scoring in the first half. Stourbridge were dominant for most passages of play and as the whistle blew, we all agreed that unless Biggleswade improved in the second half, Stourbridge would go on to win convincingly.

At half time, we ended up getting visitors passes to the social club and bar, through Alan's groundhopping charms! Every game Alan buys a programme and a home team badge as a souvenir of his visit. Prior to kick off, Alan was chatting to a steward called Jim, who he had also been chatting to up in Workington and he said Alan could get a badge from the souvenir shop at half-time, which was within the social club. As a goodwill gesture, he said if we all wanted to go along, he would meet us and get us in. Thus, half time was spent in the social club, but with so many members and season ticket holders in there, it was impossible to get a drink. At least it was an opportunity to visit a better quality of urinal, as the outdoor ones at non-League grounds tend to have a Third World look about them. Whilst I was in there, the tallest man I have ever seen at a football match walked in. The guy must have been over seven feet tall and was really thick set too. Day to day life must involve a lot of crouching for him, as the top of his head was at least six inches above the door so he had to stoop to get in. Perhaps as a child I would have felt compelled to see if he was all in proportion, but as a 42 year old, I was just happy to get out of there, in case there was an almighty splash back.

We returned to the same spot to watch the second half, but noticed a lot of the Stourbridge fans (including John my first half companion), had vacated the area, wandering up towards the goal that Stourbridge were now attacking. Keith also wandered off for a while, as he had brought an expensive camera with him and wanted to capture a few photos for posterity.

The second half started quite scrappily with both sides knowing the next goal would prove decisive. A third for Stourbridge would kill the game, whilst an equaliser from Biggleswade would probably be deemed enough for them and they would be happy to take the tie back to their place.During this dip in the quality and tempo of the game, my mind briefly wandered back to celebrity names and despite not finding any more amongst the players, I noticed there was a backwards James Bond one, as one of the Biggleswade Town players was called Craig Daniel and was also mildly amused by the 57th minute Stourbridge substitution that saw Francis replace Drake, a useful pair if Stourbridge qualify for Europe and need to tackle the Spanish.

Biggleswade were having the majority of the possession but it was Stourbridge that looked more dangerous in the final third. Benbow continued to excite and frustrate in equal measure, using his fast, bulky frame to good effect when the ball was near him, but much like at Workington, looking like a forlorn figure when not called into action.

There was another Workington 'Groundhog Day' moment in the 58th minute when Will Richards, the Stourbridge centre back wandered forward for a corner and used his aerial ability to good effect once again, sending an unstoppable header beyond Brown in the Biggleswade goal to make it 3-1. A two goal lead can often be a precarious one, but despite Biggleswade looking dangerous on occasion, from there on in, it looked equally likely they could be caught on the break as the game opened up. From one Stourbridge counter attack, Benbow had a great opportunity to roll one across the box for a Rowe tap in, to complete his hat trick, but Benbow opted to shoot himself and cursed himself as the ball ballooned over. Benbow subsequently had further chances to score that were squandered and just when it looked like it wasn't his day for personal glory, in the 85th minute, he fired a fine left foot shot into the net after a jinky run. The ever swelling gathering behind the Biggleswade goal went wild and Benbow ran to them to savour the adulation. 4-1 was a little harsh on Biggleswade who had given the game their all, it just appeared that Stourbridge had more players who posed a real goal threat.

Before the end, we started heading towards the exit, so we could make a quick dash for the car as soon the final whistle blew. Benbow's goal had been the 25th of our FA Cup trail so far and the full time whistle signified we were halfway through the fourteen rounds. If we see another twenty five goals in the next seven rounds, to reach the fifty goal mark that would be a decent return. Seven games, no replays, one sending off and an average return of over 3.5 goals per game is an excellent first half. Roll on tomorrow now to see if Stourbridge can get a decent Second Round draw and the opportunity to reach the Third Round for the first time in their history.

FINAL SCORE : Stourbridge 4 Biggleswade Town 1

Scorers :- Stourbridge – Rowe (2), Richards, Benbow. Biggleswade – Key.

Our 'Speccies':- Calvin Wade, Alan Oliver, Richard Wade, Phil Cooper, Keith Brian.

On our journey home from Stourbridge last night we discussed what draw we wanted for the F.A Cup 2nd Round. My hope was for Stourbridge to be drawn away at a ground I hadn't previously visited and that is exactly how it has worked out. This is my hope for every round really, as it is more exciting to visit somewhere new than to return to the same place. Stourbridge were the very last team to be drawn out of the hat and will be away at Stevenage, who are towards the bottom of the First Division, four leagues above Stourbridge. The game will be on Saturday 7th December, unless the game is televised. A couple of seasons ago, Stourbridge were hosts to Stevenage in the F.A Cup Second Round and Stevenage defeated them 3-0. John, the Stourbridge fan I was standing with during the first half yesterday, told me that Stevenage totally outplayed them and Stourbridge didn't manage a shot on goal. On that basis, Stevenage are going to be happier with the draw than Stourbridge, but for us it will be a long drive down, but a really interesting one too.

Stourbridge are now the lowest ranked team guaranteed a Second Round spot and will become the lowest ranked team left in the competition if Shortwood United fail to beat Port Vale in the BT Sport live game tomorrow night. These two teams are actually the only teams below Conference level (the 5th level of English football), left in the competition and with no disrespect to Shortwood, they are very unlikely to overcome Port Vale. So, Stourbridge are likely to become the sole representative of about 600 clubs that entered the Cup from lower than Tier 5. For us to see them equal their best ever F.A Cup performance in their 137 year history is really something, but if they go one step further and make the Third Round, it really will be the stuff dreams are made of.

Once the draw was made, I immediately sent a text to Alan to let him know where we would be heading next. Alan asked me to do this, as he was planning to spend the afternoon at the hospital visiting his Mum. I received a three word response which just said, "Fantastic! Phil country," as not only is Biggleswade a mile from Phil's home village, Stevenage is only ten miles down the road too. I hope this means Phil is going to come to the next round too, as he is always good company. From the outset, Phil mentioned that it would be great if our journey included Biggleswade Town, Stevenage or Luton and as luck would have it, we have had two out the three.

With Phil being an Arsenal fan, Alan a Manchester City fan and Dad and me being Evertonians, I just have a feeling we are going to see at least one of our sides in the Final. Alan went to see Manchester City play Wigan Athletic last season, but the day turned out disastrously for him. As Alan could only get tickets in the Wigan end , him and Jordan ended up leaving at half time because he looks and speaks like Mr.Mancunian and was getting a hostile reaction from the Wigan fans which was upsetting Jordan. Obviously, to make matters worse, City ended up losing 1-0. This season, I don't see a relative minnow like Wigan winning it, as there are about seven sides currently competing for the Top 4 places in the Premier League and those that miss out on the Champions League places will be busting a gut to appease their fans with some silverware. Everton v Manchester City (or Arsenal) Final – you heard it here first!

Having text Alan about the draw, I then phoned my Dad. My Dad is really up for a trip down to Stevenage! He was saying that it was a pity he no longer has Paul Fairclough's number, as he probably still has some contacts at Stourbridge. Paul is the son of a former employee of my Dad's, Eric Fairclough. Eric worked for my Dad for years, at least fifteen, but Paul was a really good semi-professional player and went on to manage Stevenage, gaining several promotions under his stewardship and famously leading them to the 4th Round of the F.A Cup in 1998, where they were eventually knocked out in a Replay at Newcastle United when Alan Shearer scored a debatable winner, when the ball did not appear to cross the line. Co-incidentally, one of the Stevenage players in those games was Steve Perkins, son of one of my Burscough managers, Russ Perkins. I played with Steve in one game for Burscough, away at Trafford, but he went on to have a long footballing career for Southern semi-professional sides, whilst my 'career' lasted little more than a season.

<u>7:30 p.m</u>

Text Alan just to tell him about the possible Paul Fairclough link and received a reply to say that he is still at the hospital as his Mum is sinking fast. Such a shame that Alan is losing his Mum to the very illness he is trying to raise money to support the fight against.

Monday 11th November 2013

Sad news. Alan posted on his Facebook site…

'Hilda Oliver Mum Nanna 1935-2013 we won't forget, love you loads xxxxxxxx'

Hope Alan goes on to raise a princely sum for Christies. He is no longer just raising money in memory of his mother-in-law, Pat, but also for his Mum, Hilda.

Wednesday 13th November 2013

After my Dad mentioned that he wished he had Paul Fairclough's contact number, he now has! Life works in mysterious ways. Yesterday, I received a Facebook message from an old school friend, Paul Cooper (for the older readers, he is not the former Ipswich Town goalkeeper). 'Coops' works as an overseas director for the recruitment company, Michael Page and currently lives in Malaysia. His message was as follows :-

'Wadey. Been reading your F.A posts – is it Stevenage next? Not sure if home or away but give me a shout if you are struggling for a ticket, I know their ex-captain who may be able to help you out if you are stuck.'

I sent a message back to Coops asking him who the captain was and when he played. It turns out it is a guy called Steve Berry, who is originally from Bootle and played for Sunderland when they reached the 1985 Milk Cup Final and subsequently went on to captain Stevenage. Coops says he is a great lad and helped arrange for Michael Page to have a work match on the Stevenage pitch, so must have some influence! I then explained that we would manage to get tickets, but my Dad would like to get Paul Fairclough's number, as he'd like to get back in touch with him. As luck would have it, Steve was managed by Paul Fairclough so Coops sent me 'Cloughies' number and I passed it on to my Dad tonight. Not sure if Paul Fairclough will be able to sort anything out for us, even if it is just access to a social club pre-match, but he will definitely be a useful contact for getting further tickets if Stevenage win and then draw a Premiership side in the next round.

As the Third Round approaches, my mind is starting to think through the possible future permutations and I do wonder whether we will manage to get tickets for every round. Hopefully having a former captain and former manager as contacts at Stevenage will help us if Stevenage get a plum draw and we can go back to the helpful Steve Hyde at Stourbridge, but if either side draws a Premiership side and then that club draws their rivals (eg Everton-Liverpool, City-United, Arsenal-Spurs), we may struggle. I think we would need my Dad to use all his influence if that sort of scenario transpired. Alan just laughs at my concerns. He says we have a nickname for the five main people on our F.A Cup journey. Alan is the 'Casual Hopper'. Phil is the 'Gunner'. Jordan is 'CSI' or 'Scully' (because of her forensics degree), my Dad is 'Director of Football' and I am the 'Risk Assessor'.Not sure they will catch on!

Just been on the phone to my Dad and he had some very positive news about the Stevenage-Stourbridge game, plus another great story about how small the football community is. My Dad gave Paul Fairclough a ring and had a good chat with him, but Paul said he didn't have a lot to do with Stevenage these days as he subsequently went on to be Director of Football at Barnet and is currently the manager of the England semi-professional team. He did say, however, that he would speak to Clive, who is Head of the Commerical team at Stevenage and see what he could do. Paul rang my Dad back and said he had spoken to Clive and he would sort us out, so to give him a ring.

Today, my Dad rang Clive at Stevenage and he said he would provide us with at least two (and possibly four) tickets for the media lounge prior to kick off, which is brilliant. My Dad got chatting with Clive and Clive was asking how he knew Paul Fairclough. My Dad explained Paul's late father, Eric, had worked for him for many years but he also knew Paul from playing football against him. Clive asked my Dad who he played for and when he said Skelmersdale United, Clive told him that he had been a boyhood Hendon Town fan and as a boy, had watched Hendon in three F.A Amateur Cup Semi Finals against 'Skem' in 1967. My Dad told Clive that he had played in those three games!

Clive also asked my Dad how we would be getting down to the game. When my Dad said we would be coming by car, Clive said it would be a long day doing a return trip on a Saturday and has offered to put us up in the Ibis Hotel in Stevenage for free in two twin rooms! The IBIS isn't a Five Star hotel by any means, it is functional like a Holiday Inn Express or a Travel Inn, but that is immaterial, this act of generosity did not need to be handed out to us, but it has been and my Dad and I are a little stunned! I am now going to see if I can get the Friday off work and I will drive us down on the Friday.

One slight issue, is that we currently have five people going and possibly four free tickets and free accommodation for four of us. Alan has said that himself, Jordan and Phil are all up for going, as well as my Dad and me. In all likelihood though, Phil will go back to stay at his parents so it will be the rest of us at the IBIS. It should be great having an overnight stay rather than just going to the football and then heading home.

The two Saturdays prior to our trip to Steveange, I will be working 2pm to 10pm at ASDA. My return to PAYE as a sales rep for World of Warranty has been a huge help in avoiding escalating financial problems, but it does not remove all my financial problems overnight, so if I want to continue to get to these F.A Cup games, I have to take on any extra work I am offered. This Saturday's shift is particularly tough as I will miss the second half of the Merseyside derby that is being broadcast on BT Sport. I still haven't been able to go to one Everton game this season, which is a real disappointment, but I am still hoping if things continue to improve, I might make a few games in the New Year.

December has started well! Just to update Merseyside derby news from last time, the game finished 3-3, with Daniel Sturridge scoring an 89th minute equaliser for Liverpool, to deprive Everton of victory. I watched the first half before going to work at ASDA and Everton were losing 2-1 at the break, so I would have taken a draw at that point, but to then go 3-2 up and lose two points in the last couple of minutes is a sickener.

Throughout this book I have tried to resist the temptation to write about Everton, as I understand for most readers it would not be entirely relevant. Having been a regular at Goodison Park for over thirty years, this season has been an odd one, as the limited monies I have for socialising have been pumped into the F.A Cup trail, so I have not been able to attend, but thankfully today I have been given two good reasons to write about Everton.

Firstly, Bill Cecil, the manager of Joel's football team, Gregson Lane, called around this afternoon at 4:01.pm. I know it was 4:01.pm as Southampton took a first minute lead at Chelsea just as he arrived (but went on to lose). I wasn't at Joel's match this morning (funnily enough against Burscough), as I am currently helping to run Brad, my eldest son's team, so Alison took Joel. Anyway, to cut a long story short, Joel's team won 4-1, he scored the fourth and one of the parents of one of the Burscough lads is an Everton scout and he had a word with Bill about Joel after the game and said he would be recommending Joel to his boss, who would probably come down and have a look at him within the next couple of months. Joel is a left footed central midfielder, who is a great passer of the ball and has a fierce shot. He still is a bit lacking in certain aspects of his game, especially when his team are in possession but he hasn't got the ball (he tends to stand behind two of the opposition and shout for a pass) but he is only eleven and would probably benefit from some specialised guidance. Bill and the lads who have run the team at Gregson Lane have really improved him, but if he does get a chance to go to Everton, I think he could improve even further. I have no idea if he will be good enough to play at a higher level, as he is by no means a unique talent, but if he does get asked it would be a good experience.

Bill, Alison and I decided it would probably be best if we did not tell Joel that he was likely to be watched, in case it stopped him playing his natural game. I have no huge aspirations for either of my boys to be footballers. I genuinely do just want them to be happy in life, but think Joel would have his confidence boosted if he went to Finch Farm (or wherever the juniors train) for a few weeks. He is not an academic genius and has to strive hard to be average, so to be aware that he is flourishing in his football would do him no harm. I really hope something comes of it, even if it is only a brief dalliance with Everton. Brad had six weeks at Manchester United when he was nine (as a goalkeeper) and as Joel sometimes gives off the impression that he feels he lives in Brad's shadow, this would be a confidence booster. I will let you know if anything transpires.

The second bit of good news relating to Everton is also linked to Bill's visit to our house. Bill has always been really kind to Alison and me. For the last couple of years, he has had a box at York races for a day and has invited us along. He runs a successful business and footballing wise, has had corporate season tickets at the club he supports, Wolverhampton Wanderers, for several years. This season however, he decided to take four corporate season tickets at Manchester United rather than Wolves. I don't know the full reason for this, perhaps it was business related, but what I do know, is that on Wednesday night, when Man U play Everton, he has asked Alison and me to be the guests of him and his wife, Karen!

On the first day of the season, when we were at West Didsbury & Chorlton versus Abbey Hey and Everton were drawing away at Norwich City, I predicted Everton would finish ninth this season. As things stand, we are fifth, having won six, drawn six and lost only one this season so far and that was away at Manchester City. Roberto Martinez is earning universal plaudits from the media, Evertonians and the wider footballing public. Our transfer deals before the deadline were great, bringing in Gareth Barry (from Man City), Romelu Lukaku (from Chelsea) and Gerard Deulofeu (from Barcelona), all on loan and signing James McCarthy from Wigan. We also sold Fellaini and Anichebe (to Man U and West Brom respectively) for more than could have been expected. The players we signed have done great, whilst the players we sold have done far less well. We go to Old Trafford on Wednesday night with Everton three places above Manchester United in the Barclays Premier League and a real belief we can win there for the first time since Ryan Giggs first Manchester United game, way back in 1992 (for which I was in the Manchester United end for the last twenty minutes). I will be there to see whether we do and then after that, on Friday, it is back on the F.A Cup trail, as we journey down to Stevenage for the F.A Cup. Bizarrely, I am looking forward to the Stevenage-Stourbridge trip just as much!

Wednesday 4ᵗʰ December 2013

As I have previously mentioned, this book is largely about my F.A Cup trail from Extra Preliminary Round to Final, but I do want to give a little focus to the other games I attend. I found the Accrington Stanley v Portsmouth game fascinating and tonight at Old Trafford found the Manchester United v Everton equally fascinating, not only because of the football on show, but also because of the contrast with every other game I have attended this season.

My Dad said that he would come over and look after the boys and he arrived at five on the dot, with Bill arriving soon after to give us a lift over to Old Trafford and allowing Alison and me the rare luxury of both being able to drink on the same night! Alison has only been to two previous Everton games. The year before our 1997 wedding, Alison came to see Everton at Goodison Park with me and my friend Jamie, for a game against Middlesbrough. It wasn't the greatest introduction to Goodison Park as after an early Craig Short goal, Middlesbrough struck back with goals from Nick Barmby (who later that season joined Everton) and the winner from the little Brazilian, Juninho. Alison has not been back to Goodison subsequently, but has been to another game, at Craven Cottage, in May 2009, to witness Everton's first away win at Fulham since 1966. This is, to date, the only Everton football match that all our four family members have attended together. We were down in London for the weekend and I booked four tickets for the Everton match and it turned out to be a master stroke as on a beautiful summer's day, Leon Osman scored a goal in each half as we strolled to victory on the banks of the Thames. The only annoying thing about that day was that I tried to put a £5 accumulator bet on all ten results in the end of season Premier League games, but was timed out just as I pressed the submit button on the internet facility in the hotel (back in 2009 WiFi was a rare commodity). All my results came in and I anxiously logged back in to my Betfred site upon returning to the hotel to find my account still had merely £5 in and not the £1500 I was expecting!

The fact that Alison was luckier with her away day trip than her only home trip, gave me hope that she may bring a bit of luck in ending another barren away spell for Everton. Bill and Karen Cecil are very good company and we had an enjoyable meal with them pre-kick off. Back in my days of working for Lloyds, they had a corporate table at Manchester United which I was able to utilise a couple of times a season. Bill and Karen's tickets in Knights Lounge were great, but not as lavish as the Lloyds ones, which were slap bang in the middle of the Main Stand. It always amazed me how much money they spent as a part nationalised company.

Bill and Karen's seats were behind the goal that faces the Stretford End. The Everton fans were situated behind one corner flag at our end and we were behind the other. Karen commented that Everton only had a small allocation and I told her to watch what happens if Everton score, as I am sure there will be people jumping up all around the home end, especially in our corporate section. They were in good spirit though, the die hard Evertonians who travel away always seem to make themselves heard and the pre-match songs were being sung with great gusto, especially a new one for this season, which goes,

"Allez, Allez, Allez oh

Allez, Allez, Allez oh

We're Everton FC

Roberto's Blue Army!"

Manchester United had had a topsy turvy start to the season, but had not lost in a twelve match run that dated back to a home defeat against West Bromwich Albion on 28th September (the day Alan, Phil and myself had been up to Workington v Burscough). It seemed strange that as an Evertonian I was so optimistic, but Everton are a stronger side than they have been for several years and it appears Manchester United are weaker, particularly in midfield, than they have been for many years, so it seemed a good time for our paths to cross.

Alison was taken aback by the grand scale of Old Trafford. Love or hate Manchester United there is no escaping that Old Trafford is a hugely impressive stadium, holding more than thirty thousand more people than Anfield or Goodison. This season the biggest attendance I have been in so far is 2531 in the Second Division game between Accrington Stanley and Portsmouth and in the F.A Cup the largest has been 1605 at Stourbridge v Biggleswade Town, so to be amongst 75 210 supporters at Old Trafford, was a little surreal. Whilst my visit to Accrington Stanley was a taster for the early F.A Cup Rounds like 1st and 2nd Round Proper, this was a taster for what we would be heading towards in the latter rounds. I keep hoping Everton will be brought into our equation at some stage and if they play with the same ability, determination and good fortune that they had tonight, it might even taken them to the Final.

To cut a long story short, Alison's good luck on away days continued and Everton won 1-0, a first victory at Old Trafford for twenty one long years. We rode our luck more than a little with Manchester United hitting the woodwork a couple of times, but Everton were never on the rack, as they had been on so many of my previous visits to Old Trafford. I thought James McCarthy was particularly impressive, reminding me of Paul Bracewell in our mid-80s title winning side, but the whole team stood up strongly to everything Manchester United threw at them and were rewarded for their guile and determination when a Lukaku cross shot in the 85th minute was turned in at the far post by the left back Bryan Oviedo.

As predicted, Everton fans jumped to their feet all over the ground, especially in the corporate sections and pandemonium broke out in the 'proper' away section. Oviedo, a Costa

Rican international signed by the former Everton manager (and now Manchester United manager), David Moyes, was only playing because Leighton Baines had broken a bone in his foot, which will sideline him for six weeks. The fact that he was lurking on the back post with five minutes remaining in a goalless game at Old Trafford, shows an attacking intent that Everton often lacked under Moyes. A statistic often trotted out is that in 46 away League games at Manchester United, Arsenal, Chelsea and Liverpool under Moyes, Everton did not win one! With five minutes to go, at Old Trafford, a Moyes managed Everton team would have been battening down the hatches and aiming to go home with a satisfactory point. Life under Martinez at Everton is different and hopefully may end our eighteen year barren spell without a trophy.

The Bryan Oviedo song broke out in the away end. To the tune of Human League's "Don't You Want Me Baby?" they sang,

"Oviedo Baby, Oviedo Ooohhhhh!"

Manchester United didn't threaten the Everton keeper. Tim Howard's goal after that and Tim and his ridiculously flourishing under chin beard, watched from afar as Everton passed the ball around midfield until the ninety minutes were up. I love going to the FA Cup games but to find yourself wholeheartedly devoted to one side is a great feeling and to see them emerge victorious from Old Trafford against a manager who jumped ship, is a wonderful feeling. I really, really hope Everton hit our radar in the F.A Cup and if not, I hope I can at least return to a game or two at Goodison before the end of the season, with my Dad or Brad.

As for Manchester United, there are a lot of supporters questioning whether David Moyes is the right man to have been chosen to succeed Sir Alex Ferguson. At this stage, I must say it is very hard to tell. By the end of this book, we will know. At the start of this book, when my Dad and I went to West Didsbury&Chorlton against Abbey Hey, the Arsenal fans were calling for

Wenger's head after a home defeat to Aston Villa. Who are top of the Premier League currently? Arsenal !

So, one half of my free footballing week comes to an end. I am hugely grateful to Bill and Karen Cecil for inviting Alison and me along. We are currently a couple with very limited resources and Bill and Karen know that, so they don't invite us along because they hope to gain something back from us, they just invite us because they enjoy our company, which is great and reflects well on them as a couple (not that they like us but that they give without expecting a return).

Roll on Friday now and our weekend away in sunny Stevenage!

During the Manchester United-Everton game yesterday, after it had finished and today, I have been exchanging text messages with Sean O'Donnell, one of my friends that I met during my days at Manchester Polytechnic. Sean is from Omagh, County Tyrone and an avid Manchester United fan. I have many fond memories of Sean, but some not so happy memories too, as back in 1993, Sean and I between us, managed to get beaten up four times in two weeks in three separate events!

Anyone who knows Sean or myself (or both of us) is aware that we like a drink. Back in 1993, aged 22, we both liked a drink far more than we do now as family men. Not surprisingly, the three events that resulted in beatings, had alcohol heavily involved. It all started on a Friday night in Crosby. When we graduated from Manchester Polytechnic in 1992, I returned home, as did the rest of the lads that we shared a house with, other than Sean who decided to stay in Manchester, possibly because he was dating a girl who was studying at Salford University. Sean continued to live in the same house in Chorlton that we had lived in for the previous two years and one of the lads who moved in after we left was from Crosby, Merseyside.

I was due to meet Sean in Manchester on the Saturday, along with a few other old Poly mates, but on the Friday, Sean went out into Crosby with his new housemate, Mark Murphy. At the end of the night, they were randomly attacked. Sean himself admits there were plenty of times he had been lucky not to be beaten up with his antics, but this time, he was just in the wrong place at the wrong time. Thus, when we arrived at our old house on the Saturday evening, Sean was already sporting a black eye.

On the Saturday night, we decided to go to 'The Cellar' bar at Manchester University. I always liked that place, it had a more intimate feel than the Polytechnic Student Union. I don't remember much about the night at all, other than when we left, the group of us had fragmented into smaller groups. My group was me and some girl I had randomly started chatting to. I doubt very much I was trying to 'pull', I was probably just randomly exchanging drunken chat, which I was very good at, whilst 'pulling' a complete stranger was something I was disastrously bad at. I was fairly shy, lacking in confidence and had an inability to gauge whether I was getting a 'come on' signal or a 'piss off' one. Anyway, whether or not I was trying to pull was immaterial as once we arrived outside, events conspired to distract me and whoever the girl was that I was speaking to, disappeared off the face of the earth, never to cross my path again.

As I stood outside the University, chatting drunkenly away, a group of about eight young local kids (seven males and one female), aged, I would guess, between fifteen and eighteen,started to give a University lad of Asian descent a hard time. He seemed to have a couple of friends with him and they appeared not to be welcoming trouble, but were finding it anyway. The young locals were becoming increasingly aggressive and whether it was a conscious decision to do the right thing or just drunken bravado, I ended up getting myself involved, and once the verbal aggression became pushing and shoving, I went over and told the local kids to 'go home and leave the lads alone'.

Next thing I knew, one of them, who was a good nine inches shorter than me, was heading my way, pushing me and questioning whether I was their mate. Within seconds, I was surrounded by about four of them who were swinging fists and kicking me. The only previous fights I had in my life, were play fights in junior school with Neil Addison (who is now well known in poetry circles!) and a grapple with Greg Brindley on Town Green train station platform when he had wiped a boot of paint on my school trousers. Even then we stopped grappling as soon as the train arrived. This was weird though as I felt like I was being attacked by a gang of angry munchkins, as they were all much younger and much smaller than me. I just tried to block their kicks and punches but eventually one of them charged at me, knocked me to the ground and the four of them started using my head and body as an oversized football.

Unbeknown to me, Sean had witnessed me being knocked to the ground and being given a good kicking and had decided to come to my rescue. This was a bold move, given there were eight of them altogether and two of us and I wasn't exactly putting up much of a fight as I curled up into a foetal position on the floor. Sean must have forgotten his cape and super powers though, as within seconds, he was on the floor too and the last thing he says he remembers seeing, was the girl in the gang's Doc Marten boot being stamped unceremoniously into his face.

Once the local lads decided to stop kicking me and head home, I got back to my feet still unaware of Sean's rescue act and the first person I saw was the lad I had gone in to help, who was unconscious on the floor. He was bleeding from the nose, mouth and ears and I was later told by the police that he had hit a concrete slab when he had been knocked out by a punch. I remember taking my top off and trying to clear the blood, then remember police and ambulance sirens. Minutes later, the ambulance was taking the seriously injured lad to hospital, whilst the police were ushering those of us with minor injuries into their van to run us down to 'Casualty'. It was in the police van that I ran into Sean and his newly acquired 'Elephant Man' face.

I am not really sure precisely how the events unfolded from there. That night, though, after our hospital visit, the police took statements from the injured parties and I was visited at work on the Monday by a police man and police lady, for a further statement. They told me that the lad who was initially attacked was still in a coma, had suffered brain injuries and they had arrested some of the gang who were responsible. I later received a letter stating that I may be called to give evidence in a 'Crown Court trial', but I never was. I don't know if this was because the testimony of a drunken 22 year old could easily have been taken to pieces or because the attackers pleaded guilty, but that was the end of it from my perspective. The police, a week after the attack, contacted me to say the main victim was out of a coma and was recovering, but I heard no more. I think Sean received a token amount of money for his criminal injuries, as his face needed stitching back together at hospital, but neither of us heeded the warning that excessive alcohol and safety don't go hand in hand and a couple of weeks later, things went spectacularly wrong again.

1993 was the first time I had ever been to Playa de Las Americas in Tenerife. Twelve months after leaving Polytechnic, four of us, Sean, myself and two of our best mates from our house in Chorlton, Jamie and Jay, decided to go on holiday together. Twenty years ago, airport security was a little more relaxed than it is today, so when we discovered our flights were at six in the morning and we had to be at Manchester Airport for four o'clock, it seemed only logical to have a few beers the night before and forget the idea of sleeping.

We arrived in 'Las Americas' bleary eyed and half-drunk, late in the morning and after checking into our appartements and grabbing an hour's sleep, we decided to head to Veronicas, the infamous local centre for partying boozers. Somehow, through the course of the day, we split into two groups and I found myself with Jay in Linekers bar. As tiredness and excess alcohol kicked into my body, I somehow managed to lose Jay and rather than do the sensible thing and head to bed, I went in search of Jamie and Sean and miraculously managed to find them. I remember dancing with them in some rooftop nightclub, I remember drinking my way through my tiredness, I remember the music no longer being different songs but merging into one continual backbeat and then....nothing.

The next thing I remember I was walking along a dark, dimly lit passageway with two African men. I was feeling ever so grateful that I had stumbled into these kindhearted men who had unselfishly volunteered to take me to the taxi rank. I was struggling to stand up, but they were standing either side of me, holding my arms, keeping me on my feet and then, as the passageway darkened further and came to a dead end, one of them tripped me up.

If you want to find something to snap you out of a drunken state in an instant, may I suggest you get someone to trip you up, lay you down horizontally, kneel on your back with a cigarette in one hand and a knife in the other, stubbing his cigarette out repeatedly on the back of your neck and cutting your neck with the blade of his knife. This sobers you up immediately. Initially, when my mugger tripped me up, I started to struggle, but once the knife and cigarettes went to work, I soon realised it was in my interest to stay still. As I lay there motionless, his thieving mate, took my watch off my wrist, rifled through my pockets and stole my wallet and then strolled off, reminding me not to come after them as they had a knife. I liked my wallet and watch but had already over indulged in stupidity so wasn't going to be chasing after the muggers in a desperate bid to retrieve them.

Penniless and, if truth be known, a little frightened, I then stumbled into a true Good Samaritan, a lad from Nottingham, who walked me up to the local medical centre. They then arranged for me to go to hospital. After checking me out, the hospital staff then arranged for me to go to the police station. It was like a Spanish déjà vu of two weeks earlier!

When I eventually arrived back at our apartment block, at about seven o'clock in the morning, Sean and Jamie were asleep on two seats in reception. They told me that the three of us had made the crazy, drunken decision to sleep on the beach and this is obviously where I had been discovered by my muggers. Jamie and Sean had woken up to find that I had gone, so had headed home, but could not get into the apartment as Jay had the key. Jay was sound asleep in the apartment and was oblivious to their knocking, but Jay had his own tale of woe, as he had attempted to hitchhike back to the apartment, had grown suspicious that his 'friendly' driver may have been taking him in the wrong direction, so had jumped out the car and made a run for it at a set of traffic lights and had then wandered round for hours trying to find his way back!

What does all this have to do with football? Nothing at all, but in a book that is semi-autobiographical, it does tell you a bit about me! Also, if Manchester United have a part to play in this year's F.A Cup and I have a feeling they might, my United mate, Sean O'Donnell may return to the story. For now, let's just say his texts were saying that he feels the job may be too much for Moyes,that Fellaini was a disaster buy and that Fellaini, Cleverly and Wellbeck are at the centre of all that is currently wrong with United. He also thought Everton were lucky, which perhaps they were.

Tomorrow, I am off to Stevenage with my Dad and Alan. We are meeting Phil there and Jordan has now opted out as her mate has bought her tickets for a gig in Manchester. Will I get completely off my face tomorrow night and end up getting picked up and mugged by two rogues? I doubt it, thankfully Alan and my Dad are both teetotal !

We are all now safely down in Stevenage and looking forward to the game tomorrow. This morning, I picked Alan up at Buckshaw Parkway station at half past ten, which has become a bit of a routine, although it has normally been a Saturday morning and from there, we drove over to Aughton to pick my Dad up. Alan and I went in for a quick coffee at my Mum and Dad's, so Alan got to meet my Mum for the first time. We are eight games in now and feel like we know Alan, Phil and Jordan fairly well, so it's strange that before today, Alan hadn't met my Mum and as yet, he hasn't met Alison. I am sure introductions will be made before this journey is over. It would be interesting to meet Alan's wife, Joanne too. She is obviously fairly easy going to allow him to spend so much of his life travelling the length and breadth of the country to watch football.

Phil has gone to his Mum and Dad's for a couple of days, so it was just my Dad, Alan and me that came down in the car. The journey was fine, not overly busy and no major delays heading South, but around Coventry I had a bit of a worry as I could feel a migraine coming on. Back in December 1986, I had labrynthitis and subsequently suffered from what a consultant in Rodney Street, Liverpool called at the time, "post viral syndrome" and has since been re-branded as M.E ('chronic fatigue syndrome'). I am pretty sure there are still medical debates about how real M.E actually is, but all I know is for six months or so, I was lacking in energy to carry out even the most simple of tasks and frequently suffered from migraines. By the summer of 1987, my energy levels gradually began to increase but I was still bothered by severe migraines on a regular basis until my mid-twenties. Since then, the migraines severity have eased, as has their regularity, but blurred vision is generally the starting point, so as soon as I felt my eyes struggling to focus properly I pulled in at a service station, quickly purchased some headache tablets and a bottle of water, keeping my fingers crossed that a migraine wouldn't develop. Alan can't drive, so my Dad would have had to take the wheel. Thankfully, the symptoms soon subsided and we were able to continue on our way after a half hour stop.

We eventually arrived at the IBIS hotel in Stevenage at around half past four after a half hour detour around Luton. Stupidly, we had relied upon an internet routefinder to get us there when we could have just asked Phil what the best route was. Had we learnt nothing from Keith Brian's crazy SatNav on the way to Stourbridge in the previous round? Obviously not!

Stevenage Football Club had, as promised, provided with us with two twin rooms in the IBIS Hotel in Stevenage town centre. Alan had a room to himself whilst my Dad and I shared the other twin. I don't ever remember sharing a room just with my Dad in my previous forty two years of existence. Once, my Dad and I had been in a tent at Tawd Vale on a Cub Scout, 'Dads and Lads' trip, but for some reason this did not involve an overnight stay. This trip back in 1981 was the only occasion my Dad and I have ever jointly won anything and, if truth be known, we cheated. Well, cheated may be a little harsh, but we certainly bent the rules. This is the only occasion in living memory that my Dad didn't quite play fair!

The directive for the 'Lads & Dads' cub scout trip competition was that you had to bring some wood and household objects and create a vehicle from the objects you brought. My Dad would probably regard himself as average at D.I.Y and I am pathetic and as a ten year old, was probably even worse than I am now, so we were up against it from the start. Once the competition began, some gifted, artistic father and son combinations were carefully crafting spitfires from a block of wood. My Dad is a painter and decorator by trade, so he brought some big empty paint tins, some small empty paint tins, some glue and three small tins of paint, green, red and black. We made a steam engine out of a large paint tin, a small paint tin, an empty tube of glue and used paint lids as wheels. Importantly, and this is where the cheat came in, we painted it. So when the judge looked at all the finished works, the spitfire, the various cars and boats, all lacked that extra ingredient – colour! Our steam engine that was cobbled together in ten minutes, beat toys that had been carefully crafted for hours to a specification that Airfix would have been proud of. There were a few grumblings from the Dads, but first prize was ours!

Back in modern day, I was a little concerned about sharing a twin room with my Dad as he is the world's lightest sleeper and I have a cough and cold currently, which leads me to cough aggressively as soon as I am horizontal and I have learnt that I have also been snoring due to my blocked nose (a few bruises resulting from kicks from Alison bear witness to that). I will let you know tomorrow how that one goes, but I am not confident he will sleep well.

Around half five, we headed out to meet Phil at the train station. The IBIS hotel is literally a five minute walk from the train station, but they are divided by a busy dual carriageway, so you have to walk along to a bridge. Having inherited my Mum's fear of heights, I was thankful it was no more than about twenty feet high, as I would have come across as a real 'big girl's blouse' if I had refused to cross.

Stevenage is a large, bustling town. I pictured, given it is a post-Second World War 'New' town like Skelmersdale, a Skelmersdale or Southport sized place. It is much bigger than I had imagined. I would say it is a similar size to Wigan. Back in April and May, when Wigan Athletic were appearing at Wembley in the 2013 FA Cup Semi Final and Final, Roberto Martinez had to defend their fans when they ony sold about 22 000 tickets for the Semi Final. To put it in perspective, it would be like Stevenage selling 22 000 tickets for a major game at Old Trafford. It is always disappointing to see empty seats at a major sporting event, but to an extent, it is understandable.

Somehow, we managed to get our wires crossed with Phil and whilst we were waiting for him at the station, he was waiting for us at the IBIS, but we each doubled back and met halfway. We then went over to the retail park by the train station for our evening meal, before heading towards the old town for a drink. On the way to Stevenage Old Town, we went past Stevenage Cricket and Hockey club, so I nipped in to ask if they would be showing the Ashes cricket from Australia overnight. The young barman, despite working at a cricket club, was obviously not a cricket fan, as he was unaware it was on and when I told him it started at midnight, he said they would be shut by then. I was desperate to watch some of it though, but he was unaware of anywhere in Stevenage that might be showing it.

Disappointed but still determined, I ran to catch up with the rest of the guys and when we passed an inviting pub called The Chequers, after about half a mile, we decided that would do for starters. Given both my Dad and Alan are teetotal, I was especially thankful that Phil had got the train to meet us. There was a band on in 'The Chequers' but it was a big old pub, so we managed to get a seat a distance away, where we could enjoy the music but not feel deafened by it. It is becoming increasingly apparent that there is a real warmth developing between the four of us. My Dad can take a little while to weigh people up and to me, it can be obvious when he doesn't like someone, as he will make little effort to converse with them (another family trait I have inherited), but his relationship with Phil and Alan is very chatty from both sides with lots of laughter and smiles. We all seem like old friends now. To Alan and especially Phil's credit, as he is a young man in his early thirties, they treat my Dad with a certain reverence.

Given my Dad doesn't drink, we rarely go for a drink together. We sometimes go for family meals but even that has become less regular because of my sons football matches and mine and Alison's recent financial plight. It is wonderful just sitting there trading stories. My

Dad has the best footballing ones as he is the man with the proper footballing career. I tee him up with one or two of my favourites, as I know Alan and Phil would like to hear them.

One of my particular favourites is about Steve McManaman. My Dad grew up on the same road, Brasenose Road, as Steve McManaman's Mum, Irene and regularly played football with Steve's Dad, Davey for the Melrose pub team. My Dad said Davey played in an almost identical manner to Steve, with great close control and that distinctive run. When Steve was thirteen or fourteen, my Dad had moved on from coaching and scouting at Everton, to work with Joe Royle at Oldham Athletic and wanted to sign Steve on schoolboy terms for Oldham. Given my Dad's Everton background, he had already recommended Mark Ward to Joe, who had moved on to Northwich Victoria from Everton. Joe bought him and then sold him on to West Ham for £250 000. My Dad saw Steve's signing as another potential big coup, as Liverpool and Everton scouts were also aware of his talents.

Having known Steve's Mum and Dad, my Dad felt he may be at an advantage, so rang Davey McManaman up and arranged to go around the following night, to talk to Steve about the merits of signing for Oldham Athletic. My Dad said he left the following evening, feeling like the meeting had gone excellently and was confident Steve would sign. Davey seemed particularly keen, telling his son that if he signed for Oldham, "Richie will look after you." Twenty four hours later, Liverpool sent their representative around, but it wasn't a scout from their Youth Development system, it was their manager, Kenny Dalglish! The rest is history! Steve went on to represent Liverpool over three hundred times, put in a 'Man of The Match' performance for Real Madrid in a Champions League victory in 2000 and then won it again two years later, becoming the first Englishman to win the 'Champions League' twice. At that time, he was regarded as the most successful Brit to ever play football abroad. He probably still retains that record to this day. He was also capped 37 times for England. I wonder if he ever had sleepless nights about not signing for Oldham?

In March 2001, I went with my Dad to Anfield to see a World Cup Qualifier between England and Finland, which England went on to win 2-1. Just inside from the Shankly Gates, my Dad spotted someone he knew and wandered over to say 'hello'.

"This is my son, Calvin," he said to the bloke.

"Hi Calvin," the guy said with a handshake and a smile, "I'm a mate of your Dad's from his footballing days. We used to play together for the Melrose."

We all had a chat for a while and only after we walked away from him, did my Dad mention that he was Steve McManaman's Dad, there to watch his son play for his country. A more down to earth bloke you could not hope to meet. My Dad says Steve is the same. He has earned himself a tidy sum, but will still turn up with his Dad in the pub for the Melrose re-unions.

By about half ten, my Dad decided he had stayed out long enough at The Chequers and wanted to head back to the IBIS and get his head down. This was probably a good plan given I would no doubt keep him up half the night coughing and snoring. I offered to walk back with him, but as it was only less than ten minutes walk, he said he was fine, said his goodbyes and headed off alone.

After my Dad left, Alan and Phil mentioned how much they have enjoyed spending time with him. I told them that it has been great for me too, getting to spend some quality time with my Dad and told them that even though he was brought up without a father, from a family of nine children and without any of the priviliges that most of us today would take for granted, he has been a great Dad and set a brilliant example to me. I would never say any of this in front of my Dad though, as it would embarrass us both.

I told Phil and Alan a story from my Manchester Polytechnic days. On 27th January 1990, three days before my 19th birthday, Rochdale played Northampton Town in the 4th Round of the F.A Cup. One of the lads in my Halls of Residence, Jeremy Davy (who we call 'Jay'), was a big Aston Villa fan, but was also excited to see his home town team, 'The Cobblers' going on an extended Cup run and when they were drawn against local side, Rochdale, a division below them at the time, he wanted all our group of friends to go along to see them progress to the dizzy heights of the 5th Round. Jay was bullish about 'The Cobblers' chances and related stories to us about their talisman, centre forward, Bobby Barnes, who had dropped down a couple of Leagues from West Ham United and was going to tear Rochdale apart. As my Dad and I had been to loads of F.A Cup games throughout my childhood, both watching Everton and as neutrals, I wanted to ask my Dad along too. So, Jay and I went over to Rochdale one day and bought six tickets for the game, for us two, my Dad, and three mates from Poly, Sean (the Manchester United fan), Jamie and Lee.

At this stage, I don't think the lads from Poly had met my Dad, so I thought I should warn them that despite his working class upbringing, he has very high morals, detests swearing with a passion and hates to see anyone dropping litter. The latter, I wasn't worried about, but the swearing was a problem, as at the time, some of the lads would curse habitually in almost every sentence. I warned them all to be on their best behaviour.

On a crisp, frosty winter's day, we headed over to Rochdale on the train and met my Dad just outside the ground. The regular warnings about language seemed to have done the trick and the lads were impeccably behaved throughout the introductions and remained so during the first half. Northampton Town had a disaster of a day though and nothing went right for them. By late in the second half, they found themselves three-nil down. Jay was extremely frustrated, but was biting his tongue, heeding the warning about my Dad's dislike of bad language.

With minutes to go, someone attempted to thread a ball through for Bobby Barnes to run on to. Barnes had had a really poor game and was obviously frustrated by 'The Cobblers' capitulation to their lower league opposition. As the intended through ball was cut out, Barnes fell to the floor and began banging the hard ground with his fists like a spoilt child.

"Jay," one of the lads shouted across, "that Bobby Barnes is an absolute c### !"

My Dad didn't react, but I knew the good impression I had wanted my friends to make on him had just been dealt a hammer blow! Thankfully my Dad must have just put it down to the impetuosity of youth, as twenty four years later, on the rare occasions he sees my old friends from Polytechnic, he is delighted to see them.

After another half hour of footballing chat, Phil announced he had to go too, to catch a train back to his parents. Alan and I walked up with him towards the station. I could tell Alan was ready to go to bed, but I wasn't, not when the Ashes cricket was about to start! Once Phil had gone for his train, I told Alan, I would walk back with him towards the IBIS and then go into town to try to find a pub that showed the cricket. Alan shook his head.

"No mate," he stated firmly, "we are in this together. If you are going to the cricket, I'm coming with you. Even though I have no idea what it is you love about the game!"

Stevenage was pretty dead but eventually we found somewhere that was showing Ashes cricket, the Holiday Inn. If a camera had followed us through town, it would have been amusing viewing, as I persuaded Alan that we could reach the hotel by vaulting over the metal railings in the middle of the dual carriageway. This wasn't a particularly difficult task for me, but Alan is almost a foot smaller than me and watching him struggle to get his legs and his body over the railings was like watching something out of 'It's A Knockout' with Eddie Waring saying, "It's a test of a lot of things: speed, strength, courage and....faith... I suppose."

Once we settled down by the TV in the Holiday Inn, Alan could hardly keep his eyes open. We watched almost an hour's play, or I did, Alan saw about six balls, in between periods of dosing, which were either left alone or blocked hesitantly by England's batsmen, Joe Root and Michael Carberry. Australia had scored a massive 570 runs in their 1st Innings and England are trying to draw the 2nd Test to avoid going 2-0 down in the Series. Having survived the fast bowlers, Joe Root for some inexplicable reason tried to hook Australia's spinner, Nathan Lyon for six and only managed to send it straight to Aussie opener, Chris Rogers in the deep, to be out for 15, leaving England wobbling at 57-2. I had had enough.

"Oi," I said shaking Alan awake, "I've had enough of this crap, come on, we're off!"

We are now back at the IBIS. A quick check on my phone has revealed Pietersen, who came into bat to replace Root has already got himself out for 4. We are 66-3 now and it's already looking like the Ashes are heading back to Australia. I am well cheesed off. I hope tomorrow's football is nowhere near as disappointing!

FA Cup 2nd Round Proper - Saturday 7th December 2013

Stevenage v Stourbridge

Attendance – 2160

Stevenage is famous for some of its modern day sportsmen. It is the birthplace of racing driver, Lewis Hamilton and golfer, Ian Poulter amongst others. The football team are known for a couple of F.A Cup ties against Newcastle. The previously mentioned ties when they were a Conference side back in 1998 and also the 3rd Round tie in 2011, when they knocked Newcastle out the competition, beating them 3-1. Bizarrely, that victory was marred by Stevenage player, Scott Laird, being knocked out by one of the team's own fans, after Stevenage supporters ran on the pitch after the final whistle. They will have gone into today's game hoping not to become the victims of an F.A CUP giantkilling act and instead hoping they could get drawn against a big team to do the David v Goliath act on, once again, next round.

Stourbridge knew a win for them would really make the sporting headlines. They were already the lowest ranked team in the competition going into the game and although they had previously reached the 2nd Round Proper, a place in the 3rd Round would re-write their history books and give them their first ever taste of life with the big boys.

We woke up early this morning. It felt like living with my Mum and Dad again, as when I was a kid, my Dad would never let me sleep in and once again this was the case! My Dad was looking for something at the bottom of the beds and as I sat up to see what was going on, my Dad asked if I had slept well.

"Pretty well," I replied.

"Well it sounded like you slept well to me with all that coughing and snoring!" my Dad responded.

It turns out, however, that I wasn't too loud or too regular with the snoring or coughing and he had had a half decent night's sleep. We gave Alan a knock, as he professes to be an early riser and sure enough he was already up, so before breakfast we all decided to go for a walk. We ended up walking all the way up to the Lamex Stadium, Stevenage's ground, which is about two miles out of town. It is a modern looking ground but every stand is really low, so I bet they get loads of balls kicked out the stadium, especially if one of the teams is clinging on to victory at the death. It looks as though it would be impossible to kick it into Row Z of any stand, possibly Row N would be as far back as it went. I looked through a gap and was surprised to see that one side of the ground, running along one side of the pitch (rather than behind a goal), is fully terraced. There is a busy dual carriageway that runs past the ground, like everywhere else in Stevenage, but across the road from that, is a massive car park, which given we were not expecting a massive crowd, seemed the ideal spot to park.

Having assessed the situation we headed back to the hotel. Alan had been to the Lamex before, on the last day of the season trip with friends from Bury Football Club and everyone on the coach had been dressed up in their fancy dress costumes. Alan decided not to get involved himself but he went to the match with a leprechaun and a pirate!

When we got back to the IBIS, we all took full advantage of the full English breakfast. As Clive Abrey and the kind people at Stevenage Football Club had put us up at the IBIS for free, we felt the least we could do was pay the £7-50 each for the 'eat as much as you like' breakfast. We thought if we had our breakfast late, then we could skip lunch. This seemed like a good plan at the time, but with hindsight, it turned out to be a rubbish one.

After breakfast my body was so full with croissants, hot chocolate, bacon, sausages and scrambled eggs, I opted to go back to bed and retrieve the sleep my Dad had stolen from me earlier! Alan and my Dad were horrified by my laziness and whilst I dozed with a full stomach for half an hour, my Dad walked over to have a look at the 'Old Town' and Alan went for a wander around the local shops. My Dad returned wishing we had opted for the 'Old Town' to eat last night, as he reported that it had a lot more character and variety than the retail park.

Pretty soon after they returned we checked out and met Phil off his train and then headed over to the Lamex. Clive Abrey had told my Dad the tickets wouldn't be available to pick up until 1:30 pm but we were at the ground by one, so Alan could go to the club shop and pick up a Stevenage badge, to continue the trend he began at West Didsbury. As we came out the club shop, a Stourbridge official supporters coach arrived and we soon established that the man who was greeting them off the coach was Clive himself. After he had sorted the Stourbridge supporters out, we made ourselves known to Clive and had a good chat with him for five minutes, thanking him warmly for his kindness and the club's incredible hospitality. At that stage, we didn't quite know the full extent of the kindness.

After our chat with Clive, he pointed us in the direction of our ticket collection point. We wandered over and to our surprise, Clive had arranged for us to be in the corporate hospitality section. This was fantastic and we were all stunned by the lengths Clive had gone to, but this now meant we were being given a full Christmas dinner! Phil was delighted as he was just thinking he was going to grab a pie for his lunch but Alan, my Dad and I looked at each other and smiled. If only we had known, I may have skipped my fifth helping of breakfast.

The four of us were on a table of eight with four of the Stourbridge fans that arrived earlier. There was a husband and wife and their adult daughter, who were all very friendly and another gentleman, in his thirties, who sat next to Alan and me, who was called Mark Craddock. He seemed to know the other three, but we didn't establish during our conversations quite how he knew them. Talking about friendly things, during our meal, we were visited by the Stevenage mascot, Boro bear, who went around the table giving everyone a hug and gave Alan's bald head a rub for luck. Whether luck from Alan would be for Stevenage or Stourbridge is debatable. When it is two teams we have no allegiance to, we always try to retain our neutrality, but the tendency is to find our allegiances tilting towards the lower club, especially if we have seen them in previous rounds.

Once Boro bear moved on to share hugs with others, Alan and I got talking to Mark. He was from Stourbridge and as well as supporting his local team, was also a big fan of Aston Villa. Over our turkey dinner, we established that Mark was an accountant and was a partner at West Midlands firm, Baldwins Accountants, in their Stourbridge office. A few years previously, they had decided to become a sponsor of Stourbridge Football Club, which paid off handsomely, as soon after, Stourbridge embarked on one of their many recent FA Cup campaigns. One game, the FA Cup 1st Round replay against Plymouth Argyle in November 2011 was televised on ESPN and Mark had arranged for the 'Baldwins Accountants' logo to be put on top of the Main Stand roof. This logo was directly opposite the vantage point of the ESPN cameras, so it was like being handed a ninety minute advertisement. When the staff of all the Baldwins offices in the Midlands returned to work the following day (after a 2-0 Stourbridge victory), they discovered they had been inundated with new enquiries from the length and breadth of Britain. Sometimes it does pay to support your local team. This season, rather than having the players names above the number on the back of the shirts, Stourbridge have the 'Baldwin Accountants' logo, so Mark was probably keener than most to see the Stourbridge 'Glassboys' progress and draw a Premier League big boy in the 3rd Round. If their offices were inundated after a 1st Round game against

Plymouth, imagine what they would be like if they played Manchester United at Old Trafford on a Sunday afternoon on ITV ?

Just before kick off, David James wandered past where we were eating, probably on reporting duty for BT Sport or ITV. My Dad went to see if he could say hello, as he had met him on a few occasions and had sat next to him at the funeral meal when Steve McManaman's mother, Irene, had tragically died of breast cancer. Dad said he always comes across as a really nice guy. I would have liked to meet him too, to give him a jovial ribbing, as he had predicted at the start of the season that Everton would face a battle against relegation and I wanted to remind him how wrong he was, now Everton were flying high in the Top Six! We didn't find him though. Maybe our paths will cross again in a later round when Everton are about to win the League and Cup double!

When we took our seats in the stand about quarter of an hour before kick off, we were a little disappointed to see the crowd wasn't going to be great. The capacity is only 6 722, but despite an excellent following from Stourbridge, of seven or eight hundred, it was looking like it would be less than half full. I guess December is an expensive time of year and Stevenage are languishing towards the bottom of the First Division, it is just a shame that more people don't get down and give them a cheer. It's a great little ground with plenty of atmosphere and those that do attend are very positive, encouraging supporters, despite their current predicament.

The game kicked off with Stourbridge looking like the more dangerous side in the early exchanges. Luke Benbow, the Stourbridge centre forward, flashed a rasping shot wide in the first few minutes and then after ten minutes, Leon Broadhurst scored from a corner, but it was disallowed for pushing. This seemed harsh as the Stevenage players were doing their fair share of holding and tugging too. Corners have become farcical these days and until the governing bodies do something about it, it will continue to be a free for all. If there is ever a whistle blown for an offence at a corner, it is always the defending team that are given the decision, like today, although in most instances, it is the defending team that tend to hold and grab more. In nearly every game there has been a major turning point and it felt, even at such an early stage, that this decision could prove costly to Stourbridge.

It is easy to forget, now they are in Division One, that Stevenage themselves were a non-League side throughout their history until 2010, so although there are four Leagues dividing the two clubs now, historically the gap would have normally been much narrower. In fact, Stevenage Borough (as they were formerly known) were only founded in 1976, as the town's former side, Stevenage Athletic had gone bankrupt in the 1970's and the ground, Broadhall Way (which was its name prior to being sponsored by Lamex Food Group) was unused for footballing purposes for three seasons. At one stage, the local businessman who owned it, had a trench dug across it, so there was no way football could be played there!

The Stevenage goalkeeper, Chris Day, looked a bit hesitant in the early stages of the half and his reluctance to come to collect the crosses Stourbridge were putting into the box, seemed to be annoying Graham Westley, the exuberant Stevenage manager. For about ten minutes, Westley wandered along the touchline, seemingly ignoring any coaching areas, to shout instructions to his keeper. As a former goalkeeper myself, I would have hated a Manager publicly criticising me in such an obvious manner, but Chris Day didn't seem to react.

As the first half progressed, Stevenage seemed to improve, with Filipe Morais, one of their two widemen, being instrumental in all their dangerous moves, putting in dangerous crosses towards their powerful forward, Francois Zoko. When Zoko initially failed to capitalise on the chances provided, he was jeered by the Stourbridge faithful behind the goal.

"Shit Emile Heskey! You're just a shit Emile Heskey," they jeered, but unfortunately for those fans, just before half-time Zoko had the last laugh, a short corner went to Luke Freeman, who was also growing into the game and his pinpoint cross was headed home by the taunted striker, Zoko.

Right from the first moments of the second half, hopes of a giantkilling began to evaporate, as Stevenage took up where they left off and dominated proceedings. Four minutes in, Stevenage scored an important second goal in bizarre circumstances. A cross came into the Stourbridge box and wasn't properly cleared and in the penalty box melee, Stevenage's Lucas Akins looped a header towards goal. The ball dropped on to the top of the bar and everyone on the Stourbridge side, including the goalkeeper, Dean Coleman, seemed to stand still, like they were playing a childhood game that required them to 'freeze'. I suspect they thought the ball was going to drop harmlessly out of play, but when it landed invitingly in the six yard box, Akins was able to follow up his own effort for a scrappy tap-in.

A player from Stevenage who is making a striking impression on my Dad and me, as the game goes on, is a small midfielder with a scampering, 'Messi like' run, called Luke Freeman. He is very good with the ball at his feet, has pace and is one of those players that makes things happen in a game. When I arrived home tonight, I was pleased to see our positive judgement on him has been shared by others. Freeman is actually the youngest player ever to play in the FA Cup 'Proper' (the FA Cup becomes 'Proper' at the 1st Round Stage), having represented Gillingham, as a substitute, against Barnet, on 10th November 2007, aged only 15 years and 233 days! From Gillingham, he ended up signing for the mighty Arsenal, but failed to break into the first team and an initial loan spell at Stevenage became a permanent deal. I have a feeling that of the Stevenage players, he is the one most likely to rise back up the ranks. He may not get to play for the likes of Arsenal in the rest of his career, but on initial evidence, could hold his own at Championship level.

Unfortunately for Stourbridge the second goal put paid to their chances and to their momentum and after that, despite their spirit and effort never dipping, it became an uphill battle. Defenders like Will Richards, who had looked rock solid in previous games, were getting stretched by professional players four leagues above them and it was Richards initial error that led to the third goal. Richards mistimed a header and Zoko, who was no longer being called a "shit Emile Heskey" by the Stourbridge fans, sprinted along the right wing before cutting into the box. His cross was deflected into the path of Heslop and although his low shot was blocked by Richards, the ball found its way back to Zoko who cleverly squared the ball across for Freeman to bundle it over the line.

It was now a case of keeping some respectability to the scoreline. Stourbridge had more than matched Stevenage for most of the first half and to be subjected to a real drubbing would have been really harsh on them. Thankfully, in the last quarter of the game, they did come into the game and spurned a couple of half chances but were still dependent on their keeper, Dean Coleman to make some great saves to keep the scoreline down. A minute from time Stevenage did manage to add a fourth goal. Luke Freeman was again the orchestrator working a one-two down the left flank before pulling the ball back towards Morais who was bundled over inside the box by Geddes. Morais was soon back on his feet and took the penalty himself, nonchalantly sending Coleman the wrong way to complete the scoring. Seconds later, it was all over and Stourbridge's epic FA Cup journey had come to an end. They were deservedly given a standing ovation by their fans, linking hands and running over to the away end to enjoy the adulation. It would have been fantastic to see them reach the Third Round for the first time in their history, but we saw them equal their best ever F.A Cup run in their 137 year history, so they could now concentrate on promotion with quite a few extra quid in the kitty. There is no doubt whatsoever that the F.A Cup is huge for teams like Stourbridge.

As for Stevenage, they will go in the hat tomorrow, with an opportunity of getting a fantastic draw against a Premier League side. We spoke to Clive after the game and from his personal perspective, he will be hoping for a plum draw at home, rather than away, as from a commercial perspective, it will bring more money into his division of the club. From my perspective, I would like a Northern Championship or Second Division club, ideally at a ground I have not previously visited. Alan and I discussed the idea of getting to see a club from each of the top four flights and we will undoubtedly see Premier League sides at the latter stages of the competition, so a Championship or Second Division side would help achieve that. A Northern option would be great, as I am still financially struggling and although Stevenage have ensured our trip there didn't tax the wallet too heavily, repeated trips to Plymouth or Southend might do!

The obvious exception to the rule is Everton. We have been to eight rounds now, before Everton have even entered the competition, so I would have no objection to watching Everton for the next six rounds! There are sixty four balls going into the draw, so it is unlikely that Stevenage will draw Everton, but they are just as likely as anyone else, so you never know!

After the game, we said goodbye to the disappointed but proud Stourbridge fans from our table, to Clive Abrey and to Phil, who was heading out to have a night out with some childhood friends before heading back to Manchester tomorrow. This game is probably the first one Phil has turned up to without a hangover, as he is normally out with friends in Manchester on a Friday night. Looks like his hangover is going to be twenty four hours late this round! I hope his hangover tomorrow is followed by a defeat for his beloved Arsenal, as they play Everton at the

Emirates ! It will once again be a real test of Everton's credentials, as Arsenal are top of the League and having an amazing season so far.

The journey home was a good one. I dropped Alan off at Crewe train station, as it would have been a drag for him to have to go to Ormskirk to drop my Dad off, then back to Buckshaw, then have to get a train to Manchester. By dropping him at Crewe, it would take a couple of hours off his journey.

When I dropped my Dad off, I went in to get Joel as he had been staying there for twenty four hours, as Alison has been on a double shift today. Brad, my eldest, at thirteen is capable of looking after himself for the day, but at eleven, Joel is a bit young to be left. He seemed to have had a great time with my Mum, as they had been out shopping into Ormskirk and he was sporting a new 'Onesie' that Alison had bought him for Christmas, but given him early because he was sleeping at his Nanna's. I had a quick coffee with my Mum and Dad and again it was great to hear my Dad enthusing about our trip.

The FA Cup trips for 2013 are now over. We have seen eight games and twenty nine goals so far. All eight have produced a result first time, helping us avoid the extra expense of replays. I will be back tomorrow to update on where we head to next in 2014, but so far the journey just seems to get better and better. This will no doubt be the case from now on, as the 'Big Boys' join the party. I have loved the non-League and lower League elements to the journey, but one of the teams that joins the competition tomorrow will ultimately win it and it is going to be fantastic watching these latter stages play out.

FINAL SCORE : Stevenage 4 Stourbridge 0

Scorers :- Zoko, Akins, Freeman, Morais.

Our 'Speccies':- Calvin Wade, Alan Oliver, Richard Wade, Phil Cooper.

Sunday 8th December 2013

Well, I got what I wished for, but Clive Abrey at Stevenage didn't get his wish, as in the Third Round of the FA Cup, Stevenage have been drawn AWAY at Doncaster Rovers! Not exactly a plum draw from either side's perspective, but for us, it is an opportunity to go to yet another new ground. We can get to Doncaster within an hour and a half and there will be no problem whatsoever getting tickets! We have to be pleased with that. The scramble for tickets will undoubtedly come as the competition progresses, so for the Third Round we can just have a pleasant Christmas, knowing we will be heading to Doncaster on the first Saturday of the New Year.

With there being a lot of replays, there are quite a few ties that are yet to be fully decided, but a couple of the plum ones are Arsenal v Tottenham Hotspur and Manchester United v Swansea. Once most of the replays have taken place, I will put the full draw details in here, as I will for each subsequent round from now on. Incidentally, Everton were drawn at Home to Queens Park Rangers, so I am confident that they should be able to get past them. At the very least, I am hoping to meet Everton at Wembley in the Semi Finals and Final! To write a book about the FA Cup as an Evertonian and not cross their path at some stage would be really disappointing, so if we avoid them and they get knocked out, it will be a particularly bitter pill to swallow this year, especially if we had to follow Liverpool for a few rounds and they ended up winning it! Everton played great today though at the Emirates, coming away with a fully deserved 1-1 draw, with our on-loan Barcelona player, Gerard Deulofeu equalising after Ozil had put Arsenal ahead. Everton have still only lost once this season, which must bode well for an extended F.A Cup run.

We now have a four week break from F.A Cup football. This will give me the opportunity to update you on a couple of things I mentioned earlier in the book, namely my disastrous attempts to lose weight and my equally disastrous footballing career!

Wishing I Was Flat Chested

Back in the summer of 2013, when this book was starting out and before a ball had been kicked in this year's F.A Cup, I was in an unhappy physical and financial place. I was losing battles with my bank account and my waistline and wanted to do something about it. Thankfully, on the financial side, my journey on the road to ruin has stopped at a service station. I would not be stupid enough to think everything in that garden is rosy just yet, but my shifts at Asda and then my permanent role at 'World Of Warranty' have certainly put me in a much better place than when I was struggling along in self-employment, waiting for that elusive 'lucky break' that was never going to arrive. Thus, from a financial perspective, the outlook is improving. From a physical perspective, the goal to be 13 stone 13 pounds on FA Cup Final day is probably further away now than it was in the summer, as I am still 16 stone and have less time to get into shape.

I have an addictive personality. Addictive in a habitual way rather than a completely reckless way but addictive nonetheless. From aged seventeen until when I was about 40, I enjoyed a bet. Enjoyed it too much really. I used to bet regularly on the horses, on the football and for a few years, on the stock market. There is a common conception that if you bet on the horses, you are likely to be out of pocket and are pretty stupid but if you play the stock markets, you are quite intelligent and have a good chance over time of coming out on top. The opposite is true for me. I have made quite a lot on the horses, lost a bit on the football and lost quite a lot on the stock markets. Primarily, I think this is because I knew more about what I was doing on the horse racing than on the stock markets and horses are honest creatures, it is humans who are not. Anyway, I stopped messing with the stock market long ago, but when money became tight, I greatly reduced my horse racing gambling too, as past performance is no guarantee of future performance and I could not afford to lose money I didn't have. I still have the occasional football bet, but it is literally a couple of pounds here and there and as I am not up to date on the horse racing, I will wait for the big days at Cheltenham, Aintree and Ascot, to put a couple of quid on them. The point is, it was a bad habit that lasted twenty three years. Since the age of about thirty five, I have also developed the habit of putting on weight and I am not going to let this one last twenty three years too.

I still have a pair of long legs that Jerry Hall would be proud of other than the hair and the football scars. As I have become greedier and lazier over the last few years, my body below the waist, has stayed exactly the same shape as it has always been throughout my adult life. Unfortunately, from the waist up everything I don't burn off gathers. When I am overweight, my beer gut swells to pregnancy proportions and even worse, I have a pair of moobs that would fit nicely into a training bra. I need to lose weight and I need to stop guzzling, but since the summer, I have taken two steps forwards and then three steps back.

Back in the summer, Alison had us on a diet regime where she would cook healthy foods (and I occasionally would!) and we would have a weekly weigh in on a Wednesday, so if we had a heavy weekend, we could still put it right by weigh-in day. This worked well for about six weeks and I was down half a stone, but since then, Alison has taken her eye off the ball and I have kicked the ball out of the park and sat in the goalmouth stuffing myself with doughnuts. After Christmas, I am going to do this properly. I am going to skip alcohol (in January anyway), bypass chocolate and exercise more. 13 stone 13 pounds by F.A Cup Final day is not beyond me, but if I don't start the New Year well, it soon will be.

My Footballing Career (Part Two) – How Life Gets In The Way!

By the time I left Burscough FC, I had aleady met the lady that would become my wife, Alison. For most of the time I was playing at Burscough, I worked at Alliance & Leicester in Church Street in Liverpool City Centre. At that time, there were two Alliance & Leicesters in town (the other one being in North John Street) so pretty often on a Friday night most of the staff would go out for a drink.

One of the girl's that worked at North John Street, Cathy, was a similar age to me and we got on well. One evening, I called around to her house in Bebington on the Wirral and her friend called around in a nurses uniform, as she was about to go into Arrowe Park hospital on a night shift. Her name was Alison and I was informed by Cathy that she was emigrating to Australia. Having backpacked around the world twelve months previously, spending a few months in Oz, I was chatting away with her, telling her she would love it, but although she was undoubtedly attractive, it was not love at first sight, as she was actually emigrating to be with her boyfriend who had already moved over there.

A couple of weeks later, Alison came out with Cathy on our Friday night out in Liverpool. At one stage, two guys in their forties, with wedding rings on made a move over to where Cathy and Alison were sitting and began a drunken attempt to chat them up. Alison was giving me a look of 'help me out here', so I walked over and sat the other side of her, and said to the bloke, jovially,

"Have you been chatting my wife up mate, whilst I've been at the bar?"

Give him his due, he was very apologetic.

"Sorry mate, I didn't know she was married. She wasn't wearing a wedding ring and I didn't see you over there."

Between us, Alison and I concocted a story about where we had met and where we were married and obviously buying into it, the guy sloped off, taking his mate with him. Cathy, Alison and I were the last ones out that night, I mustn't have had a match the following day, as the three of us went clubbing, but I was actually 'going out' with someone else at this point and it was still Alison's intention to emigrate, so although we obviously got on well, it still seemed little more than a friendship. I remember seeing Alison and Cathy getting into a taxi that night and as Alison got in saying to her,

"Do you know what, I'm sure you'd make a lovely wife!"

Alison continued to come on the occasional Friday night out, but soon after I left Alliance & Leicester and also split up from my girlfriend. I still spoke to Cathy from time to time once I started working for Yorkshire Building Society and one day, on the phone, she mentioned that she was off out into town with Alison that night.

"I thought Alison would have emigrated by now?"

"Oh no!" Cathy explained, "She didn't go. Her and her boyfriend have split up."

I tried to sound sympathetic but my mind was ticking over as to how I could engineer the conversation to ask whether I had any chance with her. I eventually just came out and asked.

"Do you think Alison would be interested in coming out with me one night?"

"On a date?"

"Yes."

Cathy said 'No'! She did give a detailed explanation as to why not. Alison had been with her boyfriend for years on and off, since their schooldays. She had gone through a lengthy emigration process and was now just wanting to enjoy herself for a while and get over the upset of her split.

The following Monday, Cathy rang me back. It was getting close to Christmas.

"I mentioned to Alison what you said," Cathy explained, "and I was wrong, she is interested. We are going out into Liverpool after work on Saturday and Alison is going to join us after she has done her early shift. Do you fancy coming across and meeting up?"

The rest, as they say, is history.

That night, Alison and I were the last two out and as we were sharing a rather drunken first kiss on the streets of Liverpool City Centre, I heard a voice in my ear.

"That's not Calvin Wade snogging the face of that girl, is it?"

I pulled out of our clinch to see Terry McPhillips, back then Burscough centre forward, nowadays, Blackburn Rovers Assistant Manager, smiling at me.

"You're a bit of a dark horse, Calvin, aren't you?!"

Alison and I were engaged six months later and married twelve months after that in June 1997. In May 1997, I was transferred by Yorkshire Building Society to become District Development Manager in the Glasgow Area. I was twenty six years old. This move pretty much signalled an end to any plans I may have had to return to semi-professional football.

I loved working in Glasgow. The people at the branch were great, the mortgage brokers I called on were great and I had a ball. Alison had moved up with me, after our honeymoon in Lake Garda, but she was twenty five and had never lived away from home before and didn't settle. The original job she did up there was on an Oncology Department of the Beatson Unit of Western Infirmary and looking after cancer patients must be emotionally draining at the best of times, let alone when you are homesick. We therefore spent the weekends when Alison wasn't working either journeying home or welcoming family and friends to our flat in the West End then later to our first house in Newton Mearns. We were there eighteen months and in that time, I think I played one game of eleven a side football and the occasional run out at five a side.

After eighteen months, we moved on again, heading South to Gloucester. I was promoted to a role called an 'Intermediary Account Manager', which was basically a 'Mortgage Rep' in a region where Yorkshire Building Society did not have a branch presence. This was another great job, as I covered Gloucestershire and Wiltshire, driving around in a company car encouraging mortgage brokers to put their business our way. We bought a new house in Longlevens, Gloucester and Alison settled quickly as one of my old schoolfriends, Andrew Moss, lived a few miles down the road in Bishop's Cleeve and Alison became great friends with his wife, Sarah. Whilst still in Glasgow, Alison had also managed to get a job as a 'Medical Sales Rep' and her best friend from that role, Judith, lived in Gloucester too. Alison managed to get another 'Medical Rep' job in Gloucestershire, so all was working out well.

With Alison more settled, we spent less time driving up and down the country at weekends so after twelve months, I returned to playing football. Having previously played for Burscough and Dingwall, a team at the higher end of the Wirral Sunday Premier League, I made my return playing for Wingate FC in the Gloucester Sunday League Division Seven! The lad next door in Longlevens, Mark Goodchild, was a really good cricketer and one of his cricketing pals, Pete Glynn, who was only seventeen at the time, was setting up a new football team with his Sixth Form pals and wanted a couple of older heads. Mark would have been around 25 at the time and I would have been about 28, so just wanting to get playing again, I decided to join. It was great to have a game and some of the young lads were good players but on reflection, I should have pushed myself to play at a higher standard.

Our first son, Brad, was born down in Gloucester on 3rd July 2000 but once we started thinking about having a second child, Alison grew increasingly keen on the idea of moving back towards our families in the North West. I am originally from Ormskirk and Alison is from Higher Bebington, Wirral, so Alison felt if we lived in the North West, our families would get to see the children more and she would get a helping hand from time to time.

As luck would have it, Yorkshire Building Society were developing a new subsidiary company at the time, Accord Mortgages and an opportunity arose for me to get a sideways career move which involved moving back to the North West. House prices were going through a New Labour boom at the time, so we couldn't afford to live in Ormskirk, but managed to find a new build plot in Euxton, just outside Chorley, that seemed ideal. We moved North when Alison was pregnant with Joel, living with my Mum and Dad for about three months whilst our house was built. I am sure it wasn't the easiest situation for my Mum and Dad having their son, daughter-in-law and eighteen month old grandson move in, but they looked after us.

About twelve months after Joel was born (on 21st June 2002), I returned to playing football. By the 2003-2004 season, I would have been 32 going on 33, so harboured no ambitions to play for a good team, I just wanted a bit of a sporting social life. One day, when I was back at my Mum and Dad's, I bumped into a lad I had been to school with, David Ainsworth. He asked if I was playing in goal for anyone and when he discovered I wasn't, he suggested I join the team he played for, Metropolitan. Although we had occasionally clashed when we had been growing up, the vast majority of the time I had got on well with David. He was very self-assured and at times, a bit of an eccentric character. He is the only person I have ever come across who swapped sides after winning the toss on a flat 5-a-side pitch! Anyway,

David said the side wasn't the greatest but were mainly aged thirty plus and included several lads I knew from schooldays so I really fancied joining.

I think in total, I played four seasons at Metropolitan and thoroughly enjoyed it. A lad who was three years below me at school, Mark Pounder, managed the side and tried to bring a few young lads in to compensate for the lack of pace in an ageing squad. At first, I was labelled 'Chris Kirkland', after the injury prone former Liverpool goalkeeper, as I started to pick up muscular injuries for the first time ever. When I was younger, I could just turn up and play but on one occasion, soon after joining them, I tore my hamstring after tearing off my line in the first minute, having arrived at the ground, put the nets up and started playing. I soon learnt that if the side were meeting half an hour before kick off, I had to arrive thirty minutes earlier to do a proper warm up and once I began that routine, the injuries were averted.

In my second season playing for Metropolitan, we actually managed to get to a Cup Final which was played at Burscough's ground, Victoria Park. We were hammered by a very good young side from Skelmersdale 5-0, but I managed to have a decent game and keep the score down to something almost respectable.

Two other incidents remain imprinted in my mind from my time at Metropolitan. One involved my Dad and the other is often spoken about by Brad, my eldest son, who was down watching when it happened.

I think the best adult performance I ever had was at Sandy Lane, Maghull in my last season for Metropolitan. About seven or eight of our team were mid-30s plus by this point and even when we started games well, we struggled to maintain the pace for ninety minutes. We were in the Division 3 (of 3) and were playing against a side that were top of the League whilst we were languishing just below mid-table. Our formation for most of the game was 9-0-1 with

Robbie Knowles, our centre forward, our only outlet. Our goal was peppered with shots, corners, crosses and free kicks but I just had a going day where I seemed to be stopping almost everything that was heading to any corner of the net. Their keeper, in contrast, had two shots from Robbie and a back pass to deal with and had a horrific display, letting all three in. So, with minutes left, we found ourselves drawing 3-3. The waves of pressure from the opposition continued and my ninety minutes of magic kept going. I must have had the spirit of Lev Yashin within me for that hour and a half, as they needed to have about three of them clean through to get past me. With seconds to go, I made a full length diving save to my right to deny their centre forward a deserved winner.

When the final whistle blew, our ten outfield players ran over to congratulate me and their players to a man came over to shake my hand and with the exception of their goalkeeper, asked if I fancied joining them. My Dad had been on the sidelines. He didn't watch many of my adult games, but this one was a couple of miles from his house, so he had driven down. After the pandemonium had died down, he walked over to me. I knew what to expect as he had always been my harshest critic.

"What happened with their second goal from that corner? You should have come and grabbed that one!" he said, berating me.

If I had been a child, this would probably have upset me, but as a man in my late thirties, it just brought my childhood memories back and I burst out laughing.

"Well played though!" he added, somewhat reluctantly.

My Dad is an undoubtedly brilliant father and role model, but praise has never been his strong point. That 'well played' was as good as it could ever get and I was a little shocked he was able to manage that. My Mum says he would tell other people how good I was or how well I had played in a game, he just found it difficult to tell me. Perhaps this is one of the reasons I have never been arrogant or over confident though. Alan Oliver finds it amusing that I will always look at the negatives as well as the positives in any scenario, but I have my Dad to thank for that!

The other incident also happened in that final season, but isn't one I am proud of, especially because Brad, who was about eight at the time, was on the touchline. Up until this day, I had always been even tempered on the football field, only ever receiving two yellow cards in my thirty years (on and off) of playing in goal. This was very much following in my father's footsteps.

In his career, my Dad was also only booked twice. Bookings weren't as prevalent back in that era, but still to be booked only twice as a tough tackling, competitive centre half, shows the character of the man. My grandfather (my Mum's father), Ernie Mack, was a showbusiness impressario in Merseyside in the fifties, sixties and seventies and ran a lot of the entertainment scene in Liverpool clubs (Melvyn Bragg once did a BBC documentary on him and his two business partners called The Impressarios). He was a mate of Ken Dodd and was an agent for Les Dennis, Frank Carson , Ricky Tomlinson, Tom O'Connor, Jimmy Cricket and many other celebrities that rose to fame via the Merseyside club scene including Stan Boardman and even booked a young Gary Barlow on to pensioners night in the Montrose Club in Anfield! Whenever my Grandad took me to Liverpool games though (my Mum's brother and Dad were big Liverpudlians), we would always run into Stan Boardman and he would always tell me a story of playing football against my Dad and thinking my Dad had gone over the top of the ball, so losing his rag and swinging a punch at him, only to discover he had gone for the wrong man, as it wasn't my Dad that had 'done'him.

"I should have realised it wasn't your Dad," Stan explained, "he was never that sort of player."

On one wet Sunday morning in February, on a muddy field at Abbey Lane, I sullied the family reputation. I would like to think I was provoked. Brad and Joel were terrible sleepers as young kids, always waking up before six, so by the time Sunday morning football kicked off at eleven, I was often tired and masking an internal irritability. This day, we were playing a team from Kirkby and we were being referreed by a fat, grey haired old man aged about one hundred and seven, who just tried to control things from the safety of the centre circle. After about ten minutes, a poor cross from their left winger was easily collected by me underneath the posts and after muted appeals from about two of their players, the referee decided in his wisdom, to give them a goal. I was incensed, as I am competitive but with a sense of fair play, so to be punished unfairly added to my poor mood. This Kirkby side were young and fiercely competitive and the game was creeping to a conclusion with us 4-1 down.

In injury time, one of their central midfielders over hit a through ball to their small, fast, teenage centre forward, so I came to the edge of my box to collect it. As I knelt down in a cricketing long barrier type position, I noticed out the corner of my eye that the small centre forward was still sprinting towards me, I picked the ball up and a second later, I saw him take off, in a two footed lunge towards my shoulder blade. He hit his intended target and I felt a sharp jolt of pain in my shoulder. I had been the victim of equally heavy challenges many times in the past, but this time I just wasn't prepared to accept it. I picked myself up off the floor, threw the ball into touch and then headed towards the little whippet of a forward who was still on the ground. If you have ever seen the Dave Mackay and Billy Bremner image of the 1960s, you will be able to imagine what I did. I grabbed his football shirt and lifted him up off the floor, in the manner of 'The Incredible Hulk' and just stared at him furiously before throwing him like he was a junior javelin back on to the grass. Despite being a foot smaller than me and twenty years younger, he was still prepared to come back at me and within ten seconds, his ten team mates (including the goalkeeper who ran the full length of the pitch) decided to join in. My team mates were not going to allow it to be eleven against one, so evened things up and pretty soon a twenty two man brawl was taking place. Their goalkeeper must have sprinted past the ref on his way to join in, as the poor old man must have taken an age to reach the edge of my box from the centre circle. When he eventually did, he managed to separate me from the twenty one other players. As the instigator of the brawl, once I was taken away from the scene, it all started to calm down.

"Right keeper," said the breathless referee, "which lad was it that you were fighting with?" he asked. I pointed out the offender. He ambled over slowly, knowing we were both in big trouble.

"By rights, I should send both of you off, you know that, don't you? I could even send the whole lot of you off and abandon the bloody game" he said.

We bowed our heads a little, feigning shame.

"But if truth be known," he went on, "there are only ten seconds left and I can't be arsed sitting down this afternoon and writing a report on this bloody shambles, so just shake hands, keeper you take the free kick and I'll blow the whistle so we can all go home."

Even after the final whistle I was half-expecting it all to kick off again, but the red mist had now disappeared. Their keeper even came over and shook my hand.

"Sorry for joining in mate," he said," I saw the twenty one of you kicking off and I thought I was missing out big time, so I had to run over and be a part of the action!"

I wandered over to Brad.

"I'm really sorry, Brad. Your Dad has never lost his temper like that before and I am sure I won't ever again."

"I don't mind, Dad, it was funny!"

"No, it wasn't Brad, I was wrong to do that. I should have been sent off and I was very lucky I wasn't. I have said sorry to everyone and now I'm saying sorry to you. Sorry."

Brad is a keeper now, but thankfully, in the last five years, he hasn't ever followed my bad example. He still reminds me of it from time to time though, when I am lecturing him about how to behave on a football pitch. I was lucky my Dad wasn't there, he would have been (rightfully) appalled.

At the end of that season, I hung up my gloves. I did once get to dust them off again to play in a 5-a-side corporate competition down in St.Albans which was a brilliant day in aid of the Anthony Nolan charity. There were about twelve work sides and each one of them was given an ex-professional player to join their squad. The professionals weren't too shabby either and included Luther Blissett, Clive Walker, Steve Sedgeley, Warren Barton and Dean Holdsworth, but we were given the best of the lot, when we were joined by ex-Arsenal and England player, Ray Parlour. Dermot Gallagher referreed the games and former Sky pundit, Matt Lorenzo did commentary over the tannoy system. Ray sooned realised he was with a load of has beens and never beens, so after our second of five games, all of us, including Ray, started to put a few pints away and by the final game, we were all half-cut! Ray seemed like a great bloke, really friendly with many great stories. He loved Arsene Wenger and said he was "before his time" regarding how he wanted the game to be played on the pitch and how he wanted players to look after themselves off it.

So, that's how my football days ended. It started out playing head tennis with 'The White Pele' (Colin Harvey) and finished playing five-a-side football with 'The Romford Pele' (Ray Parlour). I was a million miles off reaching the heights of my Dad, but I still loved playing the game and came out of it with a few good stories. I am just hoping the real talent has skipped a generation and one of my boys can make a better attempt than I ever did of emulating my Dad.

Wednesday 1st January 2014

Happy New Year! Christmas and New Year celebrations are over for another year and I overdid things once again, like every other year. I now tip the scales at my highest ever weight of 16 stone 4 and a half pounds. No alcohol in January and sensible food until F.A Cup Final Day is my New Year's resolution.

Despite the over eating and over drinking, all things considered, it has been a relatively quiet Christmas. Alison has been on a lot of nights at the hospital, including Christmas Eve and New Year's Eve, so we skipped the Christmas dinner and I also skipped the booze up on New Year's Eve, as I drove over to Bill Cecil's (the Wolverhampton fan with a Manchester United season ticket) with Joel. We both had a great night though. Bill has converted an outbuilding into a bar and pool room, so we mainly partied in there, with the kids watching 'Grown Ups 2' in the house for a while too, which Joel thinks is the funniest film he has ever seen.

Our tickets for the Doncaster Rovers against Stevenage game are all sorted out. The Keepmoat Stadium has a capacity of 15 231, but I can't see it being even half-full, despite Doncaster discounting tickets to £10 for Adults and Seniors and only £1 for children. I tried to persuade Brad and Joel to go to a game before it was going to do too much damage to my wallet, but once again this game doesn't appeal.

The main five supporters in our group, myself, my Dad, Alan, Phil and Jordan are all signed up for this one. I offered to pick them all up, but the Arsenal-Spurs game is on at 5:15p.m and they want to go into Doncaster after our game to watch it in a pub, so are going to get the train home. So, this time around, there will only be my Dad and me in the car. Dad is going to drive to my house for about 10:30 a.m and I will drive to Doncaster from here. It is an easy route, motorway all the way and won't take much more than an hour and a half.

Budweiser FA Cup Third Round Draw

Now most of the replays for 2nd Round games have been played, there is a bit of shape to the FA Cup draw, so I thought I would put it in here:-

Blackburn Rovers v Manchester City.

Barnsley v Coventry.

Yeovil v Leyton Orient.

Bristol City v Watford.

Southend United v Milwall.

Middlesbrough v Hull City.

West Bromwich Albion v Crystal Palace.

Kidderminster Harriers v Peterborough United.

** DONCASTER ROVERS v STEVENAGE **

Stoke City v Leicester City.

Southampton v Burnley.

Newcastle United v Cardiff City.

Rochdale v Leeds United.

Wigan Athletic v MK Dons.

Charlton Athletic v Oxford United.

Norwich City v Fulham.

Aston Villa v Sheffield United.

Macclesfield Town v Sheffield Wednesday.

Bolton Wanderers v Blackpool.

Everton v Queens Park Rangers.

Brighton & Hove Albion v Reading.

Grimsby Town v Huddersfield Town.

Ipswich Town v Preston North End.

Bournemouth v Burton Albion.

Arsenal v Tottenham Hotspur.

Nottingham Forest v West Ham United.

Sunderland v Carlisle United.

Derby County v Chelsea.

Liverpool v Oldham Athletic.

Port Vale v Plymouth Argyle.

Manchester United v Swansea City.

Birmingham City v Crawley or Bristol Rovers.

** There are sixty five teams left in the competition. Five of the games are all Premier League clashes, so a maximum of 15 Premier League sides will make the 4th Round (probably less). There are three non-League sides left in, Grimsby Town Macclesfield Town and Kidderminster Harriers, but all three have tough games so it would take a tremendous achievement for any of them to make it through to the 4th Round, often one non-League side does though.

The odds to win the FA Cup outright, according to various bookmakers are :-

Manchester City 5/1

Chelsea 6/1

Manchester United 7/1

Liverpool 7/1

Arsenal 9/1

Everton 12/1

Tottenham Hotspur 16/1

Southampton 25/1

Newcastle United 25/1

Aston Villa 40/1

50/1 BAR

Doncaster Rovers 300/1

Stevenage 2500/1

Is it worth a £1 on Stevenage? Only if you like donating money to bookmakers!
I think Manchester City's odds at 5/1 are generous as I can't see who is going to beat them if
they have a going day. I don't see an outsider like Wigan winning it again and predict that
someone from the top six sides will win it. Everton could, if they are lucky with the draw. We
could do with a nice home draw to the winners of Doncaster Rovers and Stevenage in the 4th
Round!

I have been checking a few things out about Doncaster Rovers prior to going there on
Saturday. One of the things that initially surprised me was that they have about 70 000 followers
of their official Twitter page (Stevenage FC has around 11 000). It was only when I went into
followers details that I understood why. About 80% of Doncaster Rovers twitter followers are
girls aged between 13 and 18. This is not because they have an unusual band of supporters at
Doncaster, it is because Doncaster signed (in an unusual marketing coup) a lad called Louis
Tomlinson from the globally successful boy band, One Direction. I would have no idea which
one Louis was, if it wasn't for Aston Villa's Gabriel Agbonlahor.

Back in September, there was a Charity game played at Celtic Park for former Celtic and Aston Villa player Stiliyan Petrov, to raise money for his cancer foundation. Petrov is a former Bulgarian international (playing 106 times for his country), who was diagnosed with leukaemia in March 2012. The game featured a Celtic XI against a Petrov XI with players such as Agbonlahor and Dimitar Berbatov playing, as well as ex-pros like Jamie Redknapp and Robert Pires. There were also a few celebrities turning out such as Tomlinson, the actor Warren Brown and the comedian John Bishop. There were over 50 000 supporters there who all took to their feet in the 19th minute to applaud Petrov, as that had been his squad number at Aston Villa and their fans had taken to applauding for sixty seconds in the 19th minute of every game, since Petrov's diagnosis. Anyway, during that game, Louis Tomlinson was tackled aggressively, but in my opinion fairly, by Agbonlahor and had to limp off the field. It made tabloid headlines because Tomlinson vomited at pitch side and incensed One Direction fans sent threats to Agbonlahor's twitter site, including one saying she would kill him and another saying she would chop his balls off. Thus, through this, I learnt what Louis Tomlinson looks like.

Tomlinson has been given a squad number at Doncaster Rovers of '28'which is no doubt the best selling shirt in the club shop, despite him not kicking a ball for them yet. He is due to turn out for the reserves for a game before the end of the season and I just hope for his sake, it isn't against an Aston Villa reserve side with Gabbi Agbonlahor turning out as he recovers from an injury!

Another famous face at Doncaster Rovers is their Manager, Paul Dickov. As a Manager he was at the helm when Oldham Athletic knocked Liverpool out the FA Cup last season, but soon resigned as their League form deteriorated. He is more famous for his playing career that took in a number of clubs including Arsenal, Manchester City, Blackburn Rovers and Leicester

City. When Joe Royle was the Manager at Manchester City, I saw Dickov play many times in a forward line with Shaun Goater, which proved fruitful as they made their way back from their Division One lows. I am not sure if Joe Royle coined the phrase or I just attributed it to Dickov myself, but he was very much a 'chaser of lost causes'. Dickov's work rate was exceptional and if there was ever an example of someone making the most of the talent they had been given, then Dickov was it. He chased goalkeepers down, defenders down, he really was like a terrier chasing a rubber ball, but he never left anything on the pitch and I admire him for that.

The season Joe Royle's City escaped from Division One via the play offs, Dickov played a huge part. He scored the last ever goal at Wigan Athletic's Springfield Park in the Play off Semi-Final and then even more importantly equalised in the 2-2 draw at Wembley with Gillingham, when City looked dead and buried. They subsequently won the match on penalties. Without Dickov's contribution, Manchester City would be unlikely to have become the prolific, multi-million pound side that they are today.

I have not seen Doncaster Rovers play, but expect them to be good enough to see off Stevenage if they play their full side. Doncaster are battling to avoid the drop to Division One, whilst Stevenage are trying to avoid the drop to Division Two, so I half-expected both sides to 'rest' key players, but statements from both Managers indicate the FA Cup could be an important financial boost for them. Doncaster's full side were good enough to win the Division One title last season, so on that basis, I have to think Doncaster will prevail. If not, it will only be the second 'shock' on our FA Cup journey, the first was when Stourbridge beat Workington, which wasn't exactly a massive shock either.

On paper, this is probably the least attractive game in the FA Cup Third Round (certainly according to both sets of supporters on Twitter anyway), so I can see it going one of two ways. It will either be our first awful game and a dull no score draw or it will be a seven goal thriller.

Fingers crossed, it will be the latter.

I am not sure quite how we are managing this, but we seem to have fallen lucky with our passage to the FA Cup Final. Every game seems to produce goals and today was no exception.

This morning, my Dad arrived as arranged at ten thirty and we set off to Doncaster. It was a dull, grey, wet day but the Northern half of England seems to have avoided the severe, consistent downpours that have hit the South and any major postponements today were South of Birmingham. Once again, I drove, but it seemed a bit strange heading off to an F.A Cup game without nipping over to Buckshaw Parkway station to pick Alan up.

My Dad was in good form and although we obviously know each other well enough not to worry about uncomfortable silences on our journeys, my Dad was very chatty, recounting tales of his previous visit to Doncaster. After reaching the F.A Amateur Cup Final in the 1966-67 season, the following season 'Skem' embarked on one of their most successful F.A Cup campaigns. In the 1st Round, they were draw away to Scunthorpe United and stayed in a bed & breakfast in Doncaster. My Dad said he was rooming with a good friend, Bobby Scott (my Dad didn't tend to room with one of my Godfather's and his good mate, Wally Bennett, as Wally snores!) They were booked in to stay for two nights, the Friday night before the game and the Saturday night after. Being in the midst of winter, the rooms were really cold but each had a gas heater in. The heaters were on a meter, so unless you regularly shelled out money, the room stayed cold. My Dad said Bobby was a gas fitter, so to avoid regularly paying to heat the room, he took the heater apart and then managed to put it back together so it constantly gave out heat but without the need to pay! They went to play on the Saturday afternoon, losing 2-0, but when they returned to the B&B on the Saturday evening, all the other lads rooms were freezing, whilst Bobby and my Dad's was almost tropical.

My Dad made me laugh with another story, but this time he did it inadvertently. We were discussing the common problem these days of defenders and forwards grappling with each other every time a corner is taken. The main culprits are the defenders and we were both agreeing that if referees started to give penalties for every misdemeanor, it would soon stop happening.

"Refs can't do that though, they would be castrated for it!" Dad decided.

"Castrated?" I queried.

"I meant castigated."

"I thought it seemed a bit harsh!"

The roads to Doncaster were very quiet and we were at the Keepmoat within an hour and a half. As is typical of the modern, out of town stadiums, it had a massive car park, but stewards were charging to park on there, so we parked a few hundred metres further away and walked up. We picked our five tickets up and then Dad and I went into the Belle Vue bar, which forms part of the stadium for some lunch. My attempts to stay 'dry' (alcohol free) have made it through the first four days, so I just had a pie and a Bovril.

Half an hour after we arrived, Alan, Jordan and Phil arrived too. They had caught the train and then grabbed a taxi at the station. Alan had arranged for us all to meet Doncaster Rovers Press Officer, Steve Uttley at around one o'clock, so we headed to the players and officials entrance. Alan had contacted Steve about Doncaster Rovers doing something to help him promote the Christie's fundraising and although he wasn't able to publicise our journey in the programme, as Doncaster have their four own chosen charities, he said to come along to meet him.

As we went to the Reception area of the 'Players and Officials' entrance and asked for Steve Uttley, it transpired he was standing right next to us! He quickly gathered together a T-Shirt that he had had signed by all the Doncaster Rovers players for Alan to raffle off for the Christie and also had Paul Dickov and his Assistant, former City manager, Brian Horton, sign a programme for Alan to keep himself as a memento.

Steve seemed like a very warm, friendly guy and said he would take us out through the tunnel to have a brief look at the stadium from the pitch. As he was doing this, he quickly went to see if Paul Dickov was around and once he found him, brought him out to meet us. Paul had his photo taken with us in the tunnel, before shaking hands with us and going on his way. Steve then showed us through to the pitch. The stadium is ultra modern and there is not a bad seat in the house. It doesn't have the obligatory obstructed views like Goodison Park, but then every side of the ground is only one tier, so to an extent, it doesn't have the same character as Goodison either. It is an impressive stadium for a club of their size though and Steve let us take a few photographs in the dugouts. We sat in the 'Home' dugouts as Graham Westley, the Stevenage manager was having a one to one chat with one of his player's in the 'Away' one.

Having had a quick look around, we said a massive thank you to Steve Uttley and headed on our way. Alan was particularly delighted, due to Dickov's Manchester City links. Phil is also very positive about developments and always adds a positive message to proceedings.
"Wow, Al, that was amazing! I can't believe that just happened."
I remembered that Dickov was at Arsenal too, so it must have been a buzz for Phil as well.

After our tour, we went back to the Belle Vue bar. Phil bought a pint, once again to aid a hangover. We discussed the fact that the only time Phil hasn't been hungover for a Saturday game was the game at Stevenage, when he was out with us the night before. We also kept an eye on Sky Sports News for updates on the score in the Blackburn Rovers v Manchester City game. City took the lead but Rovers soon equalised. If that was my team, I would have been panicking about an unexpected Third Round exit, but Alan remained calm, seeing the downside of a replay, without entertaining the thought that they could actually lose. Looking at the bigger picture, from an Everton perspective I wouldn't mind seeing City knocked out, as they are one of the sides likely to beat us. It would make a great story if it was a City-Everton F.A Cup Final, but if we played them before then, I think we would be up against it. You will have to forgive the 'we' when I refer to Everton, it is a forty year habit and it isn't going to stop now. Anyway, Alan was right, City ended up with an inconvenient one-all draw and will replay a week on Wednesday.

At about two thirty we went into the ground for a second time, but this time not through the 'Players & Officials' entrance! Our seats were slap bang on the centre circle, right behind the tunnel we emerged through earlier. At half two, the ground was looking pretty empty. Doncaster Rovers have done what they can to entice fans in, £10 for adults and a £1 for kids is an excellent deal, it just seems non-League clubs love the glamour and financial boost the F.A Cup brings, but lower League clubs fans only really buy into it if they get a glamour tie. As previously stated, unfortunately Stevenage at home is a long way from being that.

This week, it was not a lower League manager but a Premier one that has hit the headlines for his criticism of the F.A Cup. Paul Lambert, the Aston Villa manager, gave a candid interview, in which he admitted that the F.A Cup was a distraction for Premier League clubs. He did go on to say that he would try and win each game the club had in it, but the press chose to use him as a scapegoat and it was wrongly portrayed that Lambert was not interested in the F.A Cup at all. From a Villa fans perspective, this was like saying Villa were not entertaining the idea of trying to win the one trophy they realistically have a chance of winning (other than the Capital

One cup which they are already out of). I think it was a storm in a teacup, a Third Round win nets a club prize money of £67 500. Great for Stevenage, OK for Doncaster, but for Aston Villa, it would probably pay a couple of their top earners for a week. The Premier League is a cash cow and the F.A Cup is merely the bell around its neck, pleasant to see and hear, but they can survive without it. The media should try to bring more focus to the early rounds and the smaller clubs, because to them it can be that lifeline that the Premier League is to the big clubs. Stevenage are a six figure sum down on their gate money for the season so far, relative to last year, so a good Cup run could help claw that deficit back.

By three o'clock, the ground had filled a little, but we guessed that the attendance was between three and four thousand (and later discovered it was 3899). This would be our highest gate so far, but nowhere near what they would be getting at the likes of Goodison, Anfield, Emirates and Old Trafford this weekend. Still, we were hoping the quality of the contest may go some way to rewarding those attending for their loyalty. After the first forty five minutes, that hope seemed very much misplaced.

Without a doubt, the first half of this match was the worst we had witnessed in nine rounds of football. It was shockingly bad! Stevenage had set their stall out to be difficult to break down and Doncaster just couldn't work out the answer to that puzzle. Doncaster had a centre forward who appeared to be completely unfit, perhaps he was returning from injury, but the rest of the side just couldn't string two passes together and Stevenage were growing in confidence, if not really in style, as the half progressed. The Doncaster supporters were vocal in their negativity, as they seemed dumbfounded that a side that almost snatched an away point from promotion contenders, Queens Park Rangers, on New Year's Day, were now playing second fiddle to Stevenage, a side rooted to the bottom of Division One.

"Stevenage will be chuffed to buggery that they are facing a side as crap as us," moaned one nearby local.

To divert our attention from the boredom, my Dad and I started to bicker about what number the impressive Stevenage player was from the last round. Given I am writing this book, I was at an advantage. I knew the player was Luke Freeman and I knew he was number fifteen. I had also been reading several internet articles about him. They informed me that Stevenage had admitted he had attracted interest from some Championship clubs and could go for the right price.

"He's number fifteen, Dad," I stated.

"No, that's definitely not him. Is that him, number thirteen?" Dad queried.

"No, he's definitely number fifteen. His name is Luke Freeman. He was number fifteen against Stourbridge, last time and he's fifteen today."

"That doesn't look anything like him."

"Well, it's him."

"It isn't."

In the second half, when Luke Freeman played down the left wing, almost directly in front of us, my Dad sheepishly admitted,

"You're right, that is him, number fifteen."

I love winning footballing arguments with my Dad, it doesn't happen very often!

At half time, with neither keeper having been forced into a save of note, Alan and I went to get a cup of tea.

"Crap game," Alan observed.

"It's got 0-0 written all over it, Al. Are you looking forward to a trip to Stevenage a week on Tuesday?"

"Don't even joke about it, Cal," Alan chided in his thick Mancunian tones.

"Well, to be fair, we've done well to get through eight games without a replay. I just can't see a goal in this one and if there is one, that'll be all there is."

Famous last words! The second half was fantastic. If the first half was the least entertaining forty five minutes of our Cup run, the second half was the most entertaining.

As is often the case, the game was brought out of its slumber by a mistake. In the 49th minute, Paul Quinn was attempting to carry the ball out of defence and slipped as he was being closed down by Francois Zoko. Zoko, who has a look of Paolo Wanchope about him, with a similar awkward run, closed in on goal and coolly slotted away to the delight of the 324 travelling Stevenage fans and to the disgust of the majority of the crowd. We were expecting a spirited Doncaster Rovers fightback, but Stevenage continued to have the upper hand and it was no great surprise when Peter Hartley headed home from a corner in the 64th minute.

"Stevenage it is then," I shouted across to Alan, who was at one end of our row of five, whilst I was at the other. Despite there being more than a quarter of the game remaining, Doncaster had not tested Chris Day at all in the Stevenage goal and there didn't seem to be a way back for them without somebody conjuring up a moment of brilliance.

On 72 minutes, a 'moment of brilliance' arrived. A rare Doncaster corner was cleared only as far as Harry Forrester and he smashed a thunderous shot at goal from over twenty yards that was still rising when it hit the left hand station at the back of Chris Day's net. It was a beauty and the frustrated home fans suddenly found their voices as they sensed the game may not be all over after all. Unfortunately for Doncaster, the fans positivity was shortlived. Each time

Doncaster exerted some pressure, Stevenage would hold firm and then break away menacingly. In the 90th minute, one such breakaway left Donaster's defence short in numbers and the ball was played across from the right to Darius Charles, who converted a simple chance. As one, half the audience leapt up from their seats in frustration and headed home.

I don't really understand the mass evacuation routine that often takes place at matches. If you are parked in Old Trafford car park for example or have a train to catch that only runs once every couple of hours then I suppose it is acceptable to dash off, but other than that why not stick around to see what you have paid for? The fourth official had indicated there were six minutes of injury time, so who was to say they would not be incident packed? As it turned out, they were.

In the 93rd minute, Luke Freeman had a great effort for Stevenage that was superbly saved by Doncaster's former Chelsea keeper, Ross Turnbull. Then, two minutes later, Doncaster's Liam Wakefield chipped a deflected shot into the net from a tight angle to make it 3-2. Alan and I exchanged a nervous look. Stevenage had dominated possession and had the bulk of the chances, surely they weren't going to concede two injury time goals to send us back down to Stevenage on a cold January evening, a week on Tuesday?

Thankfully, Stevenage held out. In the final minute of injury time, Stevenage cleared to the halfway line and Ross Turnbull found himself alone against two breaking Stevenage players. Turnbull was already in the centre circle, as the rest of his team mates had pushed forward in a "do or die" effort, but he dashed forward towards Stevenage's Michael Doughty and clumsily took him out with a desperately mistimed tackle. Whilst Turnbull and Doughty were on the floor, Luke Freeman kicked the ball into an empty net from 45 yards. 4-2. Definitely game over now. Then, something bizarre happened. It transpired ref Scott Duncan had failed to play the advantage to Stevenage and had blown up for a foul. It seemed he had little choice but to send

Turnbull off, there was no debating that he had denied a goal scoring opportunity as Freeman had just scored! Whether he was like my Sunday League referee, who just couldn't be arsed with the paperwork or accidentally pulled out the wrong card, I do not know, but to the astonishment of every single fan left in the ground, Scott Duncan, the ref, brandished a yellow card. Everyone looked at each other in confusion. If the ref had not played advantage, surely he had to send Turnbull off? It turned out to be immaterial as seconds later he blew for full time. It was a crazy way to end the game, but it had been a crazy second half. The five goals took our FA Cup tally to a brilliant 34 goals in nine games, almost an average of four a game.

The Doncaster fans that remained let their feelings be known to Paul Dickov and the Doncaster Rovers side, whilst the jubilant Stevenage players went over to show their appreciation to their travelling fans. For the winners, the Fourth Round beckoned and with it the opportunity to get the plum tie that they had missed out on in the Third Round.

FINAL SCORE : Doncaster Rovers 2 Stevenage 3

Scorers :- Doncaster Rovers – Forrester & Wakefield.

Stevenage – Zoko, Hartley & Charles.

Our 'Speccies':- Calvin Wade, Alan Oliver, Jordan Oliver, Richard Wade, Phil Cooper.

Sunday 5th January 2014

10.00am

An Arsenal victory in the North London derby as we drove home last night guarantees that mine and my Dad's team (Everton), Alan and Jordan's team (Manchester City) and Phil's team (Arsenal) are all in the draw for the 4th Round. There are thirty two balls going into this afternoon's draw and our three teams are responsible for three of them, so the probability of Stevenage drawing one of our teams is 3 out of 31. Technically, Manchester City still have to beat Blackburn Rovers in a replay at the Etihad, but I just can't see Blackburn getting anything out of that one.

Stevenage obviously have a fifty-fifty chance of being drawn home or away. If they get a home draw, we will not be travelling down the day before again, as my Mum and Dad go to Tenerife on Friday for a fortnight and only arrive back on the Friday evening before the next game on the Saturday. At least one game will actually take place on the Friday night (a BT Sport live game), so if that is Stevenage, my Dad will have to miss a Round for the second time. All will be decided this afternoon.

From my perspective, I am hoping for (at least) one of the following scenarios :-

i) Stevenage to be drawn away from home. We have already been down to Stevenage once and I'd like to go to another ground that I haven't been to before.

ii) If Stevenage are at home, for them to face a Premier League club but not either of the Manchester clubs, Liverpool or Chelsea. We would have to follow those teams through a few rounds I reckon and having been to all four grounds, I'd rather go elsewhere. Having been to the Lamex when it is two thirds empty, it would be good to go back to see it packed to the rafters.

iii)   Stevenage to be drawn against Everton (or failing that Arsenal). I don't want to go
       through this without crossing paths with my own team. I keep saying this and Alan
       reckons it's too early, but I disagree, we have done nine rounds and there are only
       five left. Following Everton from here on in would be the fairytale ending. Arsenal
       are my 2nd choice as I haven't been to the Emirates and they play good football.

The draw will be made around two o'clock, just after the Nottingham Forest v West Ham United
game, so I will update you as soon as I know where we are heading next.

2:30 pm

To use the catchphrase of a comedy great, 'I don't believe it!' The draw for the Fourth Round took place after Nottingham Forest's thumping 5-0 victory over West Ham and Stevenage were drawn at home to EVERTON! At this stage, I cannot tell you any of the draw other than that one game because as soon as Stevenage were paired with Everton, I ran straight to the phone and rang my Dad. I can tell immediately that my Dad is equally excited about the way this has turned out. Alan is very much a believer in someone from above pulling the strings to all this and I don't believe that for a second, but it is a wonderful co-incidence. I cannot explain the emotions that are running through me currently, but they range from thrilled, excited, delirious and panicky! Getting tickets for every round so far, with the possible exception of the Stourbridge v Biggleswade game, has been a cake walk, but from now on in, it will be a challenge. No more so than trying to get five tickets for this one before my Dad goes on holiday on Friday!

My Dad is the man with the power. He has already spoken to Joe Royle about our F.A Cup journey and Joe has said he can help out for near enough all the clubs left in, but when it comes to Everton contacts, my Dad, having been involved at Everton for some time, has several. How much influence they will have at Stevenage though is a different matter, as the Everton allocation will be tiny. What we need now, is help from Clive Abrey, Stevenage's Head of Commercial, once again. It goes without saying that we would not expect the red carpet treatment like we were lucky enough to have against Stourbridge. All we want this time are paid tickets.

I discuss tactics with Dad. He says he will e-mail Clive and then follow it up with a phone call. We also discuss a priority pecking order. Dad says if he can only get two tickets, then Alan and I should go, as it was always our intention to go to every game and neither him nor Phil or Jordan have managed every Round. I have a bit of a sinking feeling thinking about going to this one without my Dad. We went to the 1984 Milk Cup Final together and the F.A Cup Finals in 1984, 1986, 1989 and 1995 and met each other there in 2009. Add into the mix probably a couple of hundred other Everton games we've been to together, lots with special memories, especially in the F.A Cup and I want to go to this game with him. We decide that if we can get three, then my Dad will take the third ticket and any more than that would be a bonus. With Phil's family being from the Biggleswade area, we are hoping he may be able to pick some tickets up as a local.

After speaking to my Dad, I speak to Alan. He is pretty excited about the draw too and knows we will have to battle to get tickets this time. Al doesn't want to curse it by mentioning it on Facebook or Twitter, but I know he envisages a Manchester City v Everton FA Cup Final or at the very least, a clash between the two at some stage. One step at a time.I am hugely excited about this, but know if Everton don't go on to win the FA Cup this year, it will make gloomy reading when I have to write about our loss. If that loss is against Stevenage, it would be disastrous. The only way I can see that happening is if we don't play anything like a full team. The Merseyside Derby is on the Tuesday after the FA Cup game, so I hope Martinez doesn't underestimate the challenge that Stevenage will pose.

7:00p.m

I had a feeling that Manchester United may win the FA Cup this year but that feeling has been well and truly been proved wrong, as they have fallen at their first hurdle this afternoon at home to Swansea City. Wilfried Bony scored a last minute winner as Manchester United were defeated 2-1 at Old Trafford. It wasn't the only shock of the weekend either. On Saturday, Sheffield United beat Aston Villa 2-1 at Villa Park, Southend beat Millwall 4-1, Cardiff won at

Newcastle 2-1, Rochdale won 2-0 at home to Leeds and two Conference sides managed replays, Kidderminster drew with Peterborough United 0-0 and Macclesfield Town drew 1-1 with Sheffield Wednesday. Once again, I won't update the draw until most of the replays are out of the way, as there are a lot of either/ors at the moment.

I keep reading through the story of the earlier rounds and shake my head in disbelief that we have stumbled across Everton! I feared getting Chelsea or Liverpool in the 3rd Round. Chelsea because of the cost of following them for a number of Rounds, Liverpool because 75% of my friends are Liverpudlians and they would have had a field day if I had had to keep watching them lot! As an agnostic, I can't really say I prayed for Everton, but I certainly hoped for Everton. I just hope they can win five more F.A Cup games for me now. Surely that's not too much to ask for!

Monday 6th January 2014

Life just keeps getting better! After a great F.A Cup match on Saturday (or great 2nd half anyway) and a great F.A Cup draw yesterday, today I had a phone call from my good friend, Carl McGovern to see if I fancied going to Goodison with him on Saturday against Norwich, as he has two free tickets.

Part of me feels guilty about taking free tickets to the match. It feels like I am not properly supporting my team but in my current situation, I'll take what's on offer. Alison and I have had to make a lot of sacrifices to keep our families financial heads above water and unfortunately, for me, not going to the match has been one of them. This F.A Cup trail has been great, as it has resurrected my passion for football, but so far, it has been at a minimal cost. I just can't afford to be an Everton regular at this time in my life but over the last 35 years I have more than put my share into the club. I was one of the 16000 or so regulars in the early 80s, one of the 8 067 at the Everton v Chesterfield Milk Cup 2nd Round 2nd Leg game in October 1983. I am not Everton's biggest fan, not by a long shot, but I have a 35 year history of regular attendance, so I'll happily bite Carl's arm off for a freebie.

Carl is not the only kindhearted soul who has ensured I have had a regular fix of football at Goodison Park since I have run into difficult times. Last season, out of nowhere, a guy called Neil Smith showed his kindness and generosity. When Neil contacted me, I was at my lowest financial point and had just witnessed a bizarre set of circumstances that had made me wonder whether I was naïve to put any trust in people I didn't know.

Prior to Neil contacting me, I was trying to make some money each month from my book writing. My first ebook, "Forever Is Over" was ticking along OK, but other than the occasional strong month, it wasn't providing enough income to live off or support a family on. I was trying to use social media to get the word out, as the reviews on the whole were excellent. One day, an author who I had not heard of, but who had been fairly successful approached me and asked me whether I would promote his book to my Twitter followers and I said I would but could he help mine along too.

Over several months, I sent a lot of tweets out about the book he was promoting and he sent the occasional one out about mine too. This seemed like a reasonable arrangement, his ebook was doing better than mine and he had more Twitter followers than I did. I didn't have a Kindle, but I downloaded the Kindle app on to my computer and downloaded my own ebook and his on to that. I even cajoled a few friends into buying his ebook. We added each other as friends on Facebook and congratulated each other when things went well and empathised when things were not so good, especially if a dreaded poor review was submitted.

One day though, someone posted a negative review of the author's ebook which went beyond the lines of acceptability. It was vicious and personal, but when I sent a message across sympathising, a bizarre reply came back suggesting that not only did this author think I had written this negative review but pretty much all his other negative reviews too! He suggested he only ever received negative reviews when I did, sometimes within minutes.Taken aback, I checked to see if there was any symmetry between his reviews and mine and there was none whatsoever. Once we had both received a negative review from different people on the same day, but other than that there was no correlation between his reviews and mine. It isn't great getting poor reviews, but I wouldn't expect everyone to love what I've written, so I take them on the chin. Unfortunately for me, this author had decided to blame me for his and told me he had reported me to Amazon.

To try to put an end to the matter, I contacted Amazon myself. I explained I had been accused of writing several poor reviews about this author's book, including a very personal one. I asked if they would remove the offending review and re-assure the author that I played no part in anything negative and had in fact, only ticked positive things on his book. Amazon replied saying that their account security policy doesn't allow them to give information about authors or reviewers, so all they could do, was remove the offensive review.

To cut a long story short, I sent a message to the author saying Amazon had agreed to remove the review but the writing of it had had nothing to do with me. I tried to explain logically why he was wrong to link me to his poor reviews. He probably had about forty reviews that were negative at the time and I would have had to buy forty different Kindles, set up forty different Amazon accounts and buy his book forty times to post those reviews! Plus, what was my motivation to be negative? We had been helping each other and for someone to buy both our ebooks would have cost them about £3 in total. He was not a rival to me in any way. Sadly, based purely on his own gut feeling, he continued to say it was me, so we blocked each other on social media, I shook my head many times in disbelief and moved on, feeling a little more sceptical about humanity. Amazon have never contacted me to say that there is an issue, as I have never done anything to create an issue, but as far as I know, in this man's mind, I am still the guilty party.

This is where Neil Smith comes in. Just after all this had happened, I was contacted by Neil Smith on Twitter. Neil was an Evertonian living down in the Midlands, who had bought and enjoyed my book. He sent me a message on Twitter saying that he couldn't make an Everton home game, but had two season tickets in the 1985 lounge and would I like to go? I replied, saying thanks very much but financially things were very tough for me at that moment in time and couldn't afford to go. Neil replied saying he did not expect a payment for them, they would just go to waste if I didn't utilise them, as he was going to be working abroad.

Thus, in the 2012-13 season, I went in the 1985 Lounge at Goodison three times courtesy of Neil. I had a meal before the game and pretty much the best tickets in the stadium. As there were three sets of tickets, twice I took my eldest son, Brad and the other time, Brad was on holiday with Alison, Joel and Alison's Mum and Dad in North Wales (being self-employed I could not afford the time off), so I took my own Dad. To make things even better, the Man of the Match comes into the Lounge after the game, so Brad got to meet and have his photograph taken firstly with England international, Phil Jagielka and then Belgian international, Kevin Mirallas. The time I went with my Dad, we bought an Everton ball and got the Man of the Match, Victor Anichebe, to sign it for Brad. To this day, I have still not met Neil Smith! Having had one person who doesn't know me jump to the conclusion that I am an absolute nutcase, it was great to have another who doesn't know me conclude that I am a good person who would really appreciate a favour. In an ideal world, one day I will get an apology from the author and have the opportunity to repay Neil for his kindness, the latter is more important to me than the former.

Really looking forward to Saturday now. I haven't been to Goodison this season and haven't seen Carl for some time, so it should be doubly good. Everton continue to be challenging for a Top 4 place and a Champions League spot, so a victory this weekend will be another step towards making that dream a reality. Roll on the weekend!

Saturday 11th January 2014

    This book is primarily about the F.A Cup journey from start to finish so I don't want to get too embroiled with the other games I've been to this season, so will just give you a quick overview.

  Today was great, Everton beat Norwich City 2-0 with Gareth Barry scoring the first with an absolute belter, running through and letting fly with a left foot shot from over twenty yards that flew into Norwich keeper, John Ruddy's, top left hand corner. The second goal came directly from a Kevin Mirallas free kick. Overall, Everton were competent rather than majestic, but to win fairly comfortably without hitting top gear is the sign of a good side. At this stage, it appears Manchester City, Chelsea and Arsenal will battle it out for the title, with Liverpool, Spurs and Everton competing for fourth spot. As I have probably said in this book before, I would settle for fourth and an F.A Cup win!

  Carl is a friend from my days as a mortgage rep. We first met about ten years ago, when another friend of mine at Yorkshire Building Society, Andy Sykes, was moving back to his Yorkshire roots after having lived in Preston for some time and wanted me to look after Carl's mortgage brokerage. Andy is a great guy (we latterly worked together at BM Solutions too) and I trust his judgement on people implicitly, so when he said Carl was a brilliant person to deal with, I was confident we would get on. It turned out we shared a love of football, Carl is a big Blackburn Rovers fan and were both into long distance running, so started to enter events together. Over the years we have run several half marathons together including Liverpool, Freckelton and Salford, as well as two marathons in London and New York. We never really ran together as I am a plodder and Carl is half decent, but spent a lot of time in each other's company, especially when we went over to New York and have never had a cross word. Carl has a lovely wife, Katie and two great children from his first marriage and now spends his life living between Lancashire and Spain where he and Katie have a home.

As well as catching up with Carl today, I also had the opportunity to briefly catch up with one of my cousin's, Paul Wharton (Paul's Mum Cathy and my Dad are brother and sister). It is safe to say Paul is an Everton fanatic. He is Chairman of the Everton Heritage Society and every home game, prior to kick off, is on the first floor of the church that backs on to Goodison selling memorabilia and also providing insight to all interested parties into the history of Everton Football Club. Carl and I popped into St. Luke's (strangely the first time I have been in there during my 37 years of visiting Goodison Park) and Paul showed us some of the F.A Cup memorabilia the Society have. He suggested that I devote a Chapter of this book to Everton's F.A Cup history, especially the early years, but I think it probably belongs to another book. If Everton progress through a few rounds, I will tap into Paul's wealth of knowledge, but if disaster strikes and we are knocked out by Stevenage, then an insight into Everton's history would be unwarranted. Hopefully, I will be returning to Paul in the final stages of the journey!

One of the particularly interesting things that Paul did tell me today was that one of the Everton players that played in the 1906 and 1907 F.A Cup Finals, Harold Hardman, ended up as a Director and subsequently Chairman of Manchester United. He was Chairman in 1958, at the time of the Munich air disaster.

We went into the ground half an hour before kick off. When I was going regularly, I must admit I took the whole day out thing for granted and didn't mind entering the ground five minutes before kick off, but once it becomes less of a regular treat, I've wanted to savour it. Carl hadn't been to Goodison for thirty years and not surprisingly said it hadn't changed much other than the away end. Still love Goodison, it has so much more character than modern stadiums but do admit to cursing if I only manage to get an obstructed view ticket. Luckily, on this occasion Carl and I have tickets at the back of the Main Stand but with a perfect view of both goals.

As mentioned previously, the game itself went well and the two goals were sheer quality. Moyes is getting a lot of stick from all quarters currently, but it shouldn't be forgotten that despite sometimes showing a lack of ambition in his tactics, he was responsible for some incredible signings. Tim Howard, Seamus Coleman, Leighton Baines, Phil Jagielka, Kevin Mirallas and Sylvain Distin amongst others are undoubtedly excellent players bought far below their actual worth, especially Coleman who was bought from Sligo Rovers for a bargain price of £65 000!

I left after the final whistle hoping my money situation continues to improve and I can soon return to Goodison every other week. Failing that, a visit in the 5th and 6th Rounds of the F.A Cup would go down nicely. I have made sure I have enough money put aside for the F.A Cup games at the very least. Hoping beyond hope that the next five games all involve Everton.

Tonight I have been back on the Wembley trail but not the F.A Cup, the F.A Trophy, as I have been down to Victory Park, Chorley with Brad, Joel and my mate, Shaun McManus to see the F.A Trophy Third Round Replay between Chorley and Skrill Conference side, Tamworth and what a great game it was too.

This season, my football finances have gone towards the F.A Cup but in the last couple of seasons, I have regularly taken the boys down to Chorley. Originally, it was £7 for me and a £1 each for the boys (or sometimes even free), but now it is £9 for me and £3 for the kids, which still represents great value. Chorley are currently second in the Evo-Stik Premier Division, four points behind top of the table, Dad's former club, Skelmersdale United, who they are playing on Saturday. Brad wants to go to that too, but I think I'll let him go to that one with his mates as my spare money won't stretch to me going twice in a few days, especially with the Stevenage-Everton game being less than two weeks away.

Chorley's F.A Trophy exploits this year have been a real money spinner for them. Managed by former Manchester City and Blackburn Rovers player, Garry Flitcroft, they have more than held their own against higher League opposition. They drew with Conference side, Forest Green Rovers at home and then also drew away, before emerging victorious on penalties and the reason for tonight's game is because they drew 1-1 away at Tamworth on Saturday. The winner's play Grimsby away in the Quarter Finals.

It was a really cold, gloomy, wet night and although a lot of Brad's mates were going, Joel was a bit more reluctant to go, as he had to miss football training. It was a one-off though and I knew there would be a good gate and great atmosphere. Joel is starting to enjoy live football more as he gets older, so I wanted to utilise this opportunity. We picked Shaun up about seven and parked up a few minutes walk away and strolled through the back streets of Chorley, dodging the deep puddles.

Shaun and I became friends through Alison, my wife, meeting Shaun's wife, Jo, collecting our eldest two children, Brad and Ellie from play school. They instantly became close friends and Shaun and I soon became pals too. They are our closest friends in Chorley and over the last ten years, we have been on numerous holidays around the UK with Shaun, Jo and their daughters, Ellie and Lucy. Shaun is a barber, at David's barbers at Pall Mall and has lived in Chorley all his life, so is guaranteed to know loads of the locals at the Chorley matches. He doesn't get to go on Saturdays, as he is working, but always tries to go to the midweek matches, especially on Tuesday nights, as he gets Wednesdays off and can nip in to the bar for a few pints. During my troubled financial times, Shaun and Jo are others that have always tried to help us in any way they can and if true friends come to the forefront during difficult periods, then Shaun and Jo truly are the best.

Once we were in the ground, we tried to nip in the bar, but it was heaving, so I said I'd take Joel over to below the Main Stand and let Shaun battle for a pint. He was meeting his mate, Martin in there too, so I didn't feel like I was abandoning him. I wasn't due to be having a pint anyway, as my 13 stone 13 pound weight target for the F.A Cup Final has led me to try to stay 'Dry' in January. It has worked well so far, the weight isn't falling off me, but I am heading in the right direction. I don't desperately miss the alcohol, but I do enjoy a pint, so I can't see me keeping off it for 45 years like my Dad. A month would be progress!

Brad walked around the ground with Joel and me, but soon spotted a few of his mates, so disappeared off with them. The good thing about local football like this, is that you can give a thirteen year old lad a free reign to go off and do his own thing and then text him five minutes from the end to arrange a meet up place. Brad likes to stand behind the goal with the older teenagers and join in with the singing. I thought Joel might ask to go off with them too, but he was happy to stand with me below the Main Stand. Actually, I don't know why I keep referring to it as 'The Main Stand'. It is 'The Only Stand', a big old thing that has wooden planks to sit on rather than seats (except in the central area which has the luxury of a seat with a back on). Chorley are riding high in the Evo Stik Premier and if they get up into the Conference North, they may have to spend some money on bringing it up to standard, but there is a certain charm in its weariness.

As the game was about to kick off, Shaun text me to say that Martin was with his brother and his Dad and they liked to stand on the embankment on the opposite side of the pitch to the stand, so did I fancy going around? I really like Martin, he is a friendly bloke and good to have a chat with, but that side of the ground is open to the elements and Joel was already dancing on the spot and rubbing his hands together to try to avoid frostbite, so I didn't think it was fair on him to take him round there. Shaun ended up splitting his time between us and them as the game progressed, but as the temperature didn't pick up and the wind and rain didn't ease off, I think I did the right thing.

On a pitch that became more and more like the proverbial farmer's field, the game itself was excellent. A fine advert for non-League football. Tamworth, as well as fielding Nick Chadwick, a former Everton player, who had scored a few goals for us back in 2002, also had Tony Capaldi, a former Norther Ireland international who had played for Cardiff City and Plymouth Argyle. The non-League these days doesn't tend to attract the very top former players, David Beckham, for example, probably never considered trudging around in his late thirties at Braintree Town or Jarrow Roofing Boldon Community Association, but I enjoy pointing out to

Joel that there is a former Premiership player and even a former international taking the field at Victory Park.

Tamworth started very brightly and in the early encounters I berated myself for including Chorley in my £1 midweek accumulator. It looked very much like Tamworth would go on to win by five or six. After ten minutes, Adam Roscoe, a player who has been at Chorley for a few years now, lost the ball in midfield which was gathered by Tamworth's Andy Haworth, who threaded a ball through to the Everton old boy, Nick Chadwick, who waltzed through the Chorley defence and neatly finished. Brad still has an Everton team poster up on his wall from the 2005-06 season and Nick Chadwick is on that, but I am sure he was cursing him when the ball hit the net. After the goal, Tamworth continued to dominate, but Chorley weathered the storm in more ways than one and after 26 minutes struck back. Josh Hine, who I had been told to watch out for by my friend since schooldays, Mark Sunderland, who is a cricketing mate of Josh's, burst down the right wing at lightning speed and put a lovely square ball into the six yard box, that Jake Cottrell beat the Tamworth defenders to, to finish in the style of Gary Lineker.

There was a crowd of 1393 in Victory Park tonight, a bumper gate for a game played in such atrocious weather and once that goal went in, it lifted the spirits of the majority. We were stood behind the Tamworth dugout and their management staff and substitutes seemed taken aback by the atmosphere.

"There's more atmosphere here than the Reebok and I genuinely mean that," one commented. In the Premier League, the fans that grab a seat closest to the away supporters are generally the ones who are as concerned about the vitriol as they are about the football. I discovered those who stand behind the away dugout at non-League games are of a similar persuasion.

"When you get a sight of goal, shoot!" shouted the Tamworth manager to one of his players, just before half time.

"I tell you what," shouted one Lancastrian wag to the Tamworth boss, "I'd like to get you in the sights of my bloody rifle and then shoot!"

Overall though, the atmosphere in the ground lifted the Chorley team and they dominated proceedings before half time, without really testing Cameron Belford in the Tamworth goal. Chorley's James Dean (yet another player this season with a famous name) did hit the cross bar but a one-one scoreline at half time was a fair reflection and Shaun and I went with Joel to the wooden hut serving food and drinks, hopeful that after our half time coffees we would witness an historic Chorley victory in the second half.

Our positive half time thoughts didn't really take into consideration that for the 45 minutes of the second half, Chorley would have to play into the face of an almost gale force wind and driving rain. Tamworth regained the superiority they had in the early stages of the first half and it was no great surprise when they also regained the lead. In a mad goalmouth scramble, Chorley keeper, Sam Ashton made two fantastic saves from close range, but Chorley just couldn't clear their lines and Wayne Thomas scored from the rebound after Ashton's second save.

Football is a game that is played with the brain, as well as the feet. Tamworth should have just continued to play in a similar manner and I am sure they would have gone on to win cosily, but they started to drop deeper, waste time and play with the sole purpose of running the clock down for a narrow victory, which allowed Chorley back into the game. In the 92nd minute, just when it looked like Tamworth's negative tactics might pay off, Chorley sent the home fans wild once more with a second equaliser. James Dean had an effort from a corner saved by the keeper, but Andrew Teague, the tall centre back who was in the box for his aerial ability, managed to smash the rebound into the net from a tight angle.

The game finished 2-2 but as it was a replay, the victors needed to be decided on the night, so the game headed into extra time. Joel and Brad were now guaranteed a very late bedtime on a school night, but there was no way I could take them home at this point. The game had been fantastic and with extra time and potentially penalties still to come, there was still a lot of drama left to witness.

If the game had started on what had soon become a farmer's field, extra time was played on a farmer's field that had just been ploughed. The middle of the pitch and both goalmouths were now devoid of grass and not surprisingly, this zapped the energy from both sets of players and it took a while for extra time to reach the peaks that had been witnessed in the first ninety minutes. Chorley were still playing into the wind though, so I was becoming cautiously optimistic when half time in extra time was reached with the match still level. Chorley now had fifteen minutes with the wind on their backs against a weary opposition. Could they make it 3-2 and earn a Quarter Final tie away at Grimsby Town?

One of the many things that I love about non-League football is that a proportion of the crowd always stand behind the goal their team is attacking. My Dad says back in the day, in the 1950s, before fans of top level teams were penned in, even supporters of the old 1st Division clubs would swop ends at half time. Thus, during the interval, a group of thousands of home fans and a group of hundreds or thousands of away fans would pass in the middle somewhere, as they headed towards the other goal! Imagine that now, it would be mayhem, although perhaps it could be argued that segregation breeds trouble. At half time in extra time, I watched one hundred or so Chorley fans dashing around the pitch to take their place behind the Tamworth keeper. I was unfortunately at the notorious game a few years ago between Chorley and Chester when troublemakers managed to create a scene reminiscent of Luton-Millwall in the early 1980s and mounted police and pepper spray were used to calm the angry mob. Thankfully tonight though, like at the huge majority of Chorley games, the supporters were enthusiastic rather than troublesome and people were only running to find the perfect position to watch the game, not for any sinister reason.

In the last fifteen minutes of this epic two hour duel, the Chorley players put their hearts and souls into one final effort. They dominated that final quarter of an hour, but just couldn't get past a resolute Tamworth defence and an inspired goalkeeper in Cameron Belford, who made a fine save from the busy James Dean. Three and a half hours of football had now passed and Chorley could not be separated from the Skrill Conference side, two leagues above them. Penalties would be needed to find a winner and although Chorley had triumphed over Forest Green on penalties in the previous round, it just felt like asking for too much to expect them to win this way again.

The penalties were at the end that Chorley had attacked last and any remaining fans at the far end, dashed around to join the masses behind the muddy goalmouth and wind battered net. Given the howling wind, rain and muddy conditions, both the standard of the penalties and the standard of the goalkeeping were fantastic. Joel and I went into the stand to get a better view and saw both sides dispatch their first two penalties with aplomb, before Chorley and then Tamworth, twice over, had penalties saved. As Chorley took their penalties first, when Adam Roscoe scored his side's fifth penalty to make it 3-2, it meant that Tamworth's Wayne Thomas had to score to take it to sudden death. Thomas struck his penalty hard and although Sam Ashton managed to get a valiant hand to the penalty, he could not keep it out. 3-3 and now it was sudden death. If one side missed and the other side scored, that would be it.

The first four sudden death penalties were all scored to take it to 5-5, but when Chorley's Jake Cottrell's penalty was saved by the magnificent Cameron Belford, Tamworth's Jordan Keane had the opportunity to win it. The pressure didn't visibly get to Keane and he finished coolly to send his fellow Tamworth players, coaching staff and travelling fans delirious and left Chorley's rain sodden fans to trudge wearily home. Chorley had made a brilliant attempt to mix it with the big boys and had only missed out on the lottery of penalties.

I found Brad and the three of us (Brad, Joel and myself) met back up with Shaun at the car to reflect on what might have been. This will be my one only F.A Trophy game of the season. The rules of following the winners through to the next round only apply to the F.A Cup, so I won't be following Tamworth across to Grimsby. I will look out for the result though.

With Chorley's adventure over, the focus is back on the F.A Cup. Next stop Stevenage. Chorley may not be going to Wembley, but Everton's F.A Cup dream is still very much alive.

Wednesday 15th January 2014

With my Mum and Dad sunning themselves in Tenerife, it has been left to me to pick up the contact with Clive Abrey, Commercial Manager at Stevenage Football Club and ensure we have tickets for the Stevenage-Everton game, a week on Saturday. BT Sport are televising it, so it will be a 5:30pm kick off on the Saturday afternoon. This works well for my Dad who is only back from Tenerife on the Friday evening.

Before heading off to sunnier climes, my Dad spoke to Clive and he said he would sort us out with three tickets and would liaise with me in my Dad's absence. I have e-mailed Clive, a couple of times, but when I phoned yesterday, to give him the card payment for the three tickets, he advised me to call back today as they had an evening game against Swindon Town (which Stevenage surprisingly won 2-0). This means that Phil would have to try to pick up the extra two tickets through the general sale, but with his Mum and Dad still living in the Stevenage area, we were always hopeful we would get them.

We are very fortunate to have the Stevenage link through Phil and even more so the link direct to Clive Abrey through associations with the former captain, Steve Berry and former manager, Paul Fairclough. The only Everton fans that can get tickets to this one are supporters who have already been to eight away games this season, also known as 'the diehards'. If Everton triumph and get a big club in the 5th Round, hopefully Dad's Everton connections will be good to us, but with this game being played at a ground with a capacity of below 7000, to get five tickets would be a right result. As I've said before, one step at a time, but based on what we have already seen, I totally expect Everton to win comfortably.

At nine o'clock this morning, I gave Clive the money for three tickets and thanked him for all his help. I then contacted Alan to let him know we have three tickets and Phil needed to put a plan into place to get the other two. From watching updates on the Stevenage FC website, it appears tickets have been selling steadily, but not like hot cakes, so we were all confident that we would get the other two and sure enough just after midday, Alan text to say Phil had managed to get them. Seating ticket prices have been put up to £32 from the normal £23, so some of the once a season supporters may have decided to keep their money and watch this one down at the pub. I can't see it not selling out eventually though, so Phil was still wise to have acted promptly.

As well as the huge gate money boost Stevenage will get from the capacity crowd at elevated prices, the BT Sport television revenue will also be gratefully received too. Both sides will pocket £144 000 from BT for this one, which is fantastic for Stevenage after having recently reported that their gate revenues are £100 000 down on those received at this point last season. Those financial difficulties have been rectified by one great FA Cup draw. The FA Cup may not be the competition it was twenty years ago, but it is still like a lucky lotto ticket to some clubs, Stevenage this season being one. Another side this year to hit the lottery is Kidderminster Harriers who beat Peterborough United 3-2 in a Third Round Replay and will now face Sunderland away in the next round. They are the last non-League survivors.

With our tickets now safely secured, the countdown to the FA Cup Fourth Round begins in earnest. Looking forward to a second trip down to the Lamex Stadium, Broadhall Way and hoping Everton put on a real show. If we win this one, Wembley is only two Rounds away! Come on you blues!

UPDATE Budweiser FA Cup Third Round Results/ Budweiser FA Cup Fourth Round Draw

3rd Round Results

Blackburn Rovers 1 Manchester City 1

Barnsley 1 Coventry City 2

Yeovil Town 4 Leyton Orient 0

Bristol City 1 Watford 1

Southend United 4 Milwall 1

Middlesbrough 0 Hull City 2

West Bromwich Albion 0 Crystal Palace 2

Kidderminster Harriers 0 Peterborough United 0

Doncaster Rovers 2 Stevenage 3

Stoke City 2 Leicester City 1

Southampton 4 Burnley 3

Newcastle United 1 Cardiff City 2

Rochdale 2 Leeds United 0

Wigan Athletic 3 Milton Keynes Dons 3

Charlton Athletic 2 Oxford United 2

Norwich City 1 Fulham 1

Aston Villa 1 Sheffield United 2

Macclesfield Town 1 Sheffield Wednesday 1

Bolton Wanderers 2 Blackpool 1

Everton 4 Queens Park Rangers 0

Brighton & Hove Albion 1 Reading 0

Grimsby Town 2 Huddersfield Town 3

Ipswich Town 1 Preston North End 1

Bournemouth 4 Burton Albion 1

Arsenal 2 Tottenham Hotspur 0

Nottingham Forest 5 West Ham United 0

Sunderland 3 Carlisle 1

Derby County 0 Chelsea 2

Liverpool 2 Oldham Athletic 0

Port Vale 2 Plymouth Argyle 2

Manchester United 1 Swansea City 2

Birmingham City 3 Bristol Rovers 0

Third Round Replays

Preston North End 3 Ipswich Town 2

Sheffield Wednesday 4 Macclesfield Town 1

Fulham 3 Norwich City 0

Plymouth Argyle 2 Port Vale 3

MK Dons 1 Wigan Athletic 3

Peterborough United 2 Kidderminster Harriers 3

Watford 2 Bristol City 0

Manchester City 5 Blackburn Rovers 0

Oxford United 0 Charlton Athletic 3

- If you are not an F.A Cup fanatic, you may find this section a bit boring, but to me, if you are a true football fan, you need to know what happened to every side from the 3rd Round onwards in the F.A Cup.

- One positive piece of news from the Third Round was that after the main weekend of F.A Cup games (4th & 5th January), the Daily Mail reported that 548 907 fans had attended 29 games, an average of 18 297 – the highest for the Third Round since 1980. On the face of it, this looks like a major fillip for the F.A Cup, but it was aided by the fact that Manchester United, Everton, Liverpool, Arsenal, Aston Villa, Sunderland and Newcastle were all at home. Still, in some quarters, the fans would dearly love to win it. I may be biased but I would hazard a guess that nowhere is it more a priority to fans than at Everton. We have won nothing for 19 years and a generation of fans have never seen us lift any silverware. This year's F.A Cup could change all that.

4th Round Draw

Nottingham Forest v Preston North End

Arsenal v Coventry Ciy

Stevenage v Everton

Birmingham City v Swansea City

Manchester City v Watford

Wigan Athletic v Crystal Palace

Rochdale v Sheffield Wednesday

Southend United v Hull City

Port Vale v Brighton & Hove Albion

Huddersfield Town v Charlton Athletic

Southampton v Yeovil Town

Bolton Wanderers v Cardiff City

Sunderland v Kidderminster Harriers

Bournemouth v Liverpool

Chelsea v Stoke City

Sheffield United v Fulham

Football sometimes brings out emotions in you that you were never expecting earlier that day when you went off cheerily to watch the game. It is gone midnight now and what should have been a great day, has left me feeling pretty hollow, because of an injury to a Costa Rican millionaire that I have never met.

Despite the kick off being at 5:30pm, I arranged to pick Alan and Jordan Oliver up at 8:30am at Buckshaw Parkway train station. It is about a four hour trip to Stevenage but the last thing I wanted, was to drive for four hours, watch the game for ninety minutes and then drive four hours back home again. I wanted a bit of chill out time on the way down and whilst we were in Stevenage, so opted for an early start. Alan had also been contacted by a researcher from BT Sport during the week and was optimistic that we might be called upon to go into the TV gantry for a quick chat before kick off. I wasn't as optimistic, as the researcher had said he would call back by Friday and hadn't done so. Still, it would have been frustrating if BT Sport had telephoned Alan to invite us all into their studio and we were still only on the M6 in Coventry.

I took Joel with me to pick Alan and Jordan up, as he was once again staying with his Nanna for the day, as Alison is on nights. We all nipped in to Tesco at Buckshaw to buy some lunch to take with us and Joel decided to buy two Galaxy Skinny Lattes.

"Joel, you won't like that, son, it's coffee," I warned him, but he refused to listen.

"It's Galaxy, Dad, I'll love it."

"Just buy one, just in case," I reasoned.

"Dad, it'll be fine."

We weren't out of Tesco's car park before he had taken a sip and decided it was disgusting! Typical.

Phil Cooper had made his own way down to Stevenage, as he was popping in to see his parents before the match, so wasn't with Jordan and Alan. Thus, there was only my Dad to pick up. With Alison on nights, a trip to the FA Cup needed good logistical planning. My Mum was going to bring Joel back to our house late in the afternoon as she doesn't like driving in the dark and then I would bring my Dad back to ours and he would drive him and Mum back home. This worked better than picking Joel up from my Mum and Dad's at midnight, as he needs his sleep.

I drove over to Aughton and we popped in to my Mum and Dad's to say hello to my Mum before setting off. My Mum had met Alan before we headed down to Stevenage last time, but hadn't met Jordan. They chatted for a while, before my Mum made an amusing error.

"Sorry," she asked, "what did you say your name was again?"

"Jordan," was the reply, but with a strong Mancunian accent, my Mum didn't grasp it.

"Jar-dan! Gosh, that's unusual, I've never heard of anyone called Jar-dan before! Is that, what you said, Jar-dan?"

Jordan didn't grasp that my Mum had lost something in translation.

"Yes, Jordan," Jordan repeated, still with the Mancunian tones.

"Jar-dan.No, I definitely haven't heard of that name before. There's a few Jordans around, aren't there, but I've never heard of Jar-dan. I like it, it's unusual."

Stifling a fit of giggles, I had to explain to my Mum and Jordan, that my Mum hadn't realised it was just 'Jordan' said in a Mancunian accent.

"Oh. Like Jordan on the TV?" Mum asked.

"Yes," Jordan and I said in unison.

"You aren't named after her, are you?" my Mum asked.

This conversation wasn't getting any better.

"Mum! Jordan's nineteen. I know Katie Price has been around a while, but not for nineteen years!"

Soon after, we were on our way. Last time we headed down to Stevenage, for the Stourbridge game, we made the trip on a Friday afternoon, so driving on a Saturday morning, it was noticeably quieter on the roads. We also knew which way to go this time, going from the end of the M6 on to the A14 then A1 rather than joining the M1. We stopped to have a coffee at the services near Huntingdon (where the A14 meets the A1) and watched the start of the Bournemouth-Liverpool game, which was the day's early kick off. Once Liverpool started to dominate, it was obvious they would run out easy winners so we all lost a bit of interest. I suspected whilst watching them, that they were one of five teams that could win the FA Cup this year, the others being Everton, Manchester City, Arsenal and Chelsea. A Liverpool victory, as an Evertonian, would be the hardest to bear. They are looking a strong side this season and although I am loath to admit it, Brendan Rodgers has done a good job. I just hope we can get a point off them in the Merseyside derby on Tuesday. A victory, I suspect, would be hoping for too much.

Even with a stop we arrived outside Stevenage's Lamex Stadium by quarter past two, more than three hours before kick off. Surprisingly, the massive car park over the road from the ground was free for the day. In these days of 'Rip off Britain', I was fully expecting someone to be charging us a tenner, so to park free was a pleasant surprise. There isn't a lot to do for three hours outside the ground, so we decided to walk into town, which is about a mile and a half away. Having missed out on Stevenage Old Town on our last visit, this seemed to be the natural place to head towards, so off we went.

The weather was clear, bright and breezy when we started walking but as we passed the IBIS hotel where we had stopped in December, we could see a mass of grey cloud heading our way.

"That looks pretty threatening," I commented, "I hope it doesn't belt down all day, that'll really play into Stevenage's hands."

"You'll beat this lot, whatever the weather," Alan observed confidently.

We had a wander around the Old Town which is really pleasant and had an array of pleasant looking restaurants. We all agreed we had made a schoolboy error not heading here for food the evening before the Stevenage-Stourbridge game. With three o'clock approaching, we decided to head into a pub with Sky Sports News and get the football score updates. Manchester City were playing Watford, so Alan and Jordan were keen to see how they were getting on.

"I can't see us losing," Alan said with his usual confidence.

"You shouldn't say that," Jordan chided her father, "you will curse them."

One thing that has always been obvious is that the Olivers are a superstitious pair.

Alan phoned Phil who was making his way into Stevenage by train and told him what our plans were. A lot of the pubs were bursting at the seams with both Stevenage and Everton fans, but we managed to find one, The Coach & Horses, that was pretty quiet.

Our order at the bar would have gone down well at an Alcoholics Anonymous meeting as it was soft drinks all round, with Alan and my Dad normally teetotal and me being dry for January. I even think Jordan opted for a soft drink to complete the set. By the time Phil arrived at about half past three, with his usual pint of lager, something amazing had happened. In fact, something amazing had happened twice, Manchester City had conceded against Watford and then, astonishingly, they had conceded again. Watford were 2-0 up at the Etihad!

"I told you, Dad, that you shouldn't have been spouting off about City winning!" Jordan said to Alan who was looking both dejected and guilty.

"I know. I know. It's my fault. I'm not saying another word."

"Don't panic, you'll win this about 4-2. Providing you score before half-time, Al, you'll be fine," I said re-assuringly and I truly believed it, but in my heart of hearts I was hoping to be wrong. I have always thought Manchester City would end up doing the double this year and if they ended up getting knocked out, it would obviously give everyone else more of a chance. If Everton win today, I thought and were then drawn away at Watford, I would fancy our chances, if we were drawn away to City, it would be curtains.

"I'm not having you saying we'll win," Alan berated me, "you're never too confident about your own team, so I don't want you to be confident about mine! That's it, we've had it. Great day this is turning out to be. BT Sport don't ring and now this."

Alan looked totally fed up and then all of a sudden his mobile rang. He looked at it and it was the researcher from BT, maybe, just maybe things were picking up. He stood up and moved away from the table slightly, but we could hear him talking. He was telling the researcher what him and Jordan look like.

"I am small and bald and Jordan has…" he pauses and looked over at Jordan thinking how best to describe her.

"Tell him I've got purple hair. If they are looking for us, a bald man and a girl with purple hair shouldn't be too hard to find," Jordan says.

After he finished the conversation, poor Alan still looked completely fed up.

"Well thanks for nothing, BT Sport," he complained, "they don't want us in the studio, they say they'll just look for us in the crowd. Our two tickets are on the terraces, they'll never bloody find us."

Yesterday, when I was arranging to pick Alan and Jordan up, he had said that he would let Phil sit with me and my Dad and he would take the two tickets that Phil had bought. These two tickets turned out to be in the standing area opposite the Main Stand. Alan was pleased about this, as it meant he had now been to Stevenage three times and been on three different sides of the ground, but with regards to a television appearance, it probably didn't help his cause. He wasn't hinting that he wanted us to swop, Alan isn't like that, he had just hoped he would get a few minutes air time off BT Sport and was frustrated that it now seemed unlikely.

Meanwhile, Manchester City reached half time and it was still two-nil to Watford. At about ten to four, we decided to walk up to the ground. Before we headed off, Alan text a few mates at the match to ask them to keep him updated. I am still torn between seeing a major competitor of Everton's being knocked out the F.A Cup and seeing Alan back in his positive mind frame. Given a choice, I must admit, I would have taken the former, Alan would get over the defeat, but I suspect we will only do this F.A Cup journey once and I want everything to fall into place to increase our chances.

We started walking and the grey clouds had now gathered ominously low in the sky. They seemed to aptly reflect Alan's mood. As most football fans know, unexpected defeats are particularly hard to take. Before we got ten minutes along on our journey, the rain started coming down. By the time we reached the IBIS Hotel and the shopping centre in the middle of Stevenage, it had turned to hail, the gusty wind throwing the hailstones into our faces so hard that they hurt. We took refuge in an indoor section of the shopping centre and for five minutes looked back out the window as the gale force winds continue to produce a huge flurry of hail,

creating a white surface similar to that at a golf driving range on a busy Saturday afternoon.

"Are you thinking what I'm thinking?" Alan asks me and my Dad.

"I hope not," my Dad replied, knowing that Alan is thinking if this hail comes down for too

much longer, the game might be called off.

"It's been dry all day, Al," I added, trying to raise Alan's spirits, which seemed to be getting

lower by the minute.

"Also," my Dad adds with a further positive insight, "it's blowing a gale out there, it'll soon pass

over."

Phil wanted to seek solace in a pie, so we waited a further five minutes whilst he ordered his pie

and then, as we reached the far exit door of the indoor market, the hail had turned to rain, still

heavy but no longer threatening enough for Noah to prepare the Ark. As the rain gradually wore

off and the skies brightened, Alan felt his phone vibrate in his pocket.

"Aguero 2-1, we're back in it! My mate says he doesn't want to tempt fate but we'll go and win

this now. 4-2, he reckons."

Jordan gives her Dad another warning stare.

"Jordan, I'm saying nothing!"

There is still half an hour left and I seriously doubt Watford's capacity to hang on against a side

that have been averaging almost four goals a game at home. City fans who used to be the most

pessimistic bunch, largely because of what their club had done to them over the years, were now

full of self-belief. For the rest of our walk which must have been a further fifteen minutes there

were no further texts. Surely Watford weren't going to pull off this season's most incredible FA

Cup victory? No, of course they bloody weren't! Just as we arrived at the Lamex and were going to head to separate sides of the ground, Alan's phone vibrated once more.

"Aguero again!2-2!"

It didn't matter that there were only twelve minutes left, we all knew Watford's chance had gone. 2-2 wouldn't have been ideal for City, as they are aiming to lift four trophies, the Capital One Cup, the F.A Cup, the European Champions League and the Premier title, but even if it had have gone to a replay at Vicarage Road, City would have won. As it turned out, no replay was necessary. By the time we were in our seats in the ground, City had scored twice more, Kolarov scoring a third and then Aguero completed his hat trick.

As far as our band of merry men (& a lady) were concerned, two of our three teams were now safely through to the 5th Round draw. Phil's team Arsenal had beaten Coventry City 4-0 in the Friday night BT Sport game and now Jordan and Alan's team, Manchester City, had survived a positive statement from their unlucky mascot, Alan, to emerge victorious from a two goal deficit. We were now relying on Everton to make it three out of three.

Once we were in our seats, the reality that we were now following Everton in the F.A Cup began to sink in. If I had designed a perfect scenario, it could not have worked out much better than this. Here we were at a tiny ground about to watch Everton taking on the bottom of the table First Division side that we had followed for the two previous rounds. I keep mentioning that to some extent the F.A Cup has lost some of its old magic, but on cold January days like this, it still seems to have a lot of magic left in the box.

When the two teams are announced, there were a few surprises in the Everton line up. Tony Hibbert, a terrific old professional who is Everton's longest serving player, has been selected at right back, his first start since he had had an operation on a recurring calf problem last season. Joel Robles, an F.A Cup winner with Wigan Athletic, was playing in goal and 19 year old John Stones, was playing at centre back. In addition, Aiden McGeady a signing in the January transfer window from Spartak Moscow, was playing right wing and Steven Naismith was playing up front which meant that Romelu Lukaku, our loan striker from Chelsea was being rested. On paper, it seemed like a strong enough side to dispense of Stevenage, but as one footballing legend once pointed out, football is not played on paper.

Phil, my Dad and myself were in the same stand, the West Stand, that we had been in for the Stourbridge game. This time, however, we were situated nearer the corner flag at the end furthest away from the away fans. BT Sport had set up their roving commentators to deliver their pitch side analysis from that very corner, so their main presenter, Jake Humphrey, along with supporting pundits of Joey Barton and David James were yards away from our seats. Phil wandered over to take some close up photos with his phone. I attempted to take a few with mine, but it is a cheap phone and made Phil's look like they have been taken by David Bailey.

As my children like to point out to their friends, Joey Barton is a distant relative of mine! My late grandfather, Ernie McGrae told me that Joey Bartons Nan and my Nan had been first cousins and she had married into the Barton family, who were already known as being tough characters back then (which must have been shortly after the Second World War). I have loads of first cousins I don't get to see too often, so it is not as though I ever run into Joey at family parties. The former Youth Development Officer at Everton, Ray Hall, once told me that Everton let Barton go, thinking he would end up having a career in football but perhaps in the lower Leagues, so were surprised when he went on to prosper at Manchester City, Newcastle and Queens Park Rangers. Scouts and coaches see so many footballers, they are bound to let the odd one go who ends up making it, but because of all the baggage he brings with him, I am not too upset that Barton didn't stay at Everton. Perhaps all the misdemeanours would not have happened if he had stayed, but we will never know.

When the game kicked off, as I was anticipating, Stevenage really went for Everton and backed by a vocal crowd, put Everton under some pressure. There was one mad early scramble in the Everton box that resulted in Robles dropping the ball under a challenge and Lucas Akins hitting a fierce shot towards goal only for it to strike John Stones near the line. Phil was looking at mine and my Dad's faces for a hint of a nervous reaction, but even if Stevenage had scored in those early exchanges, I would not have been too concerned, as we would have had eighty five minutes to put things right. If it was still nil-nil in the last five minutes and we were being put under pressure, that would have been different, I would then have been a nervous wreck!

Thankfully, from Everton's first real attack they quietened the home support by scoring in the fifth minute. I had seen Steven Naismith looking really good last season against Leyton Orient in the Capital One Cup and once again he prospered against a League One side. Mirallas had a shot on goal which was only partially cleared and McGeady put a ball across to Naismith who lifted the ball over the onrushing defenders and into the back of the net.

My Dad forgot momentarily that he was in the middle of several thousand Stevenage fans and clapped his hands, slapped his thigh and was about to triumphantly rise to his feet, when I warned him in Jordan-esque style about his behaviour! The Stevenage fans seemed a friendly bunch so I doubt they would have turned, en masse, on a 69 year old pensioner, but it only takes one idiot or an unhappy steward for a problem to be created. I was probably being overly sensitive, as moments later, pockets of Everton fans throughout the stand, some in full kit, did rise to applaud the goal.

Stevenage continued to press Everton and Phil Jagielka in particular, weathered the Stevenage storm manfully. In the 22nd minute though, the incident happened that took the joy out the day and left me with that hollow feeling. James McCarthy lost the ball in midfield and Bryan Oviedo, Everton's 23 year old Costa Rican international tracked back after Stevenage's Simon Heslop, in attempt to win back possession. Oviedo has had a real breakthrough season. He scored the winner at Old Trafford and when England international left back, Leighton Baines was out injured he deputised creditably. Oviedo can play left midfield too, as he was today and was now regularly making the first eleven. He also had the World Cup to look forward to and the fact that England were in Costa Rica's Group for Brazil, added to the focus on him.

When Heslop reached twenty five yards from goal, with Oviedo a yard behind him, he decided to shoot. Sensing this, Oviedo slid in, in an attempt to touch the ball away from Heslop's boot. As he slid past Heslop, Heslop did attempt to shoot, but instead of connecting with the ball, he connected forcefully with Oviedo's sliding leg. Oviedo's ankle snapped at a horrific angle, which scans later revealed had resulted in a double leg break, tibia and fibia. It was a complete accident but Oviedo's season was more than likely finished in an instant and perhaps his dreams of playing in the World Cup too.

The Stevenage supporters around me began to speculate who the injured man was. Giving the game away about my allegiances, I revealed it was Bryan Oviedo, but then had to scan across the other nine outfield players just to make sure. One or two Stevenage fans were concerned it could be Leighton Baines and as the players from both sides reaction indicated it was a leg break, the fans worried it may harm England's already fragile World Cup chances. "No, it's not Baines, it is definitely Bryan Oviedo," I stated, my scan around the pitch confirming this.

There was a six minute delay whilst Oviedo was stretchered off. Whilst some players could not even bear to look, John Stones, Everton's 19 year old centre back showed a maturity beyond his years by staying by Oviedo's side during his initial treatment, propping his head up off the floor with one hand and giving him a re-assuring squeeze of his hand with the other. Everton captain, Jagielka, also stayed with him, interlocking his arms around Oviedo's left leg to keep it still. At the most difficult of times, you often see people's true character.

Football is a short career anyway (unless you happen to hit the Manchester United first team at seventeen and remain there until you are forty like Ryan Giggs), but I particularly felt sorry for Oviedo, as he was seemingly basking in the best days of his blossoming career when this happened. Leon Osman came on to replace him and after sympathetic applause from all four corners of the ground, the Everton players had to forget about the terrible injury to their stricken team mate and face up to a free kick 25 yards from goal.

One of the key strengths of Graham Westley's team, is their invention from set pieces and this dangerous free kick was no different. There were two players stood, one either side of the ball and it looked like it would be pulled back to the man behind them, but instead Luke Freeeman peeled off to the left, and the ball was prodded across to him and he unleashed a fierce low shot that Robles got down well to save. Robles had to be at his best again a few minutes later to save another free kick, this time from Morais, but Stevenage's failure to capitalise on their periods of superiority were looking ominous as Everton were counter attacking dangerously.

Just after the half hour mark, Everton doubled their lead. Jon Ashton, Stevenage's centre back who had looked very solid at Doncaster Rovers, miscontrolled a bobbling ball and Steven Naismith took full advantage, running through on goal before neatly pushing the ball past the advancing keeper Day, to make it two for Everton and two for Naismith.

The Everton fans behind the goal Naismith had scored in, were finding their voices.

"Have you heard the words to that song?" Phil asked me looking amused.

"No, I can't quite make it out," I replied, "what are they singing?"

"It's to the tune of 'Give Me Joy In My Heart' and it's

Stuck with Moyes, Stuck with Moyes, Man United,

Stuck with Moyes, Stuck with Moyes, I say,

Stuck with Moyes, Stuck with Moyes, Man United,

Playing football in a negative way!"

There were no further clear cut chances before half time and as the players departed for their half time cup of tea or probably their drink filled with vitamin supplements, Jake Humphrey, Joey Barton and David James re-emerged by our corner flag. Phil went down to take some more close up photos, I nipped to the loo and my Dad who had become increasingly cold as the game progressed, shuffled around a bit to try to keep warm.

When the players came back out for the Second Half, Everton had made a change. We were not sure at the time whether it was just a move to rest Jagielka, with one eye on Tuesday's Merseyside derby, but John Heitinga came on to replace him. The post-match indication is, however, that Jagielka may have felt a twinge in his hamstring and was taken off as a precaution. Hetinga was Everton's player of the season a couple of years back, but had a notable dip in form last season. He is, however, still a Dutch international who has played in a World Cup Final. Unfortunately for Heitinga, he didn't exactly cover himself in glory in that Final as he was sent off by Howard Webb, as Spain defeated Holland 1-0.Nevertheless, as far as this game is concerned, he is an able deputy.

Phil had noticed my Dad was starting to suffer with the cold temperature. Dad had returned from Tenerife with a heavy cold so Phil kindly took his hat off and offered it to my Dad. Dad initially refused, but Phil insisted, so Dad plonked it on his head. I am not a fervent follower of fashion, so I am not sure what type of hat it was, but it was a fashionable one that didn't look quite as cool on my Dad's head as it did on Phil's! I am sure it kept him just as warm though.

Heitinga took only ten minutes to get himself on the scoresheet. A corner was cleared as far as Leighton Baines on the edge of the box. Baines shot was deflected to Kevin Mirallas, who took a couple of touches, but found himself facing away from goal, so did a spectacular overhead kick cross to the far post, where Heitinga leapt up to nod a strong header into the back of the net.

With Everton now coasting, Martinez was able to enjoy the rest of the game and with ten minutes left took off Mirallas and replaced him by Magaye Gueye. Last season, Brad and I were in the Everton souvenir shop by Goodison Park and I spotted Gueye in there, strolling around unnoticed, so asked him if he would have his photo taken with Brad, which he kindly agreed to. He has played irregularly for Everton and has been out on loan, but a few minutes after coming on, Leon Osman put a neat ball through to him in the box, he shimmied past a defender and hit a well placed but fairly tame shot into the back of the net. Everton were 4-0 up and not one of the scorers was likely to start in the Merseyside derby at Anfield on Tuesday.

The fourth goal led to a lot of Stevenage supporters deciding they had seen enough and headed for the exit. We were pleased to see them go, as we thought there might be a mad scamble to get out the car park opposite the ground, so at least the scoreline was leading to the fans leaving at intervals. When the final whistle went we made a sharp exit ourselves and I mentioned to Phil that we had now seen ten F.A Cup games with no replays and a very healthy thirty eight goals.

The local police had intelligently closed the road by the ground so there was less panic about getting out the car park on to the busy main road. We said farewell to Phil, after returning his hat. He headed back to the train station and soon after we met up with Jordan and Alan, who had returned to the car early as Jordan was feeling unwell and they were both freezing! We were able to get out the car park briskly and followed the police diversion away from the ground.

"What were you worrying about? Your lot won easily." Alan commented.

"I wasn't overly worried Al," I re-assured him.

"I tell you," he said in 'Mancunian Mystic Meg' tones, "this is written in the stars, mate!"

Everton will probably draw Manchester City now tomorrow and ruin that fantasy!

Our drive home was trouble free. We stopped for a coffee and a cake just South of Birmingham, then dropped Jordan and Alan off at Crewe station. We were back in Euxton before midnight. My Mum said Joel had been as good as gold and had been helping her with her lines, as she has a big part in a play at Southport Little Theatre at the end of February. Once my Mum and Dad set off home, I watched the game again on ITV1 plus one. Oviedo's injury was horrific. It would be great if he made a speedy recovery, recovering in time to make the squad for the FA Cup Final and the World Cup. Perhaps I am getting ahead of myself or perhaps Alan is right and it is written in the stars!

Tottenham Hotspur and England winger, Andros Townsend and his Dad, Troy have just completed the draw for the Fifth Round of the FA Cup and what a great draw it was too. Troy is a 'Mentoring and Project Leadership Manager' for football's equality organisation, Kick It Out. Before I run through the draw though, here are all the Fourth Round results from today, yesterday and Friday.

Budweiser FA Cup 4th Round Results

Arsenal 4 Coventry City 0

Nottingham Forest0 Preston North End 0

Bournemouth 0 Liverpool 2

Sunderland 1 Kidderminster Harriers 0

Bolton Wanderers 0 Cardiff City 1

Southampton 2 Yeovil Town 0

Huddersfield Town 0 Charlton Athletic 1

Port Vale 1 Brighton & Hove Albion 3

Southend United 0 Hull City 2

Rochdale 1 Sheffield Wednesday 2

Wigan Athletic 2 Crystal Palace 1

Manchester City 4 Watford 2

Birmingham City 1 Swansea City 2

Stevenage 0 Everton 4

Sheffield United 1 Fulham 1

Chelsea 1 Stoke City 0

From an Everton perspective, as the draw was made, the overwhelming desire I had was to avoid the teams in the Top 4 in the Premier League, Arsenal, Manchester City, Chelsea and Liverpool. Everton have been to the Emirates once this season and come home with a draw, so that would have been the most acceptable of the four (and I haven't been there) but I desperately didn't want us to be going to Stamford Bridge, The Etihad or Anfield.

Manchester City were the first drawn out of the hat and immediately I went into, "Not Everton, not Everton!" pleas. Amazingly, it wasn't Everton, but it turned out to be Chelsea. The two favourites for the FA Cup had just been drawn against each other! Great. Get one of the big boys out and give Everton more of a chance. I am sure Alan probably isn't too delighted with that but at least they are at home. I have more City friends than Chelsea friends, so probably want City to win that. I could also, bizarrely, see Everton coping better against City than Chelsea.

The four teams involved in replays, Fulham, Sheffield United, Preston North End and Nottingham Forest were then drawn to face each other. After that, it was Arsenal and the, "Not Everton, not Everton!" chorus started again.

Again, my chant must have worked, as Arsenal were drawn at home to Liverpool! They were the other two clubs from the Top4 and they would be facing each other too. Two of the Top4 in the Premier League would exit the competition in the Fifth Round. This would really open things up and I realised no draw for Everton could be a complete nightmare now and a victory would give us one hell of a chance in this competition.

The "Not Everton, not Everton!" chorus was by no means finished though, as the next out of the hat was Brighton & Hove Albion. Seventeen years ago, my mate Andrew Moss had his Stag Do in Brighton and it was an absolute nightmare to get to. There was no other team left in the competition that would require as long a drive as Brighton. Thankfully, we avoided them too. Hull City had that nightmare journey.

After that Cardiff City were drawn at home next. I wouldn't have minded going there. I used to travel to Cardiff on a regular basis when I worked for Lloyds Bank, as for a time the mortgage processing for the part of the company I worked for (BM Solutions), was done there. It would have been a good opportunity to meet a few old friends for a beer, but F.A Cup holders Wigan Athletic were given that journey. Cardiff have been struggling in the Premier League lately, so Wigan Athletic will fancy their chances of at least a draw. They are not letting go of their Cup too easily, despite being 150-1 outsiders before the competition started.

Sheffield Wednesday were then drawn at home and I would have been pleased to have been drawn against them too, as they are a mid-table Championship side with a massive ground, Hillsborough, so we would have managed to get tickets easily. It would once again have brought back memories of the tragedy in 1989, when 96 Liverpool supporters lost their lives there, but it is a different ground now. The year after the Hillsborough tragedy, Everton were drawn at Sheffield Wednesday in the 4th Round and my Dad and I went across to see Everton win 2-1, with both goals being scored by Norman Whiteside. We were in the stand above the Leppings Lane terrace and the tragedy was never far from our minds that day and to an extent has never been far from our minds since. I am not going to write too much about Hillsborough, but I am sure I will re-visit it when we get around to F.A Cup Semi Final day. Anyway, thoughts of returning there were soon discarded when they were drawn to play Charlton Athletic, ensuring at least one Championship side will be in the Quarter Final.

There were now only four teams left and my television screen revealed they were Everton, Sunderland, Southampton and Swansea. I've been to Sunderland and Southampton, so my preference was a trip to Swansea, if we had to go to any. Sunderland were drawn at home against Southampton, which is a tough one to call, so that just left Everton and Swansea City. Despite not having been to Swansea and having been to Goodison hundreds of times, for financial and footballing (bias) reasons, I wanted Everton to be at home and that's how it worked out, as Andros picked out the number ten ball that represented Everton, leaving Troy with the fifteen ball for Swansea. If truth be told, I have mixed feelings. Delighted from an Everton perspective, as we will be favourites to win, but with regards to the whole adventure, I am not breaking new ground. Still, the objective now is to see Everton win it and this gives us a real chance. Also, with tickets likely to be hard to come by, and expensive, for the following three rounds, this may be an opportunity to take my two boys, Brad and Joel. Overall, the glass is more than half full.

To summarise, the draw is now as follows :-

<u>Budweiser FA Cup 5th Round Proper</u>

Manchester City v Chelsea

Fulham or Sheffield United v Preston North End or Nottingham Forest

Arsenal v Liverpool

Brighton & Hove Albion v Hull City

Cardiff City v Wigan Athletic

Sheffield Wednesday v Charlton Athletic

Sunderland v Southampton

Everton v Swansea City

Saturday 1st February 2014

Tuesday night was the poorest, most miserable footballing night of an excellent footballing season. The second Merseyside derby of the season saw Liverpool beat Everton 4-0 at Anfield. Jagielka came back but didn't look fit, Alcaraz played with him at centre back and looked lacking in match fitness too, John Stones playing at right back looked a yard off the pace and Tim Howard, our goalkeeper seemed confused by our defensive high line and made some bad decisions. To be fair, Liverpool's forward pairing, Sturridge and the gifted but annoying Suarez, are in fine form and tore us apart. Liverpool looked like scoring with every attack and we looked like we could play until FA Cup Final Day and not score. It was one of those all too familiar nights when Everton have not turned up against Liverpool. Roberto Martinez, the Everton manager, has hardly put a foot wrong this season, but this wasn't his finest hour. I thought Tony Hibbert was great at Stevenage and his defensive qualities and experience would have been invaluable. I doubt he would have altered where the three points went, but he would have made a positive difference.

On a more positive note, I took Joel to Goodison Park today to see Everton against Aston Villa. Joel has a terrific record of having seen Everton win in on every occasion he has seen them play (seven out of seven before today) but unfortunately supports Manchester United like Alison's Dad, Barry. Brad, my eldest son, the Evertonian, was staying at a mates so couldn't come. Joel is good company and enjoys watching football now he's eleven more than he has ever done before, so was delighted to come along, especially when I told him I would take him to KFC before kick off!

Joel had predicted a 2-1 Everton win and a Mirallas goal, so I decided to put his good luck to use and put a bet on 2-1 (50p at 7-1) and a £1 on Mirallas scoring at some point at 6-4.

£1-50 on bets is not far off my limit! We took our seats on the second from back row of the Main Stand and soon after a familiar face and his friend took their seats behind me. I listened in to their conversation for a couple of minutes, just to be certain,then turned around.

"Excuse me," I asked, "are you Roly Howard?"

"I am."

"I'm Richie Wade's son, Calvin. You won't remember me, but I remember spending every Saturday morning when I was three and four in the Marine dressing room!"

Roly Howard, as mentioned very early in this book when detailing my Dad's playing days, was the Marine manager long enough for it to be a Guinness World Record and my Dad played and coached under him. The other bloke turned out to be Frank O'Brien, another coach that worked at Marine under Roly. I had a good chat with the pair of them. Co-incidentally, my Dad had been to a re-union of the Skelmersdale United players from their two FA Amateur Cup Finals in 1967 and 1971, a few weeks earlier, which was at Skelmersdale for the Skem-Marine clash and he had been speaking to Roly and Frank then. My Dad had been telling them all about our FA Cup journey, further evidence that he is loving every minute of it.

"I believe Stevenage gave you free hotel accommodation!" Roly pointed out with a smile.

The match itself was a good one and took Joel's Everton record to eight wins out of eight games. It started encouragingly for Everton when in the fourth minute Aidan McGeady, on the right wing, pulled the ball back on to his left foot and curled a ball from the edge of the box, which looked destined to nestle in the corner of the net, only for it to hit the inside of the post and rebound to safety.

"That McGeady is brilliant," concluded Joel, heavily influenced by his brother, Brad, who is always saying that on the Xbox FIFA game, McGeady is brilliant! Brad judges all players talents on how good they are on FIFA. It has, however, given him an in depth knowledge of top flight European football and he knows far more European players and their clubs than I do. When I was a kid, my own knowledge of top flight English and Scottish players was strengthened via the Panini sticker albums. In 1980, I all but completed it, just needing the Notts County team photo!

For the rest of the first forty five minutes, Aston Villa looked like a good side. They were at the very least a match for Everton and although they didn't often test Tim Howard, in the Everton goal, it was no great surprise when a 34th minute shot by Aston Villa's right back, Leandro Bacuna, found its way into the back of the Everton net. After the 4-0 defeat to Liverpool, it was worryingly beginning to look like the rails were coming off Everton's season. They were desperately short of striking options and when it was still 1-0 to Aston Villa at half-time, it seemed too much to hope for that Everton would score two (without reply) in the second half.

Thankfully for Everton, the second half was totally different. As Everton became more positive, Aston Villa became increasingly negative and played into Everton's hands. With the same positive mentality they had in the first half, Villa may have snatched at least a point, but Everton's confidence grew as Villa sat back. At half time, Steven Pienaar had replaced young Ross Barkley, who had given the ball away in midfield, which had then immediately led to Villa's goal. This substitution gave Everton more width and Roberto Martinez made an even bolder substitution in the 69th minute when he took off right back, John Stones and put Steven Naismith up front, in effect playing 3-5-2. Within five minutes the substitutes combined, Pienaar putting an intricate ball through to Naismith who finished confidently. One all and now it looked like Everton would go on and grab the winner.

Everton continued to press and when Kevin Mirallas was fouled ten yards outside the Aston Villa box, slightly left of centre as the Everton players looked, I commented to Joel that it should be Leighton Baines rather than Mirallas who should take the resultant free kick, as only Baines had the ferocity of shot to beat the Aston Villa keeper from such a distance. Thankfully, the players couldn't hear me, Mirallas struck a perfectly placed curling free kick, that flew into Guzan's top right hand corner, just beyond his despairing dive. Everton saw out the final few minutes and a 2-1 victory was secured.

Joel had made it eight wins out of eight watching Everton (surely there aren't many supporters who can trump that, yet unfortunately he supports Manchester United!) and to top it off, we won £6-50 from the 2-1 scoreline and Mirallas goal. I hope his luck holds out if I bring him back in a couple of weeks for the Fifth Round F.A Cup game against Swansea City.

Our family have all been out tonight to the Hop Vine in Burscough for a meal to celebrate my Dad's 70th birthday which is tomorrow. My Mum and Dad, my sister Lisa, her husband Vinny, their daughter Olivia (who shares a birthday with my Dad and is seventeen tomorrow), their son Max (who is thirteen), Alison, Brad, Joel and myself. I remember when Olivia was born saying she would be seventeen on the day my Dad was seventy, but that seemed a million miles away at the time and in the blink of an eye it is here.

It was a really enjoyable night. All the ladies sat together at one end, the three young lads at the other, with myself, my Dad and Vinny in the middle. Vinny is another Evertonian. Since long before he met my sister, Vinny, his Dad, his two brothers and his sister have had season tickets at Goodison. One of his brothers, James, is married to one of Colin Harvey's daughter's, Emma, so they certainly all have blue blood too!

Amongst many of the Everton led discussions, we discussed a disappointing one-nil defeat today, at the hands of Tottenham Hotspur (at White Hart Lane). Despite dominating possession, we were hit by an Emmanuel Adebayor goal, which was Spurs only shot on target. Our squad is looking weary and thin currently and I am just hoping we prioritise the F.A Cup slightly above the League now as a Champions League place is looking increasingly unlikely. We have two home games in a week, Crystal Palace in the Premier League on Wednesday night and then Swansea next Sunday in the F.A Cup.

ITV have decided to televise the Everton-Swansea game. It will be a half past one kick off on the Sunday, so for the first time in eleven rounds, our game is not on a Saturday afternoon. The fact it is on terrestrial TV has impacted on ticket sales, but the positive gleaned from that is a reduction in ticket prices to £30 for adults and only £5 for children, so we are going in a party of seven. Alan Oliver, Jordan Oliver, Phil Cooper, me, my Dad and both my boys, Brad and Joel are coming to his one. This will be Brad's first taste of our F.A Cup adventure, but as it is at Goodison Park, a stadium he is very familiar with, it won't seem all that big a deal to him.

I think it is a great pity that my boys don't quite have that same eagerness to go the football with their Dad, that I had when I was a boy, but they are their own strong characters and any attempts I have made to mould them into a mini-me have always been met with a firm rebuttal (see Joel's Manchester United support as a perfect example). If they had started out coming to every early round, I would have been trying to get them tickets for every round from now onwards, but I very much expect this to be Brad's first and last outing (and Joel's second and last as he went to Workington v Stourbridge). Overall though, they both play football every week, one supports Everton and they both enjoy coming to a few games a season with me, so it could well turn out that they fancy joining me on a similar adventure when they are a little older.

Today and tomorrow though are not about my children, they are about my Dad. Seventy years old. He has been a great role model, a great father and a great friend and I hope he is around for many, many more years. Short term, I hope he is with me on 17th May at Wembley when Phil Jagielka, the Everton captain, lifts the F.A Cup!

Sad news in the football world this evening, as it has been announced that Sir Tom Finney, the former Preston North End and England player has died aged 91. Throughout his career, he only ever played for his local club, Preston playing 433 times for them and scoring 187 goals. He also represented England 76 times scoring 30 times. Ex Liverpool manager, Bill Shankly and ex-Manchester United manager Tommy Docherty, both stated that the greatest player they ever played with or managed was Sir Tom Finney.

Prior to Finney's footballing career hitting the heights, he had served in Montgomery's Eighth Army in Egypt and then Italy as a tank driver. It has been widely reported that when he was in North Africa, the Army would play against local teams and in one match, Sir Tom played against the internationally famous actor, Omar Sharif!

A few people I know have had the pleasure of meeting Sir Tom and they all say he was a fantastic man.

When I was 23, I went backpacking around the world with two friends, Andrew Berry, a close friend since Primary school days who was 'Best Man' at our wedding and also Paul Bennett, son of my Dad's old Skelmersdale United team mate, Wally Bennett, who I had also spent a lot of my time with throughout my childhood years.When my Dad found out we were going to be staying in Sydney, he contacted another old football friend, John Bond, who had played for Skelmersdale United in the 1967-68 season but had emigrated to Australia soon after. When we flew into Sydney, John and his then girlfriend, now wife, Carol, were waiting for us and we spent a fantastic couple of weeks with them in the Hunter Valley, before touring around Australia for a couple of months and then returning to stay with them for a further week before moving on to New Zealand.

John and Carol, despite never having previously met us, treated us like three sons during our stay. They could not have been more friendly and hospitable and one of my biggest regrets in life is that I have not been able to afford to return to Australia since, as I would love to see them again. Anyway, the relevance to the Sir Tom Finney story, is that John was a Preston lad and actually signed for Preston North End as an apprentice.

When John was sixteen, in the first year of his Apprenticeship, in the early 1960s, he broke his toe and when he returned to training, he was initially doing sessions on his own to avoid full physical contact on his toe. Walter Crook, the first team trainer, came over to John to say that he had a training partner for him, as Walter needed to know how John's toe would handle contact. Lo and behold, the training partner turned out to be the recently retired Tom Finney, who was organising a footballing fundraising event at Fulwood Barracks and felt like he needed a training session himself. John said his jaw dropped. They trained together for half an hour, just doing general ball work between them, John feeling so excited that he soon forgot about the pain in his toe. After they finished, Tom thanked John for his time. John said he was totally in awe of the man and to be thanked by him was a special feeling. When John arrived home that night, he rushed to tell his Dad who he had had a training session with and his father refused to believe that he had trained alone with the legendary Tom Finney.

The other friends that have had the privilege of meeting Sir Tom are Richard and Robbie Knowles, who I mentioned early in this book tried to do every round of the F.A Cup in the 2009-10 season. Their story can be read at http://runcorn2wembley.blogspot.co.uk . Saturday 10th October 2009 was the day they met Sir Tom. Richard and Robbie were raising money for Cancer Research UK and found themselves at Guiseley AFC for the 3rd Qualifying Round game against Kendal Town. Sir Tom Finney was Kendal Town's President and had gone along to watch the game. Sir Tom came over to have a chat with Richard and Robbie, donated £20 to their cause and gladly lined up to have his photograph taken with them and Richard's partner, Sarah. When Sir Tom died, Richard said,

"On hearing the news of his passing it reminded me of the day over four years ago when he spared some time to speak to my brother and partner about football and put his name and image to the charity cause we were fundraising for.

He was simply a lovely man and I have no doubt that his passing will leave a hole in many lives and also the world of football and sport in this country.

If only players nowadays could follow his example and attitude to the sport. I may only have met him once, but his presence, kindness and sincerity will stay with me forever."

Both Robbie Knowles and John Bond's stories are simple stories of brief meetings with Sir Tom but they are cherished memories for each of them. The term 'legend' is ubiquitous these days, but Sir Tom Finney was a real footballing legend and his impact on the town of Preston, the people he met and the country he proudly represented both in play and in war cannot be overstated. RIP Sir Tom Finney.

Budweiser F.A Cup 5th Round Proper - Sunday 16th February 2014

Everton v Swansea City

Attendance – 31 498

Today was our 11th F.A Cup round and our first game that has not been played on a Saturday. There had been due to be four games yesterday, but the Sheffield Wednesday v Charlton Athletic game had been postponed due to a waterlogged pitch, so only three went ahead. In the early kick off, Sunderland defeated Southampton 1-0, with the ground looking fairly empty with just over 16 000 there. Sunderland are already in the Capital One Cup Final against Manchester City and an extended F.A Cup run is obviously a further stretch on many peoples tight budgets, so it appears many fans decided to watch this one on the TV.

The only traditional 3pm Saturday kick off saw holders Wigan Athletic win 2-1 away at Cardiff City and continue their participation in a tournament they started as massive 150-1 underdogs in. It is still very unlikely that they will retain their trophy, but what a story it would be if they did.

The final Saturday game was the one between the two favourites for the Premier League title, Manchester City and Chelsea. Alan will have been delighted to see that despite Chelsea winning 1-0 in the League game at the Etihad, it never appeared likely that lightning would strike twice and Manchester City ran out convincing 2-0 winners.

Today, there were three further games. Everton-Swansea was the first. The second game was between the two victors of the replayed 4th Round games, Sheffield United & Nottingham Forest and the final one was Arsenal v Liverpool. The last tie, Brighton & Hove Albion against Hull City is tomorrow night.

For several previous rounds, Alan, my Dad and I have all journeyed together but this time we all made our own ways to Goodison Park, Alan and my Dad on trains from home and me in the car with my two boys, Brad and Joel in tow. Alan phoned me at 9am to say Jordan was unwell and would not be able to make this one, so he would just be travelling over with Phil. Alison, my wife, is on nights at the moment, so was probably delighted to have the house to herself without three males clunking around whilst she is trying to get some sleep.

I grew up in Aughton, about twelve miles from Liverpool, but the city is in my blood. My two parents are from Liverpool, my four grandparents were all from Liverpool, as were my eight great grandparents. I have worked in Liverpool city centre and in the Montrose Club in Whitefield Road, Anfield, married a lady from the Wirral and spent a huge amount of time in Liverpool. There are many fantastic things about the city, the architecture and the people, so it is often frustrating to see how it is depicted in the national press and the generalisations people make about "Scousers".

If I drive to the match, I always park at The Mons pub and walk the mile and a half up. Walking up with a thirteen year old and an eleven year old takes me back to the days I used to walk up with my Dad or my Grandad ("Pop"), when I was their age. I've not noticed as many kids out asking if they can mind your car as there used to be when I was a kid, but I think they used to latch on to my Grandad as he used to give them a quid, which was a decent chunk of money to a kid in the late 70s/ early 80s.

We were all due to meet up at St.Luke's Church that backs on to Goodison Park at twelve o'clock, as Alan had said he was interested in seeing the historical items that my cousin, Paul Wharton and the rest of the EFC Heritage Society had on display. I bumped in to Alan and Phil on Goodison Road and seconds later also bumped in to another old friend, Andy Hosie and his father. Andy went to school with me at Ormskirk Grammar (he was the Head Boy in the school year below me and also played rugby with me) and I went to the occasional Everton match with him back then. He was a really intelligent lad, going to Cambridge University after Sixth Form and in his subsequent career, he worked for Everton Football Club for a number of years as Commercial Director and is now heavily involved in the emerging internet gambling site, Bet Butler. Andy must have followed our F.A Cup journey from my regular mentions on Facebook, as he explained to his Dad, how we had picked a side in the Extra Preliminary Round and followed the winners through. I made a mental note to add Andy to my list of potential useful contacts if we are struggling to get tickets in the final three rounds!

Alan, Phil, Brad, Joel and I then went in to St. Lukes to be warmly greeted by Paul, who showed Alan some of the more interesting items they have on display, including some Joe Mercer memorabilia. Joe Mercer had been an outstanding player for Everton and Arsenal, before going on to manage Manchester City in the 1960s and early 1970s, so was probably the ideal Evertonian to unite the interest of Phil as an Arsenal fan and Alan as a Manchester City fan. Paul also showed us all, what the Heritage Society had been doing to celebrate the life of one of Everton's most iconic figures, Will Cuff. Will Cuff had been secretary of Everton when they won the FA Cup for the first time in 1906 and became Chairman in 1921. Subsequently, in 1938, he became President of the Football League, a role he continued until he died aged 79 in 1949. Despite being a man that was held in incredibly high esteem in his life time, in recent years his grave at Anfield Cemetery had been unattended, so EFC Heritage Society and Everton Football Club have restored it, putting a new headstone on and a plaque detailing his achievements. A ceremony was recently held at his graveside that was attended by Everton manager, Roberto

Martinez , Chief Executive, Robert Elstone and Life President (and former Chairman) Sir Philip Carter.

My Dad arrived about half past twelve as he had been for a coffee with another ex-Skelmersdale United player, Alan McDermott, who had sorted some of the tickets out for us. We asked Paul to take a few photographs of us in the Church before we headed off to the Fanzone area behind the Park End stand in search of two blokes who have also been following the F.A Cup from the Extra Preliminary Round, who are known on Twitter as "Cup Runnings". Alan had arranged to meet them there, but as neither of us really knew what they looked like, it was a bit like searching for two needles in a haystack, so we soon gave up and decided to head to our seats in the Main Stand.

As we walked back along Goodison Road, Alan spotted an EvertonTV cameraman and collared him to ask him to do a quick interview about our F.A Cup journey so far. It was only Alan and me that were interviewed this time (not the whole group of us like at Guisborough for FATV), but although I didn't get 'camera fright' and talk random nonsense like I had last time around, I could tell pretty early on from the manner of the questions from the interviewer and the lack of interest from the cameraman, that this was not likely to ever be shown on Everton TV or anywhere else! The camera seemed to be pointing to the floor from about half way through the interview and although the interviewer passed on his Twitter address (@efc_camerman) , he hasn't replied to my tweets this evening, so once again our fifteen minutes of fame elude us. Perhaps Lady Luck is saving our good fortune for Wembley Way.

I always have a tingle of excitement going in to Everton's old ground. Some of the modern stadia are a bit characterless, but Goodison Park is crammed full of the stuff and although we probably need to move on to a bigger, more corporate focused stadium if we want to establish ourselves as a regular amongst the Premier League elite, I still love every moment I spend there (with the obvious exception of the moments when the opposition score). The fairly sparsely populated away end reflects, however, that Swansea City feel they have bigger fish to fry than the F.A Cup. They have recently sacked Michael Laudrup, their former manager, due to their close proximity to the Premier League drop zone and are due to play Napoli in the last 32 of the Europa League, home and away, over the next few weeks. Swansea's team sheet showed eight changes from their last game, a victory over Welsh rivals Cardiff City and their interim Manager, Garry Monk, was sending out a message that although Swansea would quite like to win the game, it wasn't to be at all costs. Everton, on the other hand, were after silverware and despite Joel Robles retaining his position as Everton's F.A Cup goalkeeper, the rest of the side named were first choice ones. Martinez was handing a debut to on-loan AS Monaco striker, Lacina Traore, a huge 6 feet 8 inch target man. With my lucky mascot, Joel, already having a record of eight wins from eight games when watching Everton, surely this was going to be a home banker? We are only 180 minutes from Wembley and I cannot tell you how desperate I am for Everton to get there.

Prior to kick off, a minutes silence was immaculately observed by both sets of fans for Sir Tom Finney. Some grounds this weekend have adopted a minute's applause and others a minute's silence. I think, given he lived to the grand old age of 91, perhaps a minute's applause would have been more fitting, but I have no idea who clubs take their lead on from this.

Our six tickets were in three twos, all in the same section at the front of the Main Stand towards the Park End. As Joel and Brad argue more than Neil Kinnock and Maggie Thatcher did when they were Labour and Tory leaders, I sat with Joel, my Dad sat with Brad and Alan and Phil sat in the seats closest to the front. In previous rounds, my Dad, Alan and myself, in particular, have spent several pre-match hours chewing the fat, so it seemed strange to just arrive at Goodison, have a quick look around St Luke's, wander around a bit and then go in and it seemed equally strange to have Joel as the only person I could discuss an F.A Cup game with, other than the odd mouthed message to Brad and my Dad, three rows in front.

It did not take long for Lacina Traore to endear himself to the Everton faithful. After only four minutes, Sylvain Distin, the Everton centre half went up for a free kick, found himself with the ball at his feet only six yards out and calmly passed across the goalmouth for Traore to scoop a backheel into the back of the net. The pre-match optimism seemed well served and already I was starting to think that Traore may become the first Everton player to score a debut hat trick since Tony Cottee scored three in a home debut 4-0 win over Newcastle United.

After the goal, however, Traore just wasn't very good. He has the tendency that giant forwards often have, of thinking he doesn't have to jump to win a header and as a result, he wasn't winning very many. He has had injury problems at Monaco though and has also not been getting picked even when fit, so it is probably harsh to judge him solely on this display, as he was not match fit, but he was substituted after an hour without contributing very much else.

Up to the hour mark, the game was actually very even and my optimism soon evaporated as I began to consider how I would go about getting to Swansea for a midweek replay. The reason for replay thoughts was largely due to the fact Swansea scored a well worked equaliser after fifteen minutes. A ball was played across from the Swansea left and Jonathan De Guzman rose to send a strong header past the outstretched left arm of Robles and into the back of the Everton net. For the rest of the first half, Everton had lots of possession and some neat, intricate periods of passing, but they rarely threatened the Swansea goal.

At half-time, I swopped sons. Joel went to sit with my Dad and Brad came to sit with me. Through his primary school days, Brad had always been an easier child to manage than Joel. When he was younger, Joel was the type of child you could buy one hundred ice creams for and he would then kick off if he couldn't have the 101st one. He has matured beyond that now. Joel is on the whole a happy, contented young man these days. Brad, on the other hand, was always mature beyond his years and much more accepting than Joel. Brad was still headstrong, but that is a given in our household. All four of us are headstrong people. Brad has however, become the type of 'Kevin' teenager that Harry Enfield warned us about. He is fourteen in July and is very popular amongst classmates and teachers. He has more girls after him than I ever had in my life and is brimming with confidence, but around Alison and me, his moods swing from abundantly cheerful to a monosyllabic, miserable grunter. As he sits down next to me, I automatically sense this is one of the latter days.

At half time, Swansea have made a change with Dyer replacing Routledge, but Everton remain unchanged.

"Martinez should have taken Jagielka off, he's rubbish," Brad observed.

"He's not rubbish, Brad, he's a first choice international centre back and will be playing in the World Cup in Brazil this summer," I countered.

"Poppa says he's rubbish," Brad stated.

Poppa is a family name for Grandad. I used to call my Mum's Dad, Ernie Mack, 'Poppa' or as I got older 'Pop'. My 'Pop' as mentioned earlier in the book was a showbusiness impresario. As well as managing or acting as an agent for many showbiz acts who found fame later in life, he could act, sing, play the ukulele and often acted as a compere. He was briefly in the film about Everton's Alex Young called 'The Golden Vision' and another with Albert Finney called 'Gumshoe' . He also had bit parts in Brookside, Coronation Street and Scully. Ernie was a well known figure around Merseyside in the 1960s and 1970s and was good friends with Joe Royle's Dad, Joe Royle Senior (playing in a jazz band with him called 'The Saturated Seven'), Liverpool managers Phil Taylor and Bill Shankly and Merseyside comedy legend, Ken Dodd. He even brought Prince Charles to Liverpool to see a Variety Club of Great Britain star studded evening at the Liverpool Empire in the late 1970s. Ken Dodd said we called our grandfather 'Poppa' as he had a tendency to leave his trouser zip undone! He died in January 2012, a few weeks short of his 90th birthday. The Liverpool Echo wrote 'Mr.Merseyside' had died. Poppa in our family is like 'Godfather' in the Corleones.

"Did Poppa say Jagielka is rubbish or his distribution is rubbish?" I asked Brad.

My Dad gets frustrated with Jagielka being involved in the new passing style of Martinez, as in my Dad's opinion, he can't pass.

"Same thing," Brad grunts.

"No, it isn't. Poppa thinks Jagielka is a great defender. He just doesn't think he is a good passer."

"Still should have taken him off."

The temptation is there to continue the argument, but I don't say anything else. Brad is at an age where he has to have the last word, even if it is just a sarcastic "Yeh" in reply to a statement Alison or I make. I want to watch the second half without getting into a prolonged squabble with my teenage son. I even avoid the temptation to add my own sarcastic "Yeh" to his last statement. He is a really good son and I am very proud of both Brad and Joel in so many ways, but I will be glad when Brad's 'teenager with attitude' stage ends.

The first fifteen minutes of the second half pass and I notice there are now two seats free next to my Dad and Joel so we go and sit with them. Everton are continuing to pass neatly but aren't threatening and my mind is beginning to map out a trip to the Liberty Stadium, Swansea. Just as I am deciding whether to go over the bridge or via Monmouth, Martinez makes his master stroke, taking off Traore and Barkley and replacing them with Leon Osman and Steven Naismith.

Both Naismith and Osman are seasoned pros. A lot of Evertonians moan about both of them because neither is excellent at any one particular thing, but both do most aspects of the game very well. Osman is a good passer, heads well for a relatively small player and works hard. Naismith reads a game well, is quick and can finish. If you were hoping for a Champions League spot for your side (by finishing in the Top 4 – something that Everton are aspiring to) you would be unlikely to select Osman and Naismith for ninety minutes of every game throughout the season but both regularly make telling contributions. Today was no different.

Four minutes after coming on, Steven Naismith made his first telling contribution. A poor back pass by Swansea's Taylor was latched on to by Naismith and as the Swansea keeper Tremmel raced out to narrow the angle, Naismith calmly rolled the ball past him and into the empty net. 2-1. Alan and Phil had only seen this guy play for just over ninety minutes and he had scored three goals, they must have been wondering why he didn't play all the time! Truth is, they had seen his best ninety four minutes of the season.

A sense of relief now spread around Goodison. Quarter Finals here we come! There was probably no-one more relieved than Alan and me, who were both thinking about the trip to Swansea and its financial implications. Despite now having a regular job, car warranty repping isn't the best paid job in the world and I get by from month to month, but don't have much left over for trips to South Wales. I would do it, because I am determined to go to every game, but the fact we have avoided replays thus far, has been a real help. Alan assures me he isn't loaded either!

Thankfully, once Everton regained the lead, their victory was not really threatened. Soon after Naismith's goal, Mirallas should have made it three, when he blazed over after a cross by Seamus Coleman. If Swansea had equalised, I would have been sending the bill for the replay to Kevin Mirallas, Finch Farm (Everton's training ground) as it was harder to miss than score. That 'sitter' soon proved to be immaterial. In the 72nd minute, Everton made it 3-1. Naismith was again a major contributor, as he was brought down in the box by Richards. Leighton Baines, who is probably the most lethal penalty taker to grace the Premier League since Matt Le Tissier, fired the resultant spot kick into the back of the net with his trusty left foot, taking his Everton penalty record to fifteen out of sixteen. It also pretty much guaranteed that my son, Joel's, 100% record of Everton victories continued. He has now seen Everton play nine times live and they have won them all. I need to buy the lad a season ticket!

With the score at 3-1, the game fizzled out, but Naismith's eventful period on the pitch ended poorly. Naismith turned sharply on the edge of the Swansea box and his head struck into Jordi Amat's arm, knocking him to the ground. Naismith initially picked himself up and tried to carry on, but it soon became apparent that he was suffering from concussion, so Martinez substituted him (despite Everton having already used our three subs), so Everton finished the game with only ten men.

Martinez later said Naismith was feeling dizzy, didn't really know where he was and couldn't remember that he'd scored. Naismith asked his boss what the goal was like, so Martinez told him it was a forty yard wonder goal! I bet he was disappointed when he saw the highlights on ITV.

Alan and Phil left in injury time. Today's match co-incided with Alan's wife, Jo's, 40th birthday, so he needed to get home as early as possible to take her for a celebratory meal, whilst Phil wanted to get into Liverpool City centre to watch the Arsenal-Liverpool FA Cup match. As a 'Gooner' that probably wasn't Phil's best laid plan! I will find out at a later date how that one went.

At the final whistle us 'Wades' made a quick dart too. The F.A Cup 6th Round draw was due to take place a few minutes after the end of the game and I was desperate to see who Everton would be facing next. Manchester City and the winners of the Arsenal-Liverpool game were the obvious ones to avoid, if we drew anybody else, home or away, I would fancy our chances.

Brad, Joel and I walked along briskly with my Dad for a while, but when we headed off in separate directions, Dad towards Kirkdale train station and me and the kids back towards 'The Mons' pub, I wanted the three of us to run.

"Come on lads, I want to see the F.A Cup draw, can we run?"

"I'm not running," Brad moaned.

"Why not?"

"I need a wee, it'll be worse if I run."

"But you'll be at the toilet quicker! Come on."

"No," Brad stated firmly.

"I'll run, Dad," Joel added helpfully.

Brad probably wasn't that desperate for a wee. He is very conscious currently of how he looks to other people, even if they are complete strangers, and even more concerned with how I look. I have a funny run, with arms and legs going in four separate directions, so Brad was probably more concerned about me showing him up than about wetting himself. As he is almost fourteen, he is safe to be left to walk half a mile on his own. I broke out into a run that John Cleese would have been proud of and Joel followed alongside.

"See you in the pub, Brad!"

It transpired we would see him sooner than we thought. I am still out of shape. The previously stated plan of being 13 stone 13 pounds on F.A Cup Final Day is looking well beyond me unless I contract some weird stomach bug between now and then. A bug that causes my taste buds to turn against beer and chocolate would be useful. As things stand I have lost a bit of weight, tipping the scales at slightly below sixteen stone, but I still weigh more than Robert de Niro did at the end of Raging Bull. As a result of my excess frame, we ran very slowly and when we reached a pedestrian crossing, Brad's leisurely walk managed to keep pace with us. Once, the green man shone, we were off ahead again, but I arrived at 'The Mons' gasping for breath, whilst Joel appeared like it was a mere trot and Brad caught us up ten seconds later. I stumbled into the pub with my shirt half hanging out, panting and sweating like a 1970's wrestler on the top seat in a sauna. No-one turned around. Everyone was gathered around the TV screens watching the F.A Cup draw that had already started. I stood behind a crowd of men, peering over their heads to see the screen. A young lad collecting glasses stood next to me.

"Have Everton been drawn out yet?" I asked him, still panting.

"Unfortunately," he said, his look of despair immediately telling me he was a dejected Evertonian and something had just gone terribly wrong.

"Who've we got?" I asked, anxious to be put out of the misery he had just put me into.

"Liverpool or Arsenal away."

"YOU'RE JOKING!"

I must have said this pretty loudly as a few heads turned away from the TV and my two boys told me to shush.

"I wish I was, mate."

At this point I could have done with Neil and Tim Finn walking through into 'The Mons' with the rest of Crowded House singing 'Don't Dream It's Over', as all my optimism about this journey having the fairytale ending of Everton lifting the Cup suddenly evaporated. This was now looking like a personal sporting disaster on a number of levels. Firstly, whoever Everton will now play will be favourites to win the game. Secondly, if it turns out to be Liverpool, we have already lost 4-0 at Anfield this season, so to get knocked out by our local rivals would be particularly galling. Thirdly, a Merseyside derby will be a nightmare to get tickets for. Finally, if we do face Liverpool and lose, not only would I have to suffer the frustration of that defeat, I would then have to go to the Semi-Final to watch Liverpool and even potentially have to return a month later to see them in the Final. Watching Steven Gerrard lift the F.A Cup at Wembley, would be the nightmare ending to a fourteen round journey. I don't hate Liverpool, three quarters of my friends support them, as do my Mum's side of the family. I just don't like them very much! Throughout my life, Liverpool Football Club have inflicted a lot of sporting misery on me.

When I was a young child, in the 1970's, Everton won nothing from the year I was born, 1971, until the F.A Cup win against Watford in 1984. I hate to think what Liverpool won in that time, but amongst their trophies were about ten League Championships, a UEFA cup, several European Cups, lots of League Cups, Milk Cups and they even won the Central League (reserves League) every season too. Near enough every Merseyside derby ended in defeat for Everton as well, including the 5-0 calamity at Goodison Park when Ian Rush scored four and my Dad and I tried to escape from the Upper Bullens long before the turnstiles were re-opened.

Before the new dawn at Everton, kickstarted by the F.A Cup win, there was the darkest hour. I cried when Graeme Souness scored the winner in the 1984 Milk Cup Final replay at Maine Road, giving Liverpool a 1-0 victory over Everton. I had been with my Dad to Wembley to see the first game, but he had gone on his own to the Replay and I blamed my Mum for our defeat, as she wouldn't let me go to watch it, as it was on a school night. I also blamed the ref for not giving a penalty in the first game, when Alan 'Handsen'diverted an Adrian Heath goal bound effort away with his arm. This heartbreak was the first of many. I was at the 1986 and 1989 F.A Cup Finals when we lost to Liverpool at Wembley. The 1986 Cup Final defeat handed Liverpool a League and F.A Cup double and left Everton as runners up in both. For that 1986 Final, my Dad and I, along with Wally Bennett (who worked at Anfield in 'Promotions' despite being a big Evertonian) and his son, Paul, were the only Evertonians on a Liverpool staff and family coach, so had to travel home with a load of jubilant Reds, including Stephen and Stacey Evans, Roy Evans children who I knew very well as they lived down our road. The defeat in 1989 still hurt, but it was in the shadow of the Hillsborough tragedy and even as an eighteen year old, I understood sporting disappointment meant nothing relative to the enormity of the loss suffered by Liverpool supporters and their families.

15th April 2014, will mark the twenty fifth anniversary of the Hillsborough disaster. For ninety six people to lose their lives simply by going to spectate at a football match of the team they love, illustrated a catastrophic chain of events that resulted in the worst modern era sporting disaster that our nation has ever seen. Enough has been said about Hillsborough without me needing to add my opinion.

That day, I went with my Dad to Villa Park, to watch the other F.A Cup Semi Final taking place at exactly the same time, between Everton and Norwich.Everton had won the League in 1985 and 1987 under the management of Howard Kendall, but by 1989, Kendall had left and his former playing colleague and coach, Colin Harvey had taken over. Several of the title winning side had moved on and Harvey was not enjoying the same successes as a Manager, as he had done as a coach. The opportunity to get to the F.A Cup Final was a real boost and especially as it was likely to be against Liverpool who were favourites to beat Nottingham Forest in the other Semi-Final at Hillsborough. Having lost the 1986 F.A Cup Final to Liverpool, only three years later, there was an opportunity for sporting revenge.

Everton won that day 1-0. Pat Nevin bundled in a scrappy goal and all the Everton fans were delighted that we were once again returning to Wembley. This was an era before mobile phones and satellite television, but in every group of twenty supporters, there was always one who would bring a transistor radio and the other nineteen would always be reliant on him for score updates. In our section of Villa Park, a middle aged guy revealed to us that the Liverpool game had been abandoned, there had been talk of crowd trouble and there was also talk that someone may even have died. Back in the 1980's hooliganism regularly blighted English football and there were initial thoughts that some idiots may have been to blame once again. My Dad and I were totally unaware of the scale of the catastrophe though until we reached his car, ten minutes after the final whistle.

Radio Five Live and Talk Sport did not exist in 1989. The football fan's station of choice was BBC Radio Two and on a Saturday afternoon, it was Sport on Two, presented by the wonderful Peter Jones. When we turned the radio on, Peter Jones sombre voice immediately alerted us to the fact that a huge tragedy had taken place. Part of the broadcast from that afternoon is still available to listen to on You Tube and twenty five years on, it still brings me to tears. I contacted the BBC when I was writing my first book to ask if I could use the words Peter Jones spoke, as part of a section on the Hillsborough disaster, as they are so moving and truly reflect the dark events of the day. Peter Jones died less than twelve months later, aged just sixty and there were those that suggested that he never got over the horror of Hillsborough.

Ninety six people died unnecessarily because of the injuries they sustained that day, (94 Liverpool supporters died on the day, a further two died subsequently because of the terrible injuries they suffered) all bar seventeen of them were thirty or younger. The families, the football club and the people of the city have determinedly sought justice for their loved ones for twenty five years. They are closer than they have ever been to getting it. Nothing will ever bring those lost at Hillsborough back, but if those who hid evidence or were in some way culpable for their deaths are finally brought to task, then it may provide some sort of comfort to the families of the dead.Most people who support Liverpool or Everton treat the rivalry as just the sporting rivalry that it is, but I am extremely proud that Everton Football Club and its supporters have backed Liverpool every step of the way in seeking justice for the Hillsborough families.

Back to today. The optimistic side of me is now hoping that Liverpool beat Arsenal. Hoping that I get to go to Anfield with a load of Liverpudlian mates and I exorcise a lot of sporting demons when Everton emerge victorious. I was a 13 year old boy when I sat with my Grandad ('Pop') in the Main Stand and jumped up victoriously when Graeme Sharp scored his wonder strike at the Anfield Road end to secure a tremendous away victory for Everton at Anfield in the 1984-85 season. I was also with my Dad in the Kemlyn Road when Gary Stevens scored a bobbling effort in a 1-0 League Cup victory in 1988, but since then, the only games I have seen at Anfield have been Everton draws or defeats. Twenty six years of personal hurt could end in the Quarter Finals.

The pessimistic side overpowers the optimistic side though. Pessimism is stating Sturridge and Suarez would run riot again and Everton would get tonked. I leave 'The Mons' desperate for an Arsenal victory in the late afternoon Arsenal-Liverpool game. Defeat at the Emirates would be hard to take, but defeat at Anfield would be unbearable.

After we left 'The Mons', I took the boys over to my in-laws, Barry and Paula's, in Higher Bebington on the Wirral. It is half-term this week, but with Alison and me working, the boys are going to their Nanna and Grandad's for a few days. When we arrived there, I was all set to settle down to watch the Arsenal-Liverpool game with Barry. As I walked through into the lounge, I was greeted by QPR-Reading from Loftus Road.

"Not watching the Liverpool game, Barry?"

Barry is from Chester and is a United fan. He worked for almost forty years at Vauxhall's at Ellesmere Port. He must have spent the first twenty years taking no end of stick from his Liverpudlian work colleagues and enjoyed getting his revenge in the last twenty. Fortunately for Barry he retired long before this season, as Manchester United are falling from grace and Liverpool showing signs of a resurgence.

"No, mate, Arsenal-Liverpool's on BT Sport. We don't have that."

"Are we alright to keep checking the score on Sky Sports News then?"

"No problem."

And keep checking the score we did. Liverpool hammered Arsenal 5-1 in the League last week at Anfield, going four-nil up in the first half hour and the backlash I was hoping for, duly arrived. Alex Oxlade-Chamberlain put Arsenal one-up sixteen minutes into the first half and when he set

Podolski up to put Arsenal two ahead, two minutes into the second half, I began thinking about how we were going to get tickets for the Emirates. To Liverpool's credit though, they dominated for the rest of the game. Gerrard scored a penalty after Suarez was brought down by Podolski and then should have had another penalty when Suarez was brought down by Oxlade-Chamberlain. Suarez is a terrific player, one of the greatest to have played in the Premiership, but the problem with him is that he will always be remembered for his other antics as well as his great skill. The fact Howard Webb, the referee, chose to ignore the foul, was presumably down to Suarez's reputation for going to ground very easily. I understand why Liverpudlians love him, if he played for Everton, I would no doubt love him too, but if a player does everything within his power to attain victory, then he cannot be too shocked when officials are dubious about his claims, even if they are for genuine reasons, like today. Arsenal held firm after the second penalty was turned down and their 2-1 victory means we will be heading to the Emirates next. A trip to Arsenal will be a very tricky one for Everton and not one we are expected to win, but we are capable, on our day, of producing a shock. The game is very likely to be a sell out so the quest to get ourselves tickets will begin as soon as they go on sale.

FINAL SCORE : Everton 3 Swansea City 1

Scorers :- Everton – Traore, Naismith, Baines (pen).

Swansea– de Guzman.

Our 'Speccies':- Calvin Wade, Alan Oliver, Richard Wade, Phil Cooper, Brad Wade, Joel Wade.

Monday 17th February 2014

Earlier this month, Rob Davies, the amiable Leicester City fan who gave me my job at World of Warranty (along with the Managing Director, Mike Grindle), left the company. Today and tomorrow, I have my new boss, John Wright, out with me. John seems like a decent enough guy too, but very different to Rob, especially when it comes to football. We were going to see a car dealers, Deepdale Motor Company, who are situated on Sir Tom Finney Way, just next door to Preston North End's ground. As we drove past the ground, I pointed out the Tom Finney statue and the TV crews, crowds and sporting memorabilia that have been left outside the ground since his death was announced.

"Tom Finney's died?" John asked.

"Yes, on Friday," I replied.

"That's really sad. I used to love him. Great actor." John stated.

I paused for a second, waiting for John to break out into laughter. He didn't.

"Actor?"

"Scrooge, Murder On The Orient Express...he was in loads of films."

"John, that's Albert Finney!"

Why exactly they would be commemorating Albert Finney's death at Deepdale, only John knows, but I guess since Fulham put up a statue of Michael Jackson at Craven Cottage, anything is possible! We both had a good laugh about it anyway.

The F.A Cup Quarter Final game that we are going to (touch wood), between Arsenal and Everton will be televised on ITV on Saturday 8th March, with a 12:45pm kick off. I am not sure whether the fact it is on TV will make it easier for us to get tickets, but already we are looking into the different options available to get four tickets. Jordan, Alan's daughter, has not been able to come to a few of the recent games because of various other commitments, so Alan has said just to try and get four tickets, for me, my Dad, Alan and Phil. My Dad is going to utilise his Evertonian contacts again and I am going to look into an Arsenal connection, which just may prove really useful.

When I worked at Lloyds Bank, I had a friend and colleague in London, Dave Horsman, who was (and still is) a massive Spurs fan. Dave is a small, good hearted, bald headed eccentric (a Southern version of Alan in many ways) and his Facebook photos often show him with his arms around a sporting or television personality. He seems to have a knack of being in the right place at the right time. A couple of Christmases ago, when Kim Wilde broke out into "Rockin' Around The Christmas Tree", on the Tube, when she was a little bit too full of Christmas cheer and the video went viral on You Tube, Dave was on that carriage, singing away in the background!

A few seasons ago, when I was hosting the Lloyds Bank corporate table at Old Trafford for Manchester United against Arsenal, Dave rang me up and asked if I would look after one of his mortgage brokers, Sanjay and his colleague, as Dave didn't want to come all the way up from London to watch an Arsenal game! Sanjay was an entertaining guest. He was a season ticket holder at Emirates and was very passionate about his football club, but was gracious to the United fans in defeat and was cheerful and friendly throughout. As he was leaving to head home, he said that if I ever went down to see Everton at the Emirates, to give him a call and we would have to meet up. Today, I have contacted Dave Horsman to get Sanjay's mobile number and have left a message with Sanjay to see if he can help us out. If he can't, my Dad reckons he should be able to get a couple and (like when we faced a similar scenario at Stevenage) has said he will drop out to allow Alan and me to go, if that's all the tickets we can manage to get. My Dad has been to ten of the eleven games so far though and especially with it being Everton, I don't want him to miss it. Neither of us have been to the Emirates either, so it would be fantastic to have a trip down there.

I have also spoken to Alan today about our trip down to the Emirates, if we get tickets. I have said I will drive again, but will need to leave about six, as we are going to park at Stevenage train station and get a train in from there. As there are no trains from Manchester to Buckshaw Parkway until an hour or so later, Alan has said he will get the train to Crewe and I will meet him there. I expect Phil will go to stay at his Mum and Dad's again, so it will just be the three of us going in our car. Barring a replay, this is the last game before Wembley, so it is London all the way now.

F.A CUP – UPDATE/ The 5th Round Results and 6th Round Draw

I have already mentioned Saturday's results and Everton and Arsenal's Sunday results, but, thought it best to go through all the 5th Round results and show the full 6th Round Draw.

The 5th Round results were as follows :-

Sunderland 1 Southampton 0

Cardiff City 1 Wigan Athletic 2

Man City 2 Chelsea 0

Sheff Wed P Charlton Athletic P (waterlogged pitch)

Everton 3 Swansea City 1

Sheff Utd 3 Nottingham Forest 1

Arsenal 2 Liverpool 1

Brighton 1 Hull City 1

I mentioned how amazingly Wigan Athletic have done so far in attempting to retain their trophy despite being a Championship side now, but it should also be mentioned how amazing Sheffield United have done. Nigel Clough took over earlier this season when Sheffield United were languishing in the relegation zone of Division One, but they are creeping up towards mid-table security now and to beat a strong Championship side like Nottingham Forest, is testament to the great work Clough has done. The other club I have a sneaky feeling for in this year's competition is Hull City. They were on BT Sport last night and despite being down for much of the game, 1-0, against Brighton & Hove Albion, I always had the feeling that they would get a draw. This proved to be the case with Sagbo scoring an 84th minute equaliser. In the January transfer window, Hull's manager, Steve Bruce, went out and spent £15 million on two forwards,

Jelavic and Long, both of whom are Cup tied in the FA Cup, but I still have a feeling they will get to Wembley. It would be brilliant meeting my old mate, Jamie Lowe there, if Hull City reach the Final. Jamie went to Manchester Poly with me and although he is a Forest fan, he has lived in Hull for twenty years and all his mates are Hull City fans, so I am sure he would join them for a Wembley trip. I have been in touch with one of Jamie's mates, Richard Campion, who is a massive Hull City fan, saying I expect to be seeing him at Wembley. Watch them lose the 5th Round replay now I have tipped them!

Budweiser F.A Cup 6th Round Draw

Arsenal v Everton

Manchester City v Wigan Athletic

Hull City or Brighton v Sunderland

Sheffield United v Sheffield Wednesday or Charlton

It has to be said it is a great draw (except from an Everton perspective!) Last year's two finalists meet at the Etihad. Surely it is going to be beyond Wigan to beat City again, especially as this one is at City's ground. There also a potential 'Steel City' derby between the two Sheffield clubs. That game also means that at least one club from below the Premier League will be heading to Wembley for the Semi-Finals. It is pretty amazing that we have come through eleven rounds and the three teams we support, Everton, Manchester City and Arsenal are all still in it. There is still the potential of the dream final of Manchester City and Everton, pitting my club against Alan's, but Phil's club, Arsenal are second favourites to City now and they will be desperate to end Arsene Wenger's nine year trophyless period. As Alan said in his text, minutes after the draw was made, 'Jesus, that's ramped it up somewhat!'

I have now spoken to Sanjay Gupta, the Arsenal fan I met at Old Trafford and he could not have been more helpful. He is very confident that he can sort us out with four tickets. Alan and Phil were delighted, but when I spoke to my Dad, the blue blooded Evertonian in him came to the surface and he said he would rather hold fire and see if we can get two tickets in the Everton end. I must admit I am torn. The whole thing is about seeing every round and as much as I would love to be in the Everton end, I don't want to turn down guaranteed tickets in the Arsenal end and then find out that we can't get tickets in the Everton end.

I rang Sanjay and explained to him that as Evertonians, my Dad wanted to hold out for tickets in the Everton end and said that would be the ideal scenario for me too. As a passionate fan of his club, Sanjay understood and said if necessary he could put four tickets to one side for us and if we wanted to just take two on the day of the game, he would be able to get two Arsenal fans to take them on the day. That was a great gesture, but it would be unfair of us to do that to him. My Dad is confident he can get something sorted, so I have to trust his judgement. Off the top of my head, I can't think of a moment when he has ever let me down, so I am pretty hopeful we will be OK.

Saturday 1ˢᵗ March 2014

      I have spoken to Sanjay once again today about meeting up with him next

Saturday to collect Alan and Phil's two tickets for the Arsenal-Everton Quarter Final. I am going

to leave here at 5:20 a.m, meet my Dad in Wigan at 5:50 a.m, where he is leaving his car and

then head down to Crewe to pick Alan up for around half past six. From there, I will drive down

to Stevenage and then we'll get a train from Stevenage to Finsbury Park, which on the fast trains

takes less than twenty minutes. Sanjay wants to meet up with us in a café on Holloway Road, so

suggests we jump on the tube for two stops on the Piccadilly line. We can then walk up to the

Emirates from the café. Phil Cooper, the Arsenal fan of our gang, is heading back to his Mum

and Dad's again in Hertfordshire, so we will meet him in the café too. The one potential

drawback to this masterplan is that as yet, we haven't got our tickets in the Everton end! When I

spoke to my Dad yesterday, he said he is 99.9% certain that he will be collecting them tomorrow,

from his mate Alan McDermott (another Skelmersdale United player from the 1967 Wembley

team). Alan is good friends with a lot of people involved in Merseyside football and is able to

utilise his connections to help us out. Unusually for a Liverpool lad, Alan is actually a

Manchester United supporter. There have been several times in the past that Alan has helped my

Dad out and funnily enough, having said last week that my Dad has never let me down, my Dad

said he is very confident, "as Alan McDermott has never let me down". Hopefully this is not the

'first time for everything'!

      Talking about Alan's, our very own groundhopper, Alan Oliver is doing a Wembley

dress rehearsal tomorrow, heading down to see Manchester City v Sunderland in the Capital One

Cup Final. Al wasn't initially intending on going, but a ticket has become available and he is hoping to blow away the hoodoo and roar City to victory. City are massive favourites so if they lose, he will be even more convinced than he already is, that he is the curse of the club!

All eight clubs in the Quarter Final are now known after the two final teams booked their place on Monday night. Sheffield Wednesday blew their chance of a derby with their near neighbours, Sheffield United, as they lost their re-arranged home fixture with Charlton Athletic 2-1. Hull City however, avoided the jinx I tried to put on them by tipping them to go far. They beat Brighton & Hove Albion 2-1 in their replay. Unusually, I don't think one game since the Third Round has been decided by penalties. I have just trailed through the fa.com website and had to go back to mid-October before I found a tie resolved by penalties, when Hednesford Town beat West Auckland Town 4-2 on penalties after a couple of 2-2 draws. We have gone eleven rounds without ever coming close to a draw, but I would be more than happy if our first one arrived next Saturday lunchtime.

Manuel Pellegrini has been heard having a huge sigh of relief this evening. Apparently this sigh was not because Manchester City had just won the Capital One Cup, their first trophy with Pellegrini at the helm. It was because the curse of Alan Oliver over Manchester City is over! Alan blamed himself for everything that went wrong at City for thirty years and then put the turnaround in their fortunes down to the fact that he was no longer attending, so all Manchester City fans that know Alan were cursing his attendance at Wembley today. They need not have worried. Alan's unlucky bald head no longer dazzles the City players or inspires the opposition like Fabien Barthez's used to inspire Laurent Blanc. The posters at the entrance to the Etihad requesting staff to beware of Alan are being ripped down as I type. Alan Oliver is now a lucky mascot.

At half time today, with Sunderland leading 1-0, from an excellent goal by Fabio Borini, Alan could be heard repeatedly uttering the statement Mario Balotelli proudly displayed on his T-shirt, 'Why Always Me?' (with the possible addition of an 'F' word or two). He mentioned in a text and on Facebook that he very nearly left Wembley at half time, but luckily for Al, he stuck around, as City scored three second half goals, the first two of which were something special. The first one, from Yaya Toure, was a fantastic 25 yard shot that he stroked into the keeper's top right hand corner, with a leisurely curl. The City end went wild, but moments later they had taken the lead. From a Sunderland attack, City cleared and a cross was met at the edge of the box by Samir Nasri, who was running at full pelt and struck his shot without breaking stride and saw it flash into the back of the net, past the stranded Sunderland keeper Mannone. In the dying minutes, Jesus Navas put the game beyond doubt with a third for City and Alan went delirious along with the rest of the City faithful. Facebook photos tonight show Alan drenched in champagne. I am delighted the burden of superstition has been lifted!

Having mentioned Alan's curse with my tongue in my cheek, as I am sure he is not solely responsible for their trophyless years or that his absence in the recent good times isn't the sole reason for City's success, I do think to an extent he has a point. I have already mentioned the 'Butterfly Effect' of how every action has a knock-on effect so who is to say if Alan hadn't been at last year's F.A Cup Final whether Wigan would still have won or if he had been attending City regularly in recent times, whether they would have won the Premier League, it is impossible to say. All I do know is that Alan is cock-a-hoop today and I'm really happy for him as trophies and days like today are rare for any football supporter and you have to make the most of them, as you never know when the good times may stop rolling.

This was not the only good news for our F.A Cup gang today. My Dad met up with Alan McDermott and picked up our two tickets for the Everton end for next Saturday. Everything is in place, I just hope Everton get everything right next Saturday and the dream scenario of following Everton to Wembley will be fulfilled.

I'm heading up to bed in a minute, alarm set for a 4:40a.m start in the morning. Alison is working nights at the hospital again, so I have had to take Joel over to my Mum's for the night, where he will stay until I pick him up tomorrow evening and Brad will be left in bed on his own for a few hours before Alison returns. Alison works incredibly hard and I would love to be in a position where I could say to her that she can reduce her hours, say from full-time to four days a week, but even though I have been back in regular work for five months, we are still just getting by from month to month, so as things stand, that day remains in the distant future. Currently, I am thankful the F.A Cup journey has proved relatively inexpensive and that I have been in a position to put a few quid in an envelope every pay day, so I can afford to pay for the petrol and get my ticket for the game. My Dad has helped me along once in a while too. The Arsenal tickets were thankfully £35 each, when at times they charge a lot more, so I hope the Wembley tickets don't break the bank either.

With regards to the Arsenal-Everton game tomorrow, I was hoping Arsenal may have their eyes on their Champions League game, away at Bayern Munich on Tuesday, but having lost at the Emirates 2-0 in the first leg, Arsenal have little hope of going through. Arsenal are now pretty much an also ran in the title race too, with Liverpool now emerging on the rails to join Chelsea and Manchester City, so Arsenal's greatest hope of ending their nine year trophyless period is the F.A Cup. They will come at Everton with all guns blazing, I am hoping Everton are well prepared to return fire. My biggest fear is that Roberto Martinez will opt to play Joel Robles, our second choice Spanish keeper, in goal for the game, like he has done for every other round of the F.A Cup. I hate this strategy. I know goalkeepers need experience, but once it becomes your biggest game of the season, which tomorrow is, I think man management needs to be put into action, apologies made and our strongest team fielded. Tim Howard, our first choice keeper is vastly experienced and should be playing tomorrow. I am not Tim Howard's biggest fan, he is a superb shot stopper but rarely leaves his six yard box when it comes to corners or crosses and I still blame him for Frank Lampard's winner when we last made it to the F.A Cup Final, but his experience instills confidence. I hope I am wrong, but if we lose tomorrow and we haven't played our strongest side, there will always be questions about what might have been.

Anyway, I am off to bed. Tomorrow is the type of game I dreamt about seeing when I decided to embark on this F.A Cup journey and I just hope Everton surprise a lot of people and make it into the hat for the semi-final draw. Come on you blue boys!

Sometimes when your alarm goes off at twenty to five in the morning, you dearly wish you had a few more hours in bed, but when you wake up to the prospect of an F.A Cup Quarter Final at the Emirates, adrenalin kicks in and you wake up with a spring in your step and a feeling of 'Here We Go!' The journey down to Stevenage went perfectly, I met my Dad in a side street in Wigan, where he left his car for the day, then made our way to Crewe to pick Alan up. Al was waiting for us at Crewe station when we arrived and, as has happened so many times since we met Alan, the time flew by as we discussed football for pretty much the whole journey down. It was a beautiful Spring day which added to the feeling of excitement and positivity.

The roads were quiet and we were parked up at Stevenage station just after nine. The train to Finsbury Park soon arrived and when we jumped on, I was surprised to see plenty of Arsenal fans already on their way. As the train was packed, we were all standing up and a young, Asian lad in his late teens or early twenties, with an Arsenal scarf on, kindly offered my Dad his seat. My Dad declined the offer, but we soon got chatting to the lad and within thirty seconds, Alan was telling him about our F.A Cup journey and had the lad's phone off him and was showing him how to follow him on Twitter! One thing you can guarantee is that Alan will not be backward in coming forward. If someone had given him a megaphone, he would have announced the exploits of 'The Casual Hopper' to every passenger on the train. He will not make thousands of pounds for 'The Christie' hospital by being a shy and retiring sort.

When we arrived at Finsbury Park, we had to go across to the Underground to get to Holloway Road, so Alan gave Phil a ring to see where he was. Phil was already tucking into a full English in a cafe a couple of hundred yards from Holloway Tube station. I also rang Sanjay but he said he had to do a mortgage appointment so would be a little late meeting us. We headed down to the Tube and my Dad commented that he'd not been on the underground for years. My Mum is scared of heights and won't venture into the tube stations because her fear incorporates escalators and she won't venture into the station in case she is confronted by a massive escalator that she won't go on. Her fear of heights has been passed on to me, but thankfully I haven't got the strain that also fears escalators. Anything with a sheer drop is what I don't like.

Half an hour later, Alan, my Dad and I were sitting with Phil in the Amici Cafe Deli on Holloway Road, tucking into our full English breakfasts. Sanjay called again on my mobile to say he had been delayed further and would not be there for an hour or so. There were still two hours before kick off, so there was no panic, but I could tell Alan and Phil were exchanging nervous glances. My Dad and I were in the secure position of having our tickets in our possession but having travelled down to London, having already been to eleven previous rounds, the last thing Alan wanted was to not get a ticket because of a last minute hiccup. Thankfully, there was nothing to fear and an hour later, Sanjay rang to say he had parked up by the McDonalds and to meet him there to collect the tickets.

Whilst we were waiting, Phil updated us on his experience of watching the Arsenal-Liverpool game in the previous round in a Liverpool City Centre pub. When he was in a taxi from Goodison Park to Lime Street Station with Alan, after the Everton-Swansea game, they had started up a conversation with the driver about where would be best to watch the game. The driver ended up dropping Phil at a pub full of Liverpool fanatics and Phil had nervously supped about half a dozen pints during the game, hoping no-one would cotton on to the fact that he was an Arsenal fan!

The other topic of conversation was the choice of today's match referee. Mark Clattenburg seemed a strange choice given his historic relationship with Everton Football Club. In December, he ended a six year exile from Goodison Park, which followed what can best described as a very poor performance in a Merseyside derby. I had a season ticket in the 2007-2008 season, when Clattenburg sent off two Everton players at Goodison in a Liverpool victory. It was not the sending offs that were the most controversial aspects of the game though. Liverpool's Dirk Kuyt escaped a sending off for a waist high, two footed karate chop on Phil Neville, Clattenburg appeared to take advice from Steven Gerrard before sending off Tony Hibbert and failed to give Everton a last minute penalty, which could have handed Everton an equaliser, when Jamie Carragher wrestled Joleon Lescott to the floor in the penalty box.His return in December was not without controversy either, with the visitors Southampton, accusing him of 'abusing and insulting' their player, Adam Lallana, after he failed to give them a late penalty when Everton led 2-1. Clattenburg was not subsequently found to be at fault, but he has had high profile issues when officiating at Goodison, so perhaps handing him another Everton game does not seem like the wisest of decisions. At least it was not at Goodison Park!

When we met up with Sanjay subsequently, he only stopped for a quick chat as he was racing around dropping tickets off to various friends and family members. He seems like the type of guy who will help anyone out, but as a consequence lives a hectic life, especially on Arsenal match days. We thanked him for his kindness in getting our tickets and I told him I hoped we didn't see him at Wembley, as a meeting there would indicate an Everton defeat. He pointed us in the right direction for the Emirates, before having to dash off, but as Phil was with us, a fellow Arsenal fan, we knew we wouldn't get lost.

Once we arrived at the Emirates, we did the touristy bit and had photos taken outside. Alan also kept up his routine of buying a home team badge from the souvenir shop and we laughed as a dozen or so coaches arrived from Liverpool and drove past the ground with every Everton fan inside using the opportunity to hammer against the windows in an intimidatory fashion. Football has moved on from the hooliganism that blighted the game in the eighties, but put a bunch of men together in a tribal type gathering and they still like to stick their chests out and try to act hard. Some of the fans are genuinely tough though. Last season, on the way down to White Hart Lane, one Everton fan, Chris Martin, fell out the emergency exit of the coach he was in, bounced twenty times along the M6, narrowly missing an oncoming car, broke his ankle and shattered his wrist in the fall, but still went to the match and only visited a hospital once he arrived back home in Liverpool.

Half an hour before kick off, my Dad and I went our separate ways from Alan and Phil, as they headed to their seats in the home end near Sanjay and we headed to ours in the away end, 'The Clock End'. There were big queues of Evertonians at our entrance, as the stewards were body searching us before we were allowed into the ground. I was searched but my Dad must now be beyond the age to be deemed a potential threat, as he was allowed to go in without a search.

The Emirates is a fantastic stadium. I have been inside the majority of Premier League grounds, but without doubt, the Emirates is the finest stadium I have seen at that level. It is up there with the new Wembley and the Nou Camp, in the best grounds I have been to. At the back of the stands at the very top, the seats are in a swirling design and despite having 60 000 seats, there are no obstructed views and plenty of leg room. I commented earlier in the season that some new stadia lack character, but the Emirates has it in abundance and it is only a few minutes walking distance from the hustle bustle of Holloway Road and within spitting distance of

Highbury, their previous ground. The land had previously been used as an industrial and waste disposal estate, but, if you excuse the pun, there is nothing rubbish about the Emirates. Our seats weren't the best though, about four rows from the front, just behind the left hand post of the goal, but we were in with the Evertonians and our end was a hive of excitement. This was our biggest game of the season and a victory here could signal an end to our nineteen year trophy drought.

We were surrounded by familiar faces. Next to my Dad was Paul McDermott and his wife. Paul is the brother of Alan McDermott who had sorted the tickets out for my Dad and me. Paul is obviously the more intelligent brother, as he supports Everton, whilst his brother supports Manchester United. In the row in front was Alan Wolfe, who played football with my Dad at Skelmersdale United and also played at Marine and Altrincham, as well as representing England at Amateur level. Then a few rows back was someone who did not know us, but we knew him. Former World Champion snooker player, John Parrott, an avid Evertonian was standing with his son. Parrott is one of many 'celebrity' Evertonians, but unlike many of the others, attends most games, but doesn't have to sit in the corporate section, preferring to be in amongst the diehard fans.

Just after kick off, the place next to me was taken by an old friend of mine, Toby Robinson. I first met Toby about twenty five years ago, when he was mates with Paul Cooper, the lad who kickstarted the contact with Stevenage Football Club and managed to get us former boss, Paul Fairclough's phone number. In the ten years after meeting him with 'Coops', I regularly saw Toby out and about in Ormskirk and Southport. He was a good looking young lad, who liked to party hard and always seemed to do well with the ladies. After I got married and settled down, I was more likely to see Toby at the races, as we shared a love of horses and gambling or at the football, as he is a big Evertonian. Sometimes he was with my brother-in-law

Vinny and his brothers, Mitch and James, as they were all mates. As he aged, he continued to like a drink but started to find it harder to shed the pounds. Like myself, Toby is a tall lad, probably around 6 feet 2, but at his heaviest, he must have weighed about twenty two stone. His physical frame reflects his larger than life character. He is the self-proclaimed 'King of Ormskirk' as there are not many people locally he doesn't know and in the world of horse racing, football and in boxing in particular, he has many excellent contacts. When my first ebook came out, through his contacts, he managed to get both Amir Khan and Michael Owen to send tweets out about it, on the same Friday evening, catapulting it about 10 000 places higher in the Amazon Kindle Chart! A couple of years ago, he had a horse called 'Millieonaire' running in a sprint at Haydock and left an owners badge at the entrance for me. He has a big frame, a big character, but most importantly, he has a big heart. When he took his place next to me at the 'Emirates Stadium', I was pleased to see he had shed a few stone since I met up with him at Haydock. He has had health issues, recently being diagnosed with 'Type 2 Diabetes', so has started a health kick which looks as though it is off to a good start.

To my frustration, Roberto Martinez had opted to play Joel Robles in goal and understandably he looked a little jittery. His early match nerves were not helped when the excellent Everton midfielder, James McCarthy, slipped halfway inside his own half allowing Arsenal's Santi Cazorla to bear down on the Everton goal at pace. When he was just outside the box, he placed an inch perfect pass through to Mesut Ozil, who calmly evaded Seamus Coleman's last ditch tackle and stroked the ball past Robles into the net. Everton were off to the worst possible start.

On the whole, deep down in the very depths of their souls, most football fans are optimists. We may pretend to be a pessimist or at the least a realist, but somewhere deep in our souls, no matter what team your side are facing, you expect to win. The words "mathematically impossible" have been invented to give football supporters a dose of reality. My brain told me this was going to be a tricky tie, when asked I said as much, but deep down in my soul, especially because I am writing this book, I expected Everton not to lose. Ozil's goal was a reality check for me and the six thousand Evertonians stood around me (there were 6000 unused seats behind our knees). Perhaps destiny was not on our side after all.

For the next twenty five minutes the game was fairly even but the majority of chances were falling Arsenal's way. Joel Robles seemed like a sportsman who had been told he was about to go out and face Tyson Fury in a heavyweight boxing bout as his hands were constantly in clenched fist mode beneath his gloves. One aimless ball was played high into the box by Arsenal and every player gave up on it, expecting the huge Robles to come and comfortably catch it, but despite no-one being around him, he elected to punch the ball and handed possession back to Arsenal. The defenders around him berated him and pleaded with him to catch it, but his fists remained clenched.

I love Martinez. Everton are now regarded as a side that a neutral supporter would want to watch. We pass the ball, we entertain and we offer bright hope for the future and that is down to the wisdom of Martinez. As a man with little money, I have had to watch the majority of our transformation from a television or computer screen, but in media interviews, Martinez always looks like a man you can trust to get things done right. The only real mistake he has made before today, in my opinion, is the defence he fielded at Anfield when Liverpool tore us apart. Playing Robles in the Cup games is perhaps a good long-term strategy, giving him vital experience and he certainly made some great saves at Stevenage, but right now all that matters is today's result and playing Tim Howard, our first choice keeper, would have been a safer option. Robles wasn't at fault for the goal and his errors so far have not had any repercussions, but I feel the goalkeeper's lack of confidence is resonating around the Everton side. No manager has ever won back to back F.A Cups with two different clubs and I really want Martinez to be the first man to do it.

Once we went behind, the second goal was always going to be vital. A second Arsenal goal would probably take the game beyond Everton and allow Arsenal to exploit gaps if we were forced to push forward, whilst an Everton goal could create some uncertainty in the Arsenal ranks. In the 32nd minute, the second goal came and thankfully it kept my F.A Cup dream alive.

Ross Barkley, the young Everton midfielder is a tremendous talent. He has that rare ability to run with the ball, beat players and create a goalscoring opportunity out of nothing. It was Barkley that created Everton's equaliser. He picked the ball up just outside the Everton box, after an Arteta shot was blocked by Gareth Barry and set off upon an almost full length of the pitch run, tearing down the right wing. Barkley then whipped a ball across the six yard box, which was ideal for Kevin Mirallas who was advancing towards the far post. It looked like all Mirallas had to do was tap the ball into the net, but the ball somehow got caught between his feet and his prodded shot looped up over Fabianski in the Arsenal goal and fell fortunately to Romelu Lukaku, the on-loan Everton striker who could not miss from one yard out.1-1.

Delirium struck six thousand Evertonians! At times, football unites supporters in a way they would never unite without a shared love for their football team. Without the presence of excess alcohol or a huge unanticipated win on the horses, I cannot picture any situation that would cause me to spontaneously hug and leap around with the bearded giant of a man that is Toby Robinson, other than an important Everton goal. Pulling out of my man hug with Toby, I saw my Dad on my other side with a look of jubilation that I have not seen for years. We grab hold of each other and hug tightly. I mentioned previously in this book that I only remembered

hugging my Dad twice, but as we hug, forgotten moments of shared embraces come rushing

back...Stuart McCall's last minute equaliser in the 1989 F.A Cup Final, Trevor Steven's last

minute equaliser in an F.A Cup game at Middlesbrough's Ayresome Park in 1988, Kevin

Sheedy's last minute equaliser from a free kick in the F.A Cup Semi Final against Luton Town at

Villa Park in 1985. All Everton goals in the F.A Cup. My Dad and I are very close, but without

Everton and the F.A Cup, we would have remained on firm handshake terms, other than one

teenage moment when I fell from seven feet on to my back. In rare moments of joy, football

takes our closeness to another level. A simple tap-in from a Belgian striker, on-loan from

Chelsea, has become the highlight of twelve rounds of F.A Cup football so far. The dream

seemed to be slipping away, but perhaps our unbridled joy will continue all the way to the Final

now.

Everton are buoyed by the equaliser whilst Arsenal look shell shocked. We finish the first

half as the better side, but when Mark Clattenburg blows his whistle for half time, Evertonians

realise we are fortunate to be all square. As Toby runs off to get a quick pint, my Dad and I

reflect upon an exciting first half, but know we will have to play like the last fifteen minutes

rather than the first thirty, if we are to stay in the competition.

As I am talking to my Dad, my mind jumps back to the 1998 FIFA World Cup in France

and the game that opened the tournament, Brazil versus Scotland. Back in the summer of 1998, I

was working and living up in Glasgow. I had met some brilliant people up there and without any

religious convinctions of my own, did not have to take sides in the Celtic-Rangers divide. One of

the big Rangers fans, Allan Stewart, a mortgage broker in Shawlands, would regularly contact

me after work to see if I fancied a quick beer and on the day of the Brazil-Scotland game, he rang me to see if I fancied meeting up with him to watch the match in a City centre pub. As it was an afternoon game, I had to square it with my boss, a lovely man called Charles Canning, but as Charles was a massive football fan himself, he was happy to let me go, given it was a business contact I was watching the game with.

It only took Brazil four minutes to take the lead, but against all odds, Scotland fought back and in the 38th minute, Scotland were awarded a penalty. John Collins calmly stepped up, slotted it away and sent our pub and the rest of Scotland crazy. At half time, with the score at 1-1, I will always remember Allan saying,

"I just want half time to last forever. In this moment, we are drawing one-all with the World Champions. It will never last. Brazil will batter us in the second half but if half-time lasts forever, so will this brilliant feeling I'm having now."

Brazil didn't batter Scotland in the second half, but they did end up winning and ruining the dreams of a nation of Scots. Tom Boyd scored an unfortunate own goal and Brazil won 2-1. It was a spirited display from Scotland, but they were still tasting defeat and at the end, I fully understood why Allan had wanted half time to last forever. The link to the Arsenal-Everton game was evident. Everton were not playing the World Champions, but they were the underdogs and had come back from an early goal to force their way back into the tie. At half time, I was feeling a mixture of relief and delight. The next forty five minutes could steal my dreams from me, but at half time they were very much alive and like Allan, I wanted to cling to them.

"I would be more than happy if nothing at all happens in the second half, Dad," I observed, "and we get out of here with a 1-1 draw."

Everton started the second half as they had finished the first and I started to feel my pessimism drain away. Arsenal were a great side going forward, but were not the best when teams were coming at them and the confidence of the Everton players seemed to be growing as the game progressed. I even began thinking that if we scored one more goal and could put everyone behind the ball for half an hour, then not only would me, my Dad, Phil and Alan be going to Wembley, but Everton would be coming with us.

Many of the F.A cup games we have been to, have had one pivotal moment. That decisive moment when the pendulum swings from one side to another, because of what happened in a single second of the game. Arsenal-Everton was no different. Romelu Lukaku, who had been relatively quiet other than his goal, robbed Vermaelen in the left back position, allowing Lukaku to cut in from the right wing before laying the ball back to Ross Barkley. Barkley had been the hero in the first half with his amazing run and now was his chance to stamp his name into Everton F.A Cup folklore. Barkley was twelve yards out but there were no defenders blocking his path to goal and he could virtually pick his spot. Anxiously, he struck the ball first time, trying to whip the ball with his right foot into Fabianski's top right hand corner, but every Evertonian behind the goal held his head in his hands as the ball sailed inches over the crossbar.

"We won't get a better chance than that," said the lad two seats to my left.

"Yes, we will," Toby countered, "be positive."

Sadly, Toby was wrong. Looking back now, that was the first step towards the exit door for Everton in this year's F.A Cup. Arsenal began to get back into the game and the much maligned (by me) Robles, made a fine diving save to keep out a Cazorla effort. Arsenal were breaking forward at pace and when Alex Oxlade-Chamberlain broke into the box, Gareth Barry, who has been terrific for Everton all season, needlessly stuck out a despairing leg and stopped Oxlade-

Chamberlain in his stride. Even from 100 yards away behind the Arsenal goal it looked like a penalty and to no great surprise Clattenburg pointed to the spot.

Footballing irony when it happens to your team, is particularly unpleasant, so a deflated feeling spread across my body when I saw the penalty taker was a former Everton hero, Mikel Arteta. Arteta is a Spanish dead ball specialist. As well as playing for Everton and Arsenal, he has also plied his trade at top clubs around Europe including Barcelona, Real Sociedad, Rangers and Paris St Germain. I unfortunately had every faith in him being able to smash the ball past Robles from the spot. He was so popular when he played for Everton, he had his own song that fans sang pretty much every week.

"Follow, follow, follow,

Everton is the team to follow,

And there's nobody better,

Than Mikel Arteta,

He's the best little Spaniard we know."

Sometimes, as I mentioned before, you feign pessimism, but I was not feigning.

"Arteta's bound to score," I said to my Dad.

"Most definitely," my Dad replied.

We were right. Arteta nonchalantly strode up, Robles moved early to his left and Arteta drilled the ball into Robles' right hand corner. 2-1.

Something extraordinary then happened! This season, Mark Clattenburg might subconsciously be trying to put right his wrongs against Everton. When he officiated at Goodison, earlier in the season, he missed a Southampton penalty that might have handed Southampton a point and now he correctly spotted Arsenal substitute, Olivier Giroud, encroaching in the penalty area before

Arteta took the penalty. Clattenburg ordered it to be re-taken. Had Clattenburg just handed Everton an F.A Cup lifeline? It took me about three seconds to decide that he probably hadn't . Arteta scored with ease first time and could probably take ten penalties and score nine. In the footballing comics of my childhood, they always said to go the same way with a re-taken penalty as you did the first time, but my suspicion was that Arteta would not have read English footballing magazines as a child in San Sebastian and would probably go the other way. To his credit, Robles went the right way, but Arteta is an intelligent footballer and not only did he go to the other side, he lofted his penalty rather than drilling it and it went into Robles top left corner. This time it really was 2-1 and Everton were going to have to push men forward now, which potentially could leave them vulnerable against Arsenal's speedy forwards.

Everton did push forward and had one good chance when Barry teed up Barkley. Barkley was just outside the box and struck a curling shot with his right foot, hard and low, but it drifted beyond Fabianski's right hand post. Minutes later all hopes drifted away when an Arsenal cross was met on the near post, six yards out by Olivier Giroud, who powered the ball past Robles. 3-1 and Everton's hopes of winning the F.A Cup for the first time since 1995 were over. Joe Royle would remain the last Everton manager to win it and although he is my godfather, that is one accolade I would rather he did not preserve. Probably more than any other season I wanted this to be Everton's year, but that third goal brought reality into play for the first time since August. It was not going to be our year.

Arsenal's third goal was in the 83rd minute but there was even time for an Arsenal fourth. Everton manager, Roberto Martinez had brought on Barcelona loanee, Gerard Deulofeu and when he was dispossessed on Everton's right wing, a slick passing moving involving Cazorla, Rosicky and Ozil, was neatly finished off by Giroud. 4-1 did flatter Arsenal a little but it was immaterial whether the score was 2-1 or 4-1, Arsenal would be in the F.A Cup Semi Final and Everton would not. We had to follow Arsenal to Wembley now.

Defeat is hard to swallow when you are passionate about football. When the final whistle blew, my mind became one of a petulant child. I didn't want to do this F.A Cup thing any more. Alan and Phil could finish it off. I wanted moments like the Lukaku goal, jumping around like a mad man with Toby and my Dad. Moments like that would not be possible when watching a game from a neutral perspective. My Dad was 51 when Everton last won the FA Cup, he is 70 now. We are unlikely to ever do this fourteen round journey again and I wanted it to have the perfect ending. It still will have the perfect ending for someone, just not for us.

My Dad and I stayed around long enough to applaud the Everton players off the pitch. They had given their all, it just wasn't enough.

"The thing is," I said to my Dad, "that was probably the best game we have seen, played in the best stadium with the nicest weather, but none of that matters. All that matters is that Everton are out."

We both trudged around to meet up with Phil and Alan. Phil is a complete gentleman so despite him being an Arsenal fan, I was not expecting him to rub our noses in it. Phil phoned to say that if we headed back towards Finsbury Park, over a bridge at the rear of the ground, him and Alan would meet us on the other side. As we were shuffling along, amongst a mass of jubilant Arsenal fans, there was a policeman at an elevated point directing the traffic with a megaphone. He must have been an Arsenal fan because out of nowhere, to the tune of The Beatles "Hey Jude" he started a chorus of,

"Nar, nar, nar.nonnar, nar nar,

Nonnar, nar, nar

GIR-OUD!"

Thousands of smiling, delighted Arsenal fans joined in.

Pretty soon after, we met up with Alan and Phil. Alan was sympathetic and as expected, Phil did nothing to darken our very sombre mood. He even tried to lift it.

"It must have been brilliant for you two, in the Everton end, when you scored. It went mental! Al and I looked at the away end going absolutely crazy and thought of you two being right in the middle of it. Your fans were brilliant!"

We walked past Arsenal's old ground, Highbury, which is now luxury flats called 'Highbury Square'. They have tried to retain some of the character and characteristics of the old stadium, creating four sets of apartments around the old pitch. The facades of the old East and West Stands have also been preserved. Alan says this is completely different to Manchester City's old Maine Road ground, that has been knocked down, retaining very little of the history of the club during their time there. Apparently there is something at Maine Road to signify where the old centre spot would have stood, but this is only accessible to people living in that residential area.

Soon after, once we reached the Arsenal box office on Drayton Park, Phil pointed us in the right direction for Finsbury Park. He was off to meet some friends in Camden, but was wanting to nip in to the Drayton Park pub first for a celebratory pint. With Al and my Dad not being drinkers and me being short of cash and driving anyway, we decided to head straight back to pick my car up in Stevenage. Once again, we shook Phil's hand warmly and said we would see him at Wembley. Despite sulking about Everton's defeat, I knew I would be there.

Alan knew, from a lifetime of supporting Manchester City, how footballing defeats can hit you, so understood that my Dad and I were a little quieter than usual on the journey home.

We went past Stevenage's ground on the way back and momentarily discussed nipping in to see the second half as they were playing Tranmere in a 3pm kick off and my Dad had actually coached their manager, John McMahon, when he was a schoolboy at Everton (not that we were likely to see him).

An hour or so further up, we ran into heavy traffic caused by an accident at junction 10 of the A14, so came off at Burton Latimer and headed into a pub called 'The Duke's Arms' for a quick drink. The landlady, Lorri, spotted that we were not regulars, so made an effort to make us welcome, even nipping up to the living quarters to make my Dad a cup of coffee. The Chelsea-Tottenham game was on in there (the late kick off) so we stopped and watched the first half, before thanking Lorri and her husband for their hospitality and continuing home. It was 0-0 when we left the pub, but we listened to the second half on the radio and to Alan's frustration, Chelsea (Man City's biggest title rivals) ran out 4-0 winners. Arsenal are also still in the running but surprisingly Liverpool have emerged as title contenders too, with a decent run of results. After going out the F.A Cup, Everton have to hope they go on a brilliant run and finish 4th, but in all likelihood, will have to settle for a place in the Europa League. It is still looking like a better season than I initially anticipated when Roberto Martinez took over in the summer. I predicted at the start of this book that Everton would finish 9th.

Out of our small band of supporters, my Dad and I are the first to see our team knocked out. Alan is off to see Manchester City against Wigan Athletic at the Etihad tomorrow. Surely it is very unlikely that Wigan will beat them in the F.A Cup again, especially seeing as though this one is at City's ground. A Manchester City versus Arsenal final would be ideal for both Alan and Phil and I would like to see two Premier League sides there too. I think I would rather see someone like Hull City make it though than both teams being from the usual Premier League Top Four.

As has become customary recently, we dropped Alan off at Crewe and then headed back to pick my Dad's car up in Wigan, before going to his house so I could see my Mum and collect Joel from her. As is always the case, Joel had a great twenty four hours with his Nanna.

Tomorrow, we will find out who Arsenal are playing in the F.A Cup Semi Final that we will attend, if, once again, we can find a helpful soul that can help us out with tickets. Arsenal are the first team to book their place at Wembley, as the other three Semi Finals take place at twelve o'clock (Sheffield United v Charlton Athletic), two o'clock (Hull City v Sunderland) and five past four (Man City v Wigan Athletic) tomorrow afternoon. My money (if I had any) would be on all three home sides to win.

So, I go to bed tonight knowing Everton are out the F.A Cup. I am just grateful that I have had the opportunity to follow them through three rounds. Today was the twelfth round of our F.A Cup journey and we have seen an amazing 47 goals, avoided all replays, never been to the same ground more than twice and never seen the same side more than three times. I reckon we will see Arsenal three times though. After today, I think their name is on the Cup!

FINAL SCORE: Arsenal 4 Everton 1.

Scorers : Arsenal – Ozil, Arteta (pen), Giroud (2).

Everton – Lukaku.

Our 'Speccies':- Calvin Wade, Alan Oliver, Richard Wade, Phil Cooper, Toby Robinson (Everton end), Sanjay Gupta (Arsenal end).

<u>Sunday 9th March 2014</u>

It occurred to me last night that I have yet to explain where the idea for the title of this book came from. Way back in 1971, Jack Rosenthal, a BAFTA award winning writer (and husband of Maureen Lipman), wrote a one-off television drama for Granada television called "Another Sunday & Sweet F.A". It was about a Sunday League football match between Parker Street Depot XI and Co-Op Albion XI and became a cult comedy. I am pretty sure the DVD is still available now. We certainly have a copy.

The cast was not brimming with well known stars of the era, but many of them subsequently found fame. The referee, Mr.Armistead was played by David Swift, a fine actor who was subsequently a star of Channel 4's "Drop The Dead Donkey". One of the touchline supporters was a young lady called Shirley, who was played by Anne Kirkbride and it was this role that led to her finding fame in Coronation Street as Deidre Barlow. The goalkeeper for Parker Street Depot XI was David Bradley, who has found international fame recently as Argus Filch in Harry Potter and Walder Frey in Game of Thrones. What has this all got to do with me? The captain of Parker Street Depot XI was Gordon McGrae, my Mum's brother! My "Pop" was asked by Granada to provide some local actors and some decent footballers, so although my Uncle had never done any TV acting before, he was a fine sportsman, a schoolboy footballer at Liverpool FC (and less significantly for the role an England schoolboy international Rugby Union player) so was given the part. Gordon was never going to get a Laurence Olivier award for his acting in this, but he more than held his own.

The first transmission was in January 1972, but I remember Granada repeating it in about 1978 and my Mum let me watch it. I can recall going into primary school the next day and asking all my school mates if they had seen it and plenty of them had. Thus, when thinking of a title for this book, the old TV drama sprang to mind and given most of our games would be likely to take place on a Saturday, it didn't take me to be too much of a genius to come up with "Another Saturday & Sweet F.A".

All in all, until yesterday, our journey has been pretty sweet too. I have loved the time I have had with my Dad and forming great friendships with the Olivers and Phil Cooper that will continue well beyond this year's F.A Cup. I have stopped sulking about the Everton defeat now. No-one likes losing but it was always about more than just one team and I am looking forward to this afternoon's draw now, so we can identify who we need to speak to, to get tickets for Wembley.

4:03 p.m

And then there were five. Earlier this afternoon, Sheffield United defeated Charlton Athletic 2-0 to become the second team to book their place in the F.A Cup Semi Final draw. It was a tight affair, 0-0 at half time, but two goals midway through the second half from Flynn and then Brayford, sent Sheffield United through. If Sheffield United make it to the Final, they will be the first team outside the top two Leagues to make it to an F.A Cup Final since Tottenham Hotspur won it as an Amateur side 113 years ago, in 1901! It is an amazing achievement by Nigel Clough, his players and staff to get this far.

The game at Bramall Lane was the lunchtime game and following on from that was Hull City v Sunderland. Sunderland appear to be a side who can look really good on their day and other times, they look very mediocre. I guess Premier League survival is their main priority, but the same could still be said for Hull City, so it must have been gutting for Sunderland fans to see their side go to pieces after they went behind. Hull took the lead in the 67th minute when Davies scored and this was followed by two more goals in the next ten minutes from Meyler and Fryatt.

Last week, David Meyler had been the victim of an unsavoury incident, when Newcastle United manager, Alan Pardew attempted to headbutt him, when Meyler had seemingly done nothing more than try to take a quick throw in and had bustled past Pardew. I have never met Alan Pardew, so cannot comment on whether he is a great bloke, but his actions were about as stupid as I have ever witnessed from a football manager. This is a man who is being watched by millions and has been given a role where he is supposed to set an example to everyone at his football club. What sort of example is he setting when he acts in such a petulant and aggressive manner? A terrible one. If I was his Chairman, I would have looked into sacking him for gross misconduct, not because he harmed Meyler, but because of the poor example he set. Thankfully, Meyler could see the funny side of the incident and when he scored today, he ran straight to the corner flag and pretended to headbutt it! The game finished 3-0 to Hull City and they became the third team in the Semi Finals, with the winner of the game kicking off now, Manchester City v Wigan Athletic completing the jigsaw.

The draw has just been made and it is Hull City v Sheffield United and our game is Arsenal v Manchester City or Wigan Athletic. I fully expect City to win, so it will be Arsenal v City, Phil's team versus Alan's, should be a cracker. Alan has already text me from the Etithad to find out the draw and is excited by the prospect of an Arsenal-City clash should they win today. For a change, even Alan is confident.

5:10 p.m

Football is a crazy game and the F.A Cup is an amazing competition! For the second time this season, Manchester City find themselves 2-0 down at home against Championship opposition. When we were at Stevenage for the Everton game, they went 2-0 down against Watford (before coming back to win 4-2) and now it is Wigan's turn to stun the City faithful.

The game is currently a few minutes into the second half and James Perch has just scored to make it 2-0 after Jordi Gomez had scored a first half penalty. Alan Oliver will be a nervous wreck at the Etihad and probably concluding his curse is back, but I'm expecting a rally and City to come back into this. At the least, I'm expecting it to be 2-2.

5:30 p.m

2-1 now. Nasri has scored to put City back in the tie. They are dominating the game and with a quarter of the match still left, it will take a gigantic effort from Wigan to win this one.

6:00 p.m

Cup exits are likes buses. None for ages and all of a sudden two come at once. After Everton's F.A Cup exit broke mine and my Dad's hearts yesterday, it is Alan's turn to be gutted today, as Manchester City failed to claw back the 2-1 deficit and Wigan Athletic are through to the Semi-Final against Arsenal. I may have wanted City to be knocked out when Everton were still in the competition, I must admit, but I was hoping for a Manchester City v Hull City final once Everton departed, as that would have meant there would be a lot of my friends (and even more of Alan's friends) at Wembley for the Final.

Alan has just text to say that's what he gets for counting his chickens and I must admit I did the same on City's behalf. I even text my Dad saying that the draw was Hull City v Sheffield United and Manchester City v Arsenal not expecting Wigan to win at the Etihad. Looking at the positives, Wigan Athletic deserve huge credit for getting to Wembley for the fourth time in twelve months (F.A Cup Semi & Final 2013, Charity Shield 2013 and now F.A Cup Semi Final 2014). For any side it is hugely impressive, but for a small town team it is incredible.

I know a lot of Wigan fans and a couple of Wigan Athletic "legends" so hopefully we should be able to get tickets easily enough. I will wait to see if the game is on the Saturday or the

Sunday and then start putting plans into action to ensure we get all the tickets we need. An added difficulty may be Alan's ticket. He has already text to say it would be better for him and Phil to be in the Arsenal end, but I think getting tickets in that end will be a 100 times harder. I will wait until he gets over the disappointment of defeat and then see if I can persuade him to be an honourary Wiganner for the day. Might need the persuasive powers of Kofi Annan to pull that one off!

My Dad rang tonight for a chat and he said until he saw the scores on BBC One News at ten o'clock last night, he had presumed Manchester City had already played and beaten Wigan Athletic based on my text, telling him we were going to Arsenal-City! He was as shocked as the rest of us by Wigan's victory.

It has been a tough weekend for our little gang. Alan said in a text that the dream is over, but I pointed out that although our dream finale has not come about, the dream is very much alive for fans of Arsenal, Wigan, Hull and Sheffield United. When I first started writing this book, last summer, I questioned whether the F.A Cup is now past its best, but if you are a Hull City fan going to Wembley to see your club in their first Semi Final since 1930, then you would no doubt say it has never been better. The F.A Cup may not be what it once was, but football isn't either. The vast riches paid to the biggest clubs and the best players has ensured the major focus has been on the clubs at the very top of the pyramid, but once again the F.A Cup has not just been dominated by the top clubs. The only "BIG" club left in the competition are Arsenal and they haven't won a trophy for nine years, so it will mean a huge amount to their fans if they win it and if any of the other three win it, it will be another shock winner. When I showed the odds before the 3rd Round, none of Hull City, Wigan Athletic or Sheffield United were even in the frame.

I used to watch Wigan Athletic occasionally as a child in the mid-1980s and back then, I would never have guessed in a million years how the club would evolve. At weekends, I would either go to a match with my Dad or go with my friends to Everton, but several times I went to Wigan Athletic night matches at Springfield Park with lads from school. Ormskirk, my hometown, is probably only twelve miles from Wigan, so a few of the lads in my year supported them, so I was happy to tag along to the odd game.

In the mid-1980s, Dave Whelan had not yet used his commercial influence to help take them to a fancy new stadium and to the higher levels of the English footballing pyramid. Back then, about 16000 would go to Central Park to watch their all conquering Rugby League side, but on the football front, the average crowd was, as far as I recall, only five or six thousand for their Division 3 encounters. I particularly remember three players, Neill Rimmer, the former Everton and England schoolboy, who I mentioned played for my village team, Town Green and then Warren Aspinall and Kevin Langley, who both went on to join Everton, but neither played more than a handful of first team games. Aspinall and Langley did have decent professional careers though, I remember Langley played at Birmingham before rejoining Wigan and Aspinall had a decent spell at Aston Villa before spending a few years at Portsmouth.

Neill Rimmer joined Wigan Athletic from Ipswich Town when I was in Sixth Form in the late 1980s. As someone I vaguely knew, I was keen for him to do well and thankfully he prospered at Wigan, making over 200 appearances for them. My sister, Lisa, remembers Neill Rimmer for entirely different reasons. The first night Lisa first met her now husband, Vin, he was out with his mate, the aforementioned, Neill Rimmer!

These days, I live probably just as close to Wigan, if not closer. I have never been inside the DW stadium though, but intend to rectify that once my financial circumstances improve. My favourite recent story involving Wigan, however, is a non-sporting one. About seven or eight years ago, I had been to the Grand National meeting on the Thursday or Friday and caught the last train out of Liverpool Lime Street to Wigan, deciding to get a taxi home from there (it must have been a reasonably successful day). I was a little worse for wear and stuck up a conversation with the driver who looked a similar age to me. It turned out taxi driving was a secondary job for him, he was just doing it to help make ends meet. When we started talking about his primary job of photography, it transpired he was principally involved in designing album covers for the music industry.

"Done any famous ones?" I asked naively.

"I did the first two Oasis albums and The Verve's Urban Hymns," came the reply.

The guy was called Brian Cannon and had created three of the most well known and iconic album sleeves of the 1990's. He seemed very genuine and I can normally spot a tall tale a mile off. Around the same period of time, when we were in New York for the marathon, Carl McGovern and I had another taxi driver tell us he had run the marathon in 2 hours 15 minutes when he was 61! Brian, however, seemed to know the intricate details of what ideas went into the creation of the covers and at the time I was convinced he was telling the truth. The following morning, when I was sober, I was a little more dubious, but a check on the internet and of the sleeve designs, convinced me once more.

Back on to the football, as well as Neill Rimmer, I know one other former Wigan Athletic player very well. Another one of my Dad's 1967 F.A Amateur Cup Final team mates at Skelmersdale United, Mick Worswick went on to play for Chorley after leaving Skem and then subsequently joined Wigan Athletic in the early 1970s and stayed until they were promoted out of the Northern Premier League into the old Division Four in 1978. Amazingly, Wigan didn't even win the League the year they were transformed from a non-League to a League side. They finished second in the old Northern Premier to Boston United but because Boston's ground wasn't up to League standards and Wigan's old Springfield Park was. Wigan were accepted in by default. When fans of other clubs mock Wigan for not taking their full allocation of tickets at

Wembley, they need to remember that Wigan is not a huge town and less than forty years ago were a non-League side. Their transformation in a relatively short space of time (in footballing terms) is incredible.

Mick Worswick played a huge part in that transformation as he helped them achieve League status. He played 249 times for Wigan and scored 73 goals. I have seen several Facebook comments and forum comments from older Wigan Athletic fans that suggest he was one of the best non-league players Wigan ever had.

Mick wasn't the only ex-Skem player from that era to go on to bigger and better things, several of them did. The most famous from the 1967 Amateur Cup team was Mickey Burns who went on to play almost 400 times for Blackpool, Newcastle United, Cardiff City and Middlesbrough. There was an ever more famous Skelmersdale United player though. Steve Heighway played for Skelmersdale United with my Dad in the 1969-70 season and ended up signing for Liverpool at the end of the season, subsequently playing over 300 times for Liverpool and 34 times for Republic of Ireland, making his debut only months after leaving Skem.

My Dad has always kept in touch with Mick Worswick over the years (nearly all the Skem 1967 team have stayed in regular contact). As a child, I used to see a lot of Mick's two boys, Steven and Martin and they would regularly come and stay at our house for a week during the summer holidays. I have always got along great with my sister, Lisa, but I used to love Steven and Martin coming to stay as for that week they were like the brothers I never had. Steven was only a year younger than me and Martin three years younger and they were both into football and cricket, so we did lots of sporty things, playing sport in the garden or at the park, camping out and having a great laugh. Being Preston lads, I remember Steven saying I had a 'funny voice' but never quite worked out whether that was because I had a lispy voice as a child or because I had a strange combination of a Scouse and Lancastrian accent which I still retain to this day!

Facebook has helped resurrect my contact with Steven, Martin and Mick. Mick, in particular, has taken a great interest in our F.A Cup journey this year. With them all being from Preston and mad North End fans, Mick was hoping our paths would cross with Preston's on this Cup trail. Unfortunately that did not happen, but we have now fallen upon the team that Mick spent five years with, so it's not a bad second best. I don't know if Mick retains any contact with the club, but I suspect we will not need him to get our tickets anyway. I went on the Wigan Athletic website today and sent an e-mail to them explaining that we have been to every Round and would love tickets in the Wigan end so hopefully they will be in touch once the ticket arrangements are announced.

Alan has now recovered from the disappointment of Manchester City's defeat and is happy to go in the Wigan end for the Semi-Final. We just need to ensure we complete every Round now, whether we are sat on the back row of the Top Tier or on the first row behind the corner flag, the priority is to attend.

Tuesday 11th March 2014

The Semi Final order of play has been announced by the F.A today and the Arsenal versus Wigan Athletic game will be on Saturday 12th April at 5 p.m with the Sheffield United versus Hull City game taking place the following day at 4 p.m. With our game kicking off late in the afternoon on the Saturday, it means we have plenty of time to get down there, but it will be a late arrival home. I spoke to my Dad tonight and he suggested that we might be best staying in a bed & breakfast somewhere around Watford, as it will be a long day otherwise. I just scrape by from month to month financially, the Wembley ticket money is going to be difficult to find, so the additional cost of a night in a cheap hotel might be beyond me.

On a more positive note, I have managed to start communications via e-mail with Ed Jones, Wigan Athletic's Head of Media and Player Liasion and he is confident of getting us four tickets for the Wigan end. He obviously has to wait until ticket distribution details are announced and season ticket holders and regular fans are looked after, but he does not expect there to be any problems getting out tickets. Phil might not be too happy sitting in the Wigan end as an Arsenal fan, but I know, like us, his priority is just to be there.

I took a day off work today to watch the Cheltenham Gold Cup on TV. I have many happy memories of going down to Cheltenham for the Festival with my mates, but this year, as they headed down, I made do with a day off work to watch the final day on Channel4. The repping job has been a huge plus in stopping a potentially calamitous situation arising financially, but this F.A Cup journey is the only luxury I can manage for now. I didn't even have a bet today, but did make those who text me for a selection very happy as I said to back Bobs Worth to win the Gold Cup and Lord Windermere each way. One of my mates, Dave Pilkington, stuck a fiver each way at Lord Windermere at 33-1 this morning, so was more than delighted when it came from last to first to grab a shock win. Despite not having a bet, I love watching the big races and it still gives me a buzz to see my selctions come in and other people making a bit of money from it. Perhaps next year I will be able to go down for a day with my Dad and my friends again, that would be fantastic.

On the football front, I have mentioned to Alan that my Dad is looking to stop over after the Semi Final but Alan is keen to get back home on the night of the game. The reason for this is related to his fundraising for The Christie hospital. So far, he has raised over £2000 solely from the F.A Cup endeavours but has decided to incorporate other fundraising events into the project. Two weeks after the F.A Cup Semi Final, he has organised a Manchester City Legends team to play against a Manchester City Supporters Club team at Droylesden F.C. Then, the day after the Final, he is arranging a musical event with various bands in a local pub and calling it 'Cancer Beats'. With two events being planned, there is a lot of organisation to be done, especially at weekends, so understandably Alan wants to get home quickly after the game. The last train out of Euston to Manchester is at nine o'clock, so it may be a bit of a mad dash for Alan if the game goes to extra time. Think Arsenal will win in ninety minutes, but I remember giving Wigan no chance in the last round and they proved me wrong then, so they may well do again!

A couple of weeks since my last entry and my Dad's plans to stop overnight after the Arsenal-Wigan game have been boosted by the assistance of family. My Mum's cousin, Carol and her husband, John live in Hemel Hempstead and have said we can stop at theirs after the game. Carol's father Bill, (my Pop's brother) was involved at Hemel Hempstead Town, as a player, coach, manager and secretary for many years so it will be great to hear a bit more about him. My Mum says she will come down in the car with us too and spend the day with Carol and John, so the Semi Final will bring a few more family members into the fold, although not to the game itself.

Alan has said he may need a lift down now. He was hoping to go to watch Barnet prior to the Semi Final, but has now put that down as a bad idea, as it would have been logistically impossible. He is still going to get the last train home though. Our plan is now to drive to Hemel Hempstead, leave the car at Carol and John's and get the train to Wembley from there.

This is all arranged on the basis that we actually get our tickets. Ed Jones, the Head of Media at Wigan Athletic has been a big help in sorting tickets out for us but has probably got a million and one things on his plate, so his communications have not been great.Alan has passed his card details on to Ed to pay for the tickets, but as yet the money has not been taken and Ed has not told us where we are to due to pick the tickets up from, nor has he told us which category of tickets he can get us (there are three categories priced at £30, £40 and £50).Both Alan and I have been in touch with Ed and although he assures us that everything will be fine, as each day passes a bit of nervousness creeps in to both my mind and Alan's. I have been in touch with Ed today, to suggest I go to the Wigan ticket office to pick them up, so just need to know when they will be there.

Thursday 3rd April 2014

      Wembley here we come! I went down to the DW Stadium today to pick up our four Wembley tickets and we are now all set for a week on Saturday. Once again, we have been dependent on the helping hand of a staff member at a club involved (this time a big thanks goes to Ed Jones at Wigan Athletic) but luckily due to the size of the club and to an extent their regular trips to Wembley, I don't think there was a major demand and supply issue in the Wigan end. The F.A have sensibly made allowances for the demands of each club allocating Arsenal 42 882 and Wigan only 22 807. The other Semi Final is a more even split with Sheffield United being allocated 31 796 and Hull City 32 011.

      When I arrived at Wigan's ticket office, there were a few issues as Ed Jones was at a funeral and the manager of the office Steve Reeves was on a course, so the ladies on the front desks knew nothing about my tickets. I was hoping they could trace them back to me or even to Alan, but after several minutes of looking, all they could come up with, was that Alan had attended a 2-2 draw at the DW Stadium between Wigan and Hull back in 2010! I wondered if that was a strange omen telling us who this year's finalists would be! As they could not trace the tickets, I said I would call back again tomorrow.

      A few minutes later, however, the ticketing issue was rectified and as I was driving away from the ground, I had a call to say to head back to pick them up. We have three tickets at £50 each and a concessionary ticket at £40 for my Dad (a £50 ticket but £10 off as he is a pensioner). It is a relief to have them as it is only nine days to the game now.

      All the pressure for the game is likely to be on Arsenal. Since they beat Everton in the 5th Round, they have had a real dip in form. Unsurprisingly, they were knocked out of the Champions League by Bayern Munich, but Ozil limped off during the away leg at the Allianz and without him, their form has really dipped. In fact, Arsenal go to Goodison this Sunday and if Everton beat them, Everton will take over fourth spot, in the battle for Champions League places. Most sensible Arsenal fans are pointing out that 4th spot and an F.A Cup victory should be recognised as a successful season, but then the panic merchants and doom merchants are pointing out that 5th spot and a failure to win the F.A Cup would be disastrous and if that is the case, Wenger should not be allowed to renew the contract that ends at the end of this season. Personally, I think Wenger will go down in history as a great Arsenal manager and the key injuries to Theo Walcott, Mesut Ozil and Aaron Ramsey have really killed their title chances. Manchester United have really struggled to replace Sir Alex Ferguson, with David Moyes looking very unlikely to get Manchester United into a Champions League spot, so the negative Arsenal fans should, in my opinion, be careful what they wish for.

Wigan Athletic, on the other hand, are flying high. After Roberto Martinez left for Everton, he was replaced by former Burnley and Bolton manager, Owen Coyle, but a less than mediocre start to the season led to a swift parting of the ways and he was replaced by former Manchester City striker, Uwe Rosler, who had been doing a fine job at Brentford. Rosler seems to have brought the magic touch to Wigan too, as they look like they are heading towards a play off place in the Championship. Wigan's priority is obviously a return to the Premier League so the F.A Cup Semi Final is purely a bonus and their players will be under no pressure to succeed.

Arsenal's season seems to be going off the rails. Today, in a crunch game in the battle for fourth position and the lucrative Champions League spot, Everton beat Arsenal 3-0, a six goal swing since their F.A Cup Sixth Round clash at the Emirates. From an Arsenal perspective, the worrying thing was that they succumbed without much of a fight. Arsenal retained a lot of possession but rarely looked dangerous. Everton have a tougher run in to the season than Arsenal but have climbed above the Gunners into fourth. The amount of dissenting voices amongst the Arsenal fans seems to be growing after a nine year gap without a trophy win. To many, fourth spot and an F.A Cup victory is now the minimum expected, so next Saturday's Semi Final against Wigan is vital. A Wigan victory and the clamour for Wenger's managerial exit will only intensify.

Today has been a fabulous day. Our thirteenth round of the F.A Cup took us for our first taste of Wembley stadium. One more visit and the whole fantastic journey will be all over and the new F.A Cup "Champions" will be crowned. I have never called the F.A Cup winners "Champions" before in my life! To me, the winners of a League are crowned "Champions" and the winners of a Cup are simply "winners" but a proper explanation will follow.

Today's kick off was put back seven minutes further from the original 5 p.m to 5.07 p.m as a tribute to the 96 people who lost their lives at Hillsborough, twenty five years ago this coming Tuesday. Six minutes past three has always been deemed the most significant time, as that was the time Ray Lewis, the referee, abandoned the game. For both Semi Finals, 96 seats are also to be left empty in tribute to the Hillsborough victims.

This morning, I picked Alan up at Buckshaw Parkway, as I have done at least half a dozen times before, at half past eight. Before leaving Buckshaw Parkway, I quickly rang Alison's Grandma, Joan up to wish her a 'Happy Birthday'. Alison's Mum and Dad were hosting a 90th birthday party for her today at their house in Bebington, that Alison and the boys were attending, but I was missing because of my F.A Cup commitments. Joan is 90 and her husband, Michael (Alison's Grandad) nine months older, but they still live in the house they have lived in, in Chester, since they were married, 67 years ago! They are both still sound of mind, but their bodies are beginning to falter now, Joan's eyesight is poor and Michael had a stroke a few months ago, but they have done incredibly well to retain their home and independence for so long.

After speaking to Joan for five minutes we set off to my Mum and Dad's in Aughton. For once, instead of just saying a quick hello to my Mum, she was coming with us.

My Mum and Dad are not polar opposites but they are definitely very different personalities. Whilst my Dad is from a working class background, is reserved, relatively quiet other than in footballing circles and hides his emotions. My Mum is very talkative, benefitted from a wealthy upbringing (due to her working class father making money from showbusiness), is tactile and is emotionally very open. My Dad might bottle things up. My Mum lets you know her concerns. My Dad is very sporty. My Mum is very dramatic. They have been very happily married for 45 years so their differences have led to a wonderful partnership. I guess my Dad is a calming influence on my Mum, whilst my Mum has a confidence, an openess and a warmth that my Dad must cherish.

Whilst my Dad and I have been going all over the country watching the F.A Cup, my Mum has been learning her lines. Mum has been in Southport Dramatic Club for about twenty years and is regularly on stage at the Southport Little Theatre. At the end of February, she starred as Lettice Douffet in a Peter Shaffer play called "Lettice and Lovage", a role that was written for Dame Maggie Smith. There are only two ladies on stage for the majority of the play, with a few other minor roles. My Mum's part of Lettice Douffet required her to memorise about eight hundred lines. Not only did she learn the lines perfectly, she played the role brilliantly too. I consider myself a reasonably intelligent person, but under pressure I think I would struggle to remember eight lines, let alone eight hundred, how she does it is beyond me.

My Mum's presence on our overnight trip led to my car boot being crammed full, although she assured me this is her "packing light"! Mum sat in the passenger seat and Dad sat with Alan in the back. My Dad and Alan chatted away busily about football the whole way down, whilst I chatted about family, television, life and ambition with my Mum. For an F.A Cup Saturday it was a refreshing change!

We arrived down in Hemel Hempstead around lunchtime. The hardest part of the journey was the final mile from the main road into Hemel to Carol and John's house, as my Dad had taken directions from John and we somehow missed the church that we should have turned left at. We ended up having do a U-turn at Hemel Hempstead's magic roundabout, five roundabouts all on top of each other, very similar to the one I regularly had to make my way through when I lived in Gloucester and had to journey into Swindon. Once we doubled back, we rang Carol and John and they stayed on the phone and directed us to their front door.

John and Carol are lovely, kindhearted people and as soon as we arrived we were fed and watered and John told us he would drive us to Watford as there would be a lot more connecting trains to Wembley from there than Hemel. Half an hour later we set off, John taking us the back way in, avoiding the major roads but taking us past the Warner Bros. Studio where all the Harry Potter films were made, which now attracts 5000 visitors a day for the studio tour. When John dropped us at the station, he said he would come back for us after the game and take us back to theirs as Carol would be cooking us a roast dinner. Alan said farewell to John, as he was heading back to Manchester after the game with Phil.

Once we arrived in Wembley, Alan rang Phil who had come down by train and we soon met him outside one of the trendy bars by Wembley Arena that he had been enjoying a pint in. Once this F.A Cup journey is over, if my finances pick up, I must arrange a night out on the beer with Phil in Manchester sometime, as it always feels inappropriate to stand around drinking pints when my Dad and Alan are teetotal. Given I had no further driving to do until the following day,

I had a real thirst for a pint, but we didn't head back into the busy bars that Phil had emerged out from.

The whole area around the new Wembley is vastly different to the antiquated surroundings that circled the old Wembley. When we came to Wembley in the 1980's and 1990's it was not only the stadium that was dated, but all the shops around it looked unappealing and there was a large car park that was always crammed full of coaches. Now, the surroundings are very 21st Century, with expensive new flats, attractive restaurants and bars, hotels and open areas for supporters to mingle whilst enjoying a pint. I said to my Dad when we return for the Final, we should arrive with enough time to spare to spend a few hours there. I doubt we will be staying overnight anywhere for the Final, so I won't be able to have more than a pint, but it'd be good to just savour the atmosphere.

Before heading into the stadium, Alan and I bought our obligatory programmes outside the ground. We were quite relieved that it was only £5 but if memory serves me right, 'Rip Off Britain' kicks in for the F.A Cup Final programme, which has similar content but is twice the price. Alan also bought himself a miniature replica of the F.A Cup!

Out of the four of us, Phil was the only one who had not been to the 'new' Wembley before, but despite him being keen to get to our seats and see the stadium in all its glory, he must have sensed that I was desperate for a pint. Once we passed through the turnstiles, Phil suggested that we grab a swift one before taking our seats and despite my Dad and Alan tutting their (mocking) disapproval, I took him up on the offer. As we struck up a conversation, it became obvious that Phil didn't actually have a sixth sense, he just wanted another pint to soothe his nerves. For Alan, my Dad and me, this was just another game, but for Phil, the Gooner, it was season defining.

We knew the stadium would not quite be full and there would be around 80 000 in attendance. It seemed strange to think that my Dad had played in front of a similar number at the 'old Wembley'. Last week, I had spotted a photograph on 'historicimages.com' from the 1967 F.A Amateur Cup Final. It showed a scramble in the Skelmersdale United goalmouth, with an Enfield player shooting towards goal, with the Skem goalkeeper and two defenders diving to block the shot. On the six yard line, protecting the goal, was centre half, Richie Wade! The stands were crammed full. It is a sensational image and makes me well up with pride when I see it.

Being at Wembley, all be it the new one, we started to question my Dad about his day there. Inevitably, with the game finishing goalless, the conversation came around to the last minute of extra time penalty that Skelmersdale United missed that denied them a victory. Alan Bermingham, Skem's regular penalty taker that season took it. My Dad said he normally blasted them, but took it more tentatively than usual, trying to pick his spot and the Enfield keeper, Ian Wolstenholme, dived to his right and made a fine save. Enfield went on to win the Cup after a replay at Maine Road. Perhaps Enfield's name was on the F.A Amateur Cup that year, like Liverpool's in the F.A Cup in 1989, because of the tragedy that had gone before.

This season, as Liverpool have gone on a brilliant run in the Premier League to emerge as title favourites, many people in the media and supporters in general say that it would be a fitting way to commemorate the 25th Anniversary of the Hillsborough tragedy. It is a valid point and even as an Evertonian, I have found myself less anxious than normal for the title to head anywhere other than Anfield. It takes me back to the 1989 F.A Cup Final where Everton's defeat to Liverpool was still a bitter blow but it was dampened because of the tragedy Liverpool Football Club and its supporters had suffered at Hillsborough. Back in 1967, there was also tragedy behind Enfield's F.A Amateur Cup victory, not on such a massive scale, but a tragedy nonetheless.

In the Quarter Final, on 25th February 1967, Enfield faced Worcester Combination League side, Highgate United, who had done brilliantly to reach the latter stages of the competition. The game was played at Highgate's Tythe Barn Lane ground, in front of 2000 spectators. Enfield were favourites and scored an early goal, but in the 27th minute, as the match was being played in heavy rain and a thunderstorm, lightning hit the centre circle, knocking several players and the referee to the ground. Tony Allden, the Highgate United centre half, had been struck. The game was immediately abandoned and Tony Allden was rushed to Solihull hospital, but he never regained consciousness and died the following day.

The game had to be played again, but because of the public interest in it, after Tony Allden's death, rather than it being played at Highgate United's ground, the replayed game was switched to Villa Park. 31 000 fans turned up to watch the re-arranged fixture, to pay tribute to Tony Allden, with Enfield emerging 6-0 victors. I guess it would have been even more fitting if Highgate United had won the 1967 F.A Amateur Cup, but given Enfield had been playing in the game that had witnessed the tragedy, it was fitting that they, as Highgate's conquerors, had gone on to lift the Cup.

Highgate United donated a trophy to the Worcester Combination League (subsequently the Midland Football Combination) in Tony Allden's memory and subsequently each year their League winners and Cup winners meet up in a Charity Shield type one-off game called the Tony Allden Memorial Cup.

Having recounted his tales from 1967, my Dad and the rest of us, were brought back to thoughts of today's game by the beating of a very large drum. A young Wigan Athletic supporter, strapped to a massive drum, was banging away with gusto and leading a group of about thirty young Wigan fans in song. They parked themselves about two feet away from us and my pint of lager shook in my hand with the noise they created. This would have been brilliant if we had been Wigan fans, but as three neutrals and an Arsenal fan, we felt a little out of place. The drummer looked a little worse for wear, so often repeated the same song, which was,

"We know what we are,

We know what we are,

F.A Cup Champions,

That's what we are!"

It does not take Sherlock Holmes to deduce that Alan Oliver doesn't take Manchester City defeats all that well and given Manchester City have been knocked out of the F.A Cup, in successive seasons, by Wigan Athletic, this song was getting his back up!

"What the hell is an F.A Cup CHAMPION, Cal?" he asked.

"I don't know. We've only ever been F.A Cup winners!"

"Exactly."

It must be said though, the Wigan Athletic fans were fantastic and all just looked like it was a day to be cherished. After last season's heroics, they probably never expected to be back to Wembley again, so to be returning the following season was just amazing and they were treating it as such. Other than this group of thirty lads who made up a bizarre male voice choir, seeping alcohol and testosterone out from their veins, most of the other groups of Wigan fans looked like families who had decided to have a wonderful day out, no matter what the result. We left the young lads singing and banging their drum and went to find our seats.

If Arsenal's Emirates stadium is the best Premier League ground I have been to, the new Wembley stadium is the best ground, bar none and that includes the Nou Camp. This is my fifth visit, but I am no less impressed this time than any previous visit. Despite being vast, it feels much more compact than the old Wembley and although we were behind the Wigan goal, it did not feel like we were miles away. There is plenty of room between each row and our view of the pitch was excellent. Phil was suitably impressed too, but it soon became evident that he was a little uncomfortable being an Arsenal fan in the Wigan end, as everything he said was spoken in hushed tones.

"Awesome stadium!" he barely whispered.

Despite Arsenal's ticket allocation only being approximately double Wigan's, it appeared that the vast majority of corporate and neutral tickets had been snapped up by Arsenal fans too. Wigan had two out of three tiers behind one goal and the two sides of the pitch, plus the three tiers down the other end were all Arsenal. Numbers wise, it felt a bit like being Michael Caine and his men being surrounded by the warriors in the 1960s film "Zulu". Not that in our scenario we were actually on Michael Caine's side, using that analogy we were three neutrals and a Zulu warrior!

"Who do you want to win, Dad?" I asked just before kick off.

"I'm not bothered," my Dad replied, "I'm just hoping it finishes in ninety minutes so we don't get back to Carol's for the Roast dinner too late!"

Prior to kick off the minute's silence to commemorate the Hillsborough dead became a minute's applause. I don't really agree with a minute's applause in such circumstances. My view on the silence/applause debate is that silence should greet a tragedy, applause should greet the end of a full life. If it is a minute to commemorate the Bradford fire, the disaster at Ibrox,

Munich or Hillsborough, it should be silence. If a player dies tragically young, silence too. If Sir Tom Finney or any other legend dies after having a great career and a full life, then it should be applause. An old great dying is sad but not tragic. I'm not sure my views will come to pass at stadiums around Britain, but given they are my views, I hope they are!

After the applause the game soon kicked off and unfortunately the first half of the game was up there with the first half between Doncaster Rovers and Stevenage as the dullest, most inconsequential half of football that we have witnessed in thirteen rounds! Wigan looked competent, well organised and difficult to break down, whilst Arsenal looked to have more class but looked wary of commiting too many men forward, their cautious play probably reflecting their run of poor results and a lack of confidence.

Arsenal had the better of most of the half but their best chance was an effort by Arsenal centre forward Yaya Sanogo that was well saved by Wigan's former England international keeper, Scott Carson. Sanogo is not a player I know much about at all, but during the first half his touch looked poor and he did not look dangerous. My Dad, Alan and Phil informed me that he played in the Quarter Final against Everton, but if he did, he made no impression on me whatsoever! Admittedly, when Everton are playing, I only tend to notice the star performers from the other side, as I am too busy watching how our eleven players perform. From the evidence of his forgettable performance against Everton and the first forty five minutes at Wembley, he is not a patch on Olivier Giroud. My Dad also commented on how unimpressive Sanogo looked, which led on to us forecasting that he may go the same way as Christopher Wreh, who was playing occasionally for Arsenal until 2000 and within four years was playing for Bishop's Stortford and Buckingham Town. Perhaps Yaya will turn out to be the best Yaya in the Premier League and prove us both wrong, but he will need to improve.

Just before half time, Callum McManaman had a shot just over the bar for Wigan, which resulted in me striking up a conversation with the guy on my right, who had only arrived at his seat, along with a few of his mates, about five minutes into the game. His name was Geoff and although he was very excited by McManaman's run and shot, it transpired he was actually a Manchester United fan living in Shrewsbury. His mate next to him was an avid Birmingham City fan and from what I could make out, one of the group of four lived in Wigan, so they had all adopted them as their second team.

"We were all here in the Wigan end last year when they beat City," Geoff explained.

"It was brilliant beating that lot," he went on, "I went to Old Trafford for the last home game of the season after the Final in a Wigan top! It was superb!"

As Geoff said this, I was relieved it was me he was recounting this tale too. Alan was finding it hard enough to be sitting in amongst the fans of Manchester City's conquerors, but if he had been sat next to a United fan gloating about City's defeat, that would really have tested his resolve.

To me though, Geoff was alright. He was a proper United fan and a fan of football. He had been to Munich in midweek to watch United succumb to Bayern Munich in the Champions League Quarter Finals.

"Moyes is a poor boss for United. He seems a nice bloke but that's not what we need. Fergie was a git a lot of the time, but he won things," Geoff concluded.

At half time, Phil and I nipped down to see if we could get another £5 pint each, but gave up when we saw the size of the queue. Geoff and his mates must have been more persistent as they arrived back about fifteen minutes into the second half.

Thankfully, as a spectacle the game gathered pace after the interval. Both sides seemed to decide extra time was not ideal for them, as they headed towards an important run in to the season, so each adopted a more gung-ho approach than their caution of the first 45 minutes.

Callum McManaman had not had the sort of game that had brought him to prominence in last year's F.A Cup run, but he does have the ability to run with the ball at pace and in the 63rd minute when he jinked his way into the Arsenal box, Per Mertesacker, the tall Arsenal defender stuck out a long leg and took some of the ball and some of the man. Michael Oliver, the referee, took a long look at it, before pointing to the penalty spot. The Wigan fans around us went wild, whilst I raised my eyebrows at my Dad. Both of us tend to feel that referees shy out of giving as many penalties as they should do.

"What did you think, Dad?" I asked.

"I didn't think it was a penalty."

"No, me neither. It will certainly liven things up a bit though!"

Jordi Gomez is the Wigan penalty taker, but he had to wait an age before taking this one. Nacho Monreal, a name that sounds like it belongs to a Mexican restaurant in a French Canadian province rather than an Arsenal footballer, was injured in the build up to the goal and after being tended to for some time, he was eventually stretchered off. Gomez was unperturbed by the delay and calmly stroked his penalty past Lukasz Fabianski and into the back of the net. ONE-NIL to Wigan! The Wigan fans went crazy and three quarters of the stadium, clad in red and white, went into massive shock. Arsenal had thirty minutes to rescue their season or it would be another year without a trophy and would give even more ammunition to Wenger's detractors.

For the last thirty minutes, Wigan sat deep and invited Arsenal to try to break them down and Arsenal gave it a real go. Oxlade-Chamberlain had a shot saved. Sanogo was bearing down on goal when Crainey made an excellent tackle on him and Crainey was the Wigan hero again when a Kieran Gibbs header beat Carson in the Wigan goal, only for Crainey to clear off the line. It was starting to feel like Arsenal may not be able to break Wigan down and I was starting, prematurely, to consider how I would feel about a Wigan Athletic F.A Cup Final once again. To be honest, I found myself wanting Arsenal to equalise. Phil Cooper had been through eleven rounds of the thirteen with us, had never been anything other than excellent company and had felt up until now that the Gods were writing this F.A Cup script just for him. If Arsenal lost, we would all be neutrals for the Final and it would not be as fitting a finale as having a team winner or at the very least, a team in the final. Prior to this journey, I would not have anticipated finding myself wanting an Arsenal equaliser, when Wigan is just down the road from us, but as Arsenal attacked in waves, in my mind, I was urging them to score.

In the 81st minute, Arsenal had one of several corners cleared, but it only fell to Alex Oxlade-Chamberlain, the Arsenal midfielder on the edge of the box. He attempted a relatively poor shot that was heading wide but thankfully for Arsenal, Per Mertesacker, the Arsenal defender who had given away the Wigan penalty, was still in the box and from close range sent a header into the corner of the net. It looked miles offside but apparently TV replays have shown it was borderline and in that case the decision was the right one. Mertesacker and the whole Arsenal contingent in the ground (except Phil Cooper in the Wigan end!) went crazy, as I would have done in their position. It may have only been an equaliser against a Championship side, but it kept the dream alive of ending their nine year period without a trophy. ONE-ALL and everything to play for.

I thought Wigan may succumb to tiredness after the body blow of the Arsenal equaliser, but they were not willing to give up the F.A Cup trophy easily. Arsenal substitute Olivier

Giroud, who has scored twice in the previous round, as a substitute, against Everton, almost got himself on the score sheet again, but Scott Carson, who had performed admirably, made a fine low save.Soon after the full-time whistle went and the game now had to go to extra time. For the first time in thirteen rounds, we witnessed a game that was level after ninety minutes, but thankfully there are no replays at the Semi Final or Final stage. We knew the game must be decided in Extra Time or, if that failed to find a winner, then there would be penalties. "Looks like we'll be having that roast dinner at Carol's late then," my Dad reminded me.

Extra time was tough on both sets of players as both sides had had a long season, Wigan had been involved in the Europa League, Arsenal in the Champions League, as well as all the domestic football, but the standard of football was similar to the excellent second half, rather than the dire first forty five. For some reason, Arsene Wenger chose to replace Podolski in the second half rather than Yaya Sanogo who had continued his poor form of the first half and he looked like a player who would never score on the day even if he had a million chances. He spurned several, but Oxlade-Chamberlain almost won it for Arsenal with a long range effort that rattled the corner of the post and bar. Wigan had the occasional chance on the break too, but failed to test Arsenal keeper Fabianski with any of them. After two hours of football, a winner could not be found and Michael Oliver blew his whistle to signal penalties.

Penalties are not down to pure luck. If it was just pure luck, the England football team would probably win half of theirs. Penalties are down to the confidence and ability of the penalty takers and pretty often down to the shot stopping ability of the goalkeepers. I have no statistics to back me up, but my gut feeling is that pretty often, certainly more than fifty per cent of the time, the side with the greater footballing ability, 'the favourites', win the shoot out. On that basis, I thought Arsenal would win.

When picking penalty takers, I think it is important to get off to a good start, so I would always choose my regular penalty taker to take the first one. Using that logic, Mikel Arteta would take Arsenal's first and Jordi Gomez, who had already scored from the spot in the contest, would take Wigan's first. Uwe Rosler, Wigan's manager, adopted different tactics and Gary Caldwell stepped up to take their first. Caldwell had only come on late in the original 90 minutes to replace the excellent Ivan Ramis, who was injured, so despite Caldwell's experience, it seemed like a strange choice. Fabianski looked huge in the Arsenal goal and although Caldwell struck his shot hard and low to the keeper's right, Fabianski got down well to make an excellent save.

Mikel Arteta then stepped up for Arsenal. The Spaniard had looked nerveless in the Quarter Final when scoring both times from the spot after Giroud had encroached on his initial penalty. As he stepped up to take this one, Carson ran across his line frantically in his yellow jersey, trying to irritate Arteta, like a bearded wasp, but Arteta was as cool as gloveless hands at the top of Everest and sent Carson the wrong way, firing it to the keeper's left as he went right.ONE-NIL to Arsenal on penalties.

Being a goal down after one penalty is not a disaster, as there are still four for each side left and plenty of opportunities are still there for things to swing back in your favour. Wigan's second penalty was important though, as they needed to score it, to ensure they kept some pressure on Arsenal. Jack Collison was the taker, but he lofted his penalty to Fabianski's right, at a nice height for the keeper and Fabianski saved comfortably. When Arsenal substitute Kim Kallstrom scored a composed left footed penalty, low to Carson's right, it was TWO-NIL to Arsenal after two penalties each. The Arsenal fans went wild as they knew there was no coming back for Wigan now. Jean Beausejour scored Wigan's third but Olivier Giroud scored Arsenal's third too, so it was 3-1 after three penalties and despite James McArthur scoring Wigan's fourth, to make it 3-2, Santi Cazorla had the opportunity to make it 4-2 and win it for Arsenal, as Wigan only had one penalty taker left (presumably Gomez had been saved until last). Like Arteta. Cazorla was unfazed by Carson running around his line and although perhaps not the best of penalties, it was struck fairly centrally and sailed high into the roof of the net beyond the despairing right hand of the keeper. It was not the most convincing of performances but Arsenal were in the F.A Cup Final and to their players, staff and supporters, that was all that mattered. Actually, that comment isn't strictly true! As my Dad and I subsequently waited in the queue for a tube at Wembley station, there was a minority of Arsenal supporters who were dwelling on the average performance rather than the victory. After nineteen years without a trophy for Everton, I would have swopped positions with them in a heartbeat. If they win the final in style, only the most negative of supporters will continue to recall that the manner of the semi-final victory was unconvincing.

After the final whistle, Alan and Phil departed quickly as they needed to be at Euston station by nine for the final train home. My Dad and I made our way through masses of delighted Arsenal fans to the tube station and thankfully, when we arrived back at Watford, John was already there in his car waiting for us. We had a great turkey roast dinner, fine company and a few beers, but I am shattered now, so will tell you more about it tomorrow!

FINAL SCORE : Arsenal 1 Wigan Athletic 1 (4-2 to Arsenal on penalties)

Scorers :- Arsenal – Mertesacker . Wigan Athletic – Gomez (pen).

Our 'Speccies':- Calvin Wade, Alan Oliver, Richard Wade, Phil Cooper.

Sunday 13th April 2014

I really enjoyed last night at John and Carol's in Hemel Hempstead. My Mum and Dad see them every year in Tenerife in January, but the last time I saw them was at my Nan's funeral back in 2002, so it was good to catch up. I asked about Bill McGrae, Carol's father and my Pop's brother, and thanks to Carol and John and also via Marc Willmore, the programme editor and historian for Hemel FC, who I have been in touch with via Twitter, I was able to discover a little more about family links to amateur football. It is a further illustration that football is in my blood both on my Mum and Dad's side of the family.

Having been stationed down South from Liverpool during the War, Bill stayed in Hemel Hempstead for the rest of his life and always described himself as a Scouser, despite developing a fairly strong Hemel Hempstead accent! He made his debut for Hemel Hempstead Town FC in 1947 and played for five seasons. Hemel competed in the Spartan League back then and were consistently in the top half of the Division One West table. In 1950/51, they finished runners up and were promoted to the Premier Division. Hemel finished a respectable fifth in the Premier League in their first season and then moved to the Delphinian League. It appears Bill then stopped playing, having scored 9 goals in his 109 appearances.

Bill remained involved at the club and had several spells as manager, including two spells in the late 1960's/early 1970's when he stepped in as Caretaker Manager. In the 1970/71 season he guided Hemel to the St Mary's Cup Final, which they won 2-0 defeating local rivals Berkhamstead Town at Hemel's old Crabtree Lane ground, which they moved out of a year later to their current home at Vauxhall Road.

Following on from his roles as manager, Bill became Secretary of the club for fifteen years. He is credited as being the brains behind Hemel's change of colours to an all Red strip in the early 1980's, which are still the club colours today. I wonder if that had anything to do with his Liverpool roots, as most of the McGrae family are avid Liverpudlians? Hopefully the idea went down better than Vincent Tan's decision to swop Cardiff Ciy's colours to red! When Bill died, aged 83 in November 2001, Carol said her Mum was heartbroken to lose him after 55 years of marriage and died herself within a couple of days. They had a joint funeral.

This morning, we left Hemel mid-morning and I was home in time to watch the other Semi-Final between Sheffield United and Hull City. Hull ran out 5-3 winners in an entertaining goal fest. Jamie Lowe, my mate from my Manchester Poly days, took his daughter, Megan, as he knew, should Hull make the final, that he couldn't be there, as he will be in Liverpool on a work weekend. At one stage, the camera captured his mate, Richard Campion, one of the few Hull fans I know, with a few of their mates and their kids, partying wildly to celebrate one of the Hull goals. I have seen on Facebook how much Hull City's F.A Cup run means to Richard as he has followed them through all four Divisions and to finally see them reach an F.A Cup Final is beyond his wildest dreams. I will make every effort to meet up with Richard at the Final, because he is the type of fan who truly appreciates the magical effects of this wonderful competition.

I was pleased to see Hull City reach the final. Sheffield United is a similar sized club to Hull, but have been through tough times recently, until Nigel Clough's managerial reign has given them a real boost. I just felt that despite Clough's heroics, Sheffield United, as a First Division side, would be unable to compete with Arsenal and it could have led to a one-sided final. It is going to be a tough ask for Hull City too, but Steve Bruce has them playing good football and as a mid-table Premier League side, they go into the Final with real hopes of victory. It should also be an entertaining game, as Hull City will certainly not defend deeply and just hope for a lucky break. They will attempt to trade punches with Arsenal, so I am hoping for plenty of goals. Including the six penalty shoot out goals yesterday, we have now seen 55 goals in 13 matches, so it would be great to reach sixty!

Within 48 hours of our Semi Final and with about five weeks to go until the Final on Saturday 17th May, I think we may have our four F.A Cup Final tickets sorted out! They are coming from two different people, but one of the two is an unexpected source.

I have explained earlier in the book that I walked away from the world of banking because of the unpleasant way some of the Sales Management staff treated some of the Business Development Managers, including myself, when I worked for BM Solutions. I think I also mentioned that other than a couple of Sales Managers/Regional Managers, the staff there were excellent and the service provided was great, so it was a real shame. Anyway, one of the many good guys, Mitch Pomfret, who was the Head of Underwriting at their Head Office at Pendeford, when I worked for them, has been in touch via Facebook to say he should be able to sort tickets out for the F.A Cup Final for me.

I used to see Mitch on a fairly regular basis at corporate events and internal team meetings and we always got on well because of our mutual love of football.Mitch is a big Manchester City fan and I will always remember him taking the stage at a presentation at Old Trafford to the sound of the Manchester City anthem, Blue Moon!

After I left BM Solutions, I kept in touch with Mitch on an occasional basis via Facebook, but I was not really aware that he was following our F.A Cup journey or that he was aware that Alan and I were intending on trying to raise as much money as possible for The Christie Hospital via Alan's various fundraising events and 50p from each sale of this book going into the pot.

It transpires that Mitch's father, Mel Pomfret, has had prostate cancer, has been a regular at The Christie in recent years and is hugely appreciative of the wonderful care he has received.

Mel just happens to be District Secretary for Stockport F.A and a Director of Cheshire F.A, so Mitch feels he should be in a position, once the allocations are announced to get us at least a couple of tickets.

I also spoke to my Dad tonight, who has been speaking to Joe Royle. Joe has a very good relationship with the Hull City manager, Steve Bruce, so Joe has very kindly said he will speak to Steve and see if he can sort us a couple of tickets out. Just to point out, in case there are any misconceptions, none of these tickets are free. The only free tickets we have received along the way were from Burscough, when they let me in for free as an ex-player and Stevenage, who allowed us all in for free for the game against Stourbridge. Neither time did we ask for free tickets, but as a man of limited financial means, I must admit they were greatly appreciated!

It is now just a case of waiting to see if these tickets come through, but there are no reasons to doubt the integrity of either source, so it very much looks like it will be mission accomplished and we will have been to every round, from start to finish.

Today was a brilliant day and with regards to Alan's fundraising for 'The Christie' hospital, the most significant day so far this season. Alan had organised a Manchester City Legends v Manchester City Supporters Club game to take place at Droylesden Football Club's Butchers Arms Ground and I wanted to go down to show my support.

It seems to be a theme of this book to say my wife, Alison, was working and once again she was. As a midwife, she works incredibly hard and does an incredible job. It is an emotionally draining job, but it must be great coming home from your shift knowing that you have had a positive impact on people's lives and although you may not remember them, a significant amount of them will remember you until their dying day.

Brad, my eldest, was at a sleepover, so I needed Joel to join me on my trip to Droylesden. He took the news much better than I had anticipated. I did throw in the offer of a hot chocolate on the way and coke and crisps at the ground, which may have made the day out a little more enticing.

The reason we were stopping on the way to Droylesden, which is only a forty minute drive away was to meet up with a second cousin of mine, Daniel Rintoul and his girlfriend, Louise Dunn at the Bolton service station. I had never previously met Daniel, but over the last couple of years, he has passionately traced his family tree using ancestry.co.uk and made contact with me a few months ago using Facebook. Daniel is the grandson of another of my Pop's brothers, Ken. Daniel told me that they were from a family of fifteen brothers and sisters, including half brothers and sisters!

It was great meeting Daniel and Louise. Not surprisingly, I discovered Daniel is another football fanatic. He is a teacher in his early 30s and was originally from Chorley but moved up to

Scotland as a child and after spending a couple of years in his young adult life in Birmingham he developed an affiliation to Aston Villa. Thus, his three teams are Hibernian, Aston Villa and Chorley, a threesome that must have led to some torturous Saturday afternoons over the years! On the positive side though, his weekend back in Chorley to see family, co-incided with Chorley Football Club's opportunity to clinch the Evo Stik Premier Division. He went over to Buxton yesterday to see them win the title with a 2-0 victory.

Daniel provided me with another gem of sporting trivia from our family history. My Pop always mentioned his brother Joseph had played for Everton, but I have never been able to find anything on the internet to show that he ever played for the first team. Daniel said he has discovered Joseph was a defender, who played between the wars. He moved from Everton to Tranmere Rovers but then significantly made a move to Norwich City where he became a first team regular, making 124 appearances and scoring three goals. He is one of the Norwich City players mentioned in a book called Canary Citizens, which I must see if I can get a copy of.

After a coffee and Joel's hot chocolate, which he wasn't overly keen on, we headed down to Droylesden. The sun was shining, a rarity in Manchester and we found the ground easily, as it is only a stone's throw from Manchester City's Etithad stadium. Alan and Jordan Oliver were at the turnstile entrance to collect the entrance money and welcome everyone to the event. Alan was proudly holding a mango pink F.A Cup football. Since the new F.A Cup balls had been introduced, Alan had been desperate to get hold of one and he had obviously managed it and told me it was going to be used as the match ball for the game. When I went into the ground itself, it is a great little ground with a fantastic Main stand but there were some areas where the surrounding walls were pretty low and I started to wonder whether Alan's ball would survive the ninety minutes! There were other match balls, but only one F.A Cup ball. Through the game it did disappear into back gardens and surrounding roads, but thanks to the good people of Droylesden it always came back.

The game between City Legends and City supporters club was watched by over 300 people and was really entertaining, the City Legends side won 3-2 with recent legend Ian Brightwell, 1980s legend, Jim Melrose and 1970s legend, Peter Barnes in the side. Barnes is in his late fifties now and doesn't move like he did when I was a kid and has, as you would expect, put on a bit of timber, but he was still involved in a lot of the good stuff the Legends played and he scored an excellent goal from a free kick, with an equisite chip that floated past the Supporters Club keeper, Nathan Foy and into the corner of the net.

I spoke to Alan this evening and they raised a superb £3000 for 'The Christie' on the day, which takes the total fundraising pot to over £5000. Alan said he didn't see a single goal, as he was too busy organsing to watch much of the game, but is overwhelmed by the money made. The game started at 12 p.m because of two important Premier League games and he was delighted how they had transpired too.

The Premier League has become, in recent weeks, a three horse race, between Liverpool, Manchester City and Chelsea. Whilst their title rivals have been faltering, Liverpool have surprised many pundits and football supporters by going on a winning run of eleven games, including a defeat of Manchester City. Victory in their last three games would have ensured the title returned to Anfield for the first time in 24 years and 25 years since the Hillsborough tragedy. Over in Manchester, David Moyes has paid the price for a season when Manchester United have failed to join the title race and are languishing in seventh place. He was sacked last week and Ryan Giggs has stepped in until the end of the season in a caretaker manager role.

The two games that all the people at the City Legends v Supporters game wanted to watch were Liverpool v Chelsea followed by Crystal Palace v Manchester City. Many of them remained in the bar for both encounters, which saw Chelsea defeat Liverpool 2-0 after a Steven Gerrard slip allowed Demba Ba to open the scoring, followed by a last minute tap in from Willian. This was followed by a 2-0 victory for City at Palace with Dzeko and the excellent Yaya Toure scoring. This leaves Liverpool with 80 points from 36 games, Chelsea with 78 points from 36 games and Manchester City with 77 points from 35 games. As Manchester City have a superior goal difference, if they now win their last three games, they win the title. Interestingly their last two games are at home to Aston Villa and West Ham but their final away game is at Goodison Park against Everton. Everton have blown their chance of fourth spot with two defeats against Crystal Palace at home and Southampton away recently and with Arsenal back in form since their F.A Cup Semi Final win, they look nailed on for fourth spot. A minority of Evertonians want City to beat us, to hand the title to Manchester City but most fans just want us to win our games, regardless of the consequences. Funny how it has worked out this way though, I don't think Alan will speak to me at Wembley if Everton beat City!

I use Facebook and Twitter a lot. Facebook allows me to keep up to date with friends from all over the world and even locally, that family life and a tight financial position mean I don't get to see as often as I would like to. Twitter allows me to keep up to date with people who have similar interests to me and also to publicise my books to people I only know through social media. Some people get offended by tweets trying to flog them something, so I've learnt to restrict my book tweets to new launches, promotions and give aways. There are still some people who object to that, but the vast majority are incredibly supportive.

Once in a while, someone on Twitter will do something kindhearted, like Neil Smith, the Evertonian who gave me his two tickets a few times to the 1985 Lounge when he couldn't go or send me something unexpectedly, which puts a smile on my face. Today, someone with a Twitter name of @leonnezza sent me a copy of a Burscough v Preston team sheet from Monday 31st July 1995 and asked "Is that you?" I was in the Burscough squad for a game against Preston North End and amongst the PNE players that day, was subsequent Everton player and 110 cap winning Republic of Ireland international, Kevin Kilbane and also a certain David Moyes! I would love to say I have a vivid recollection of them both, saved a Kevin Kilbane penalty and had a chat with David Moyes about Glasgow and future careers in coaching, but if truth be known, I don't remember the game at all. I contacted Stan Strickland, the secretary of Burscough at the time, to see if I got on the pitch, but he doesn't know (but imagines that I did as it was a friendly). According to my Facebook friend, Gordon Johnson, who was linesman that day, it was two days after the 6-0 defeat to Everton and Preston won 4-1. Irrespective of whether I played or not, little did anyone know that day what a stellar playing career Kevin Kilbane would have or that David

Moyes, who was turning out in front of a few hundred at Victoria Park, Burscough,would go on to manage Preston, Everton and Manchester United.

Gordon Johnson has also provided me with a back up plan for tickets for the F.A Cup Final. The arrangements to get two tickets from Joe Royle via Steve Bruce and the others from Mel Pomfret from Stockport F.A are seemingly going to plan. Alan asked me if I could ask Mel, if he could get three instead of two, as Jordan would also love to come, so I have put that request in and Mel is hopeful. If there is any hiccup with either option, Gordon said he will do what he can to get us tickets, which is really great of him as we know of each other really, through our mutual passion for football, rather than being close friends.

Gordon was a copper in Greater Manchester for thirty years from 1983 to 2013 but I know him as a local ref/linesman. A football related high point of his police career was receiving a Chief Constables High Commendation, "For Bravery, Courage and Professionalism, when faced with extreme violence" during the 2008 UEFA Cup Final.

Referree and linesman wise, he is always posting on Facebook about games he is officiating at, that I would love to watch. Until the end of last season, he was a Level 2B referee, which meant he could officiate at Conference North level or for Premier League reserve or Under 21 games. Gordon ran the line all the way up to Championship level. His first Championship linesman role was at Burnley v Crystal Palace at Turf Moor, which will be a Premier League fixture next season. Gordon said the ref that day was Andy D'Urso, who he felt was a quality ref to work with. He has reffed at Wembley Stadium and officiated at the National Stadium in Jamor, Lisbon where Celtic became the first British side to win the European Cup in 1967. A lot of the time running the line or being a ref is a thankless task, but without people like Gordon wanting to do it, the game would be in a right mess. It would be great if one day the media, managers and fans started to give the officials a break and granted them the respect given to officials in other sports like rugby and cricket.

Saturday 3rd May 2014

2:15 p.m

      Crunch game in the race for the Premier League takes place between Everton and Manchester City at half five this afternoon. I posted the following on Facebook earlier to let my views be known, prior to kick off :-

"Weird day. I support Everton and irrespective of the implications, I want Everton to win. Does it bother me if Liverpool win the League? To be honest, not as much as I thought it would. Rodgers seems a decent bloke, they play attractive football and I admit there would be something fitting about it on the 25th Anniversary of Hillsborough. OK, Suarez still winds me up more than any other player on earth with his theatrics and the odd biased armchair Liverpool fan raises my blood pressure from time to time, but most of my mates are Reds and I know how delighted they would be. So, Liverpudlians will support Everton today and perhaps half of Evertonians are saying they won't (unless Arsenal lose earlier and 4th place is back up for grabs). I reckon though, once the game kicks off, some Blues who have said all week that they want City to win, will find themselves screaming for the side they support rather than the opposition. It's our team, we support them no matter what. In my mind, anything else is just wrong."

8:00 p.m

      It very much looks like it is Manchester City's title now. They beat Everton 3-2. Barkley scored a screamer for Everton early on, but then goals from Aguero and two from Dzeko took the game away from Everton, despite a late rally after a Lukaku header from a Leighton Baines cross. As expected, Everton fans did get behind their team despite Martin Tyler and Gary Neville implying on Sky TV that they were happy with a City victory. I didn't go, as I need every penny for the F.A Cup Final, but my Dad went and he said the atmosphere was good, the fans got behind the team and the only reason it may have been slightly more subdued than recent games, was because we have lost out on the battle for fourth. I have always liked Martin Tyler in the past, but was annoyed today that he was trying to make a story out of nothing. Liverpool have to win now on Monday night to keep the pressure on City, but it seems unlikely that City will drop points at home to Villa or West Ham.

<u>**Monday 5th May 2014**</u>

Liverpool only drew 3-3 tonight at Crystal Palace after throwing away a three goal lead late on. Despite being nine goals inferior on goal difference, once Liverpool went three up (still six goals down) they were rushing to get the ball out of the net with the implied aim of scoring more goals. It seemed a naïve tactic to me, as City are likely to win each of their games by at least a goal or two, so two goal wins against each of Villa and West Ham would mean Liverpool needing to beat Newcastle 8-0 even if they had beaten Palace 5-0. Anyway, hindsight I guess is a wonderful thing. Liverpool went on an eleven match winning run playing open, expansive football, so I suppose they were just trying to do what they do best. What the Palace comeback means though, is that City now only need four points from their two home games to clinch the title. Chelsea are out of it after a goalless draw with Norwich City.

Wednesday 7th May 2014

The title race is almost over. Manchester City beat Aston Villa 4-0 tonight with goals from Dzeko (2), Jovetic and a sublime late effort from Yaya Toure. It was nervy stuff for over an hour, with the first goal not coming until the 64th minute, but after that the floodgates opened. Alan and my old mate, Howard Slack from my Yorkshire Building Society days will be over the (blue) moon as a point at home against West Ham on Sunday will clinch their second title in three years. Liverpool would need to beat Newcastle at Anfield and West Ham beat City at the Etihad for the title to go to Anfield. Liverpool have had a great season in the Premier League but look like they will just fall short. Suarez has deservedly won the Football Writers and Players Player of the Year award for the Premier League and has been on fire (as has Sturridge and several other Liverpool attacking players like Sterling) but their defensive frailties look like they will cost them. They were seventh last season though, so it cannot be argued that Rodgers hasn't done brilliantly.

Sunday 11th May 2014

The conclusion to the Premier League was not the unbelievable ending of 2012 when Aguero scored a last minute winner against Q.P.R to grasp the title from Manchester United. This time around Manchester City beat West Ham United comfortably 2-0, so despite Liverpool coming from behind to beat Newcastle United 2-1, the Premier league title is Manchester City's, with Liverpool as runners up. The rest of the Top Six were Chelsea (3rd), Arsenal (4th), Everton (5th) and Tottenham Hotspur (6th). Norwich City, Fulham and Cardiff City were relegated.

Arsenal warmed up for the F.A Cup Final with a 2-0 away to Norwich City whilst Hull City lost their final League game 2-0 at home to Everton. It has been a great Premier League season for all but the relegated sides and I hope the English season now finishes with a fantastic F.A Cup Final next Saturday!

737 teams entered the 2013-14 F.A Cup. These clubs range from unpaid amateur sides to professional outfits who pay their players millions. After fourteen eventful rounds, the competition will conclude on Saturday at Wembley Stadium with the F.A Cup Final between Arsenal and Hull City and our gang of five are now in possession of our full allocation of tickets. My Dad picked up two tickets from Joe Royle today, which are in the Hull City end and I picked up three tickets from Mel Pomfret in Stockport which are in the Arsenal end.

It was lovely to meet Mitch's Dad, Mel as he is a real gentleman. I was invited into Mel's house in Bramhall, Stockport and spent a fascinating ten minutes with him. It is always great to meet people who live and breathe football and Mel is no exception.

Mel Pomfret has spent all of his adult life involved with local amateur football, progressing from his involvement with a local amateur team, through to the 'heady' heights of being a Director of Cheshire F.A. Throughout the years he has selflessly offered his time and expertise, in the interests of helping anyone with the slightest interest in indulging their passion in football. Mel first became involved in football administration as Secretary of Woodley FC in 1966, which turned out to be quite a good year for English football, all things considered. It proved to be the start of a life long involvement with the local amateur game. As a result of this involvement, Mel subsequently took a call from the local Sunday League who asked him to join their Committee as Treasurer, and he then subsequently went on to be Secretary. He then became Assistant Secretary of Cheshire F.A, and following the sudden and untimely death of Harold Bates, Cheshire F.A Secretary, Mel took over this role, as well as that of Secretary of Stockport F.A.Alongside these roles, Mel has been a regular member of local F.A disciplinary committees, and has overseen numerous Stockport & District F.A local cup finals, many of which have held their finals at Stockport County's famous Edgeley Park ground.

People like Mel Pomfret and Gordon Johnson are cogs in the wheel that make English football so interesting to so many. Without the hard work of selfless people like them, the sport would fail to function. When fans of the teams that reach the F.A Cup final feel aggrieved that so many tickets are given to the F.A, they tend to forget that the likes of Gordon and Mel are sacrificing huge chunks of their leisure time for the good of their community. Gordon will be paid very little for this sacrifice, Mel will not be paid at all, I wouldn't have thought. They will either use the tickets themselves or pass them to someone they feel is deserving and in our case, I am delighted and honoured Mel Pomfret has passed his tickets to us.

It is an unfortunate fact that F.A Cup Final's don't tend to be the best of games, especially in recent years. The supporters of the team that wins are not overly concerned about the quality of the game, they are more concerned with the outcome but for the millions of neutrals around the world, a quality F.A Cup Final is long overdue. When I woke this morning to see a cloudless sky on a glorious day, I felt a surge of optimism that our fourteen round adventure was going to finish in style. It had been announced that a new F.A Cup trophy, only the third ever, would be presented to the winners and I just had a sneaky feeling they would lift it after an excellent game. I was not disappointed.

I must admit my sense of optimism did get the better of me a little. I was feeling so optimistic, I sprang out of bed at half past six and even spent a few minutes picking six horses for a racing competition called Scoop 6 which would net me £10 million if all my six horses won and I was the only one to select them! Very unlikely indeed, but as I say, I was feeling optimistic so it was worth a £2 punt! The Christie would certainly benefit from a tidy sum then.

I was only travelling down with my Dad for the Final. Alan, Jordan and Phil were getting the train together from Manchester but Alan didn't want a lift, as he wanted to rush back post game, to sort out the final arrangements for 'Cancer Beats', the musical Charity event he is putting on tomorrow in aid of 'The Christie'. My Dad said he would meet me in a side street in Wigan at nine (I was only up at half six through excitement rather than necessity) and then I would drive to Banbury and we would then get the Chiltern Railways train to Wembley Stadium from there.

On the way down, we alternated between my Dad's choice, BBC Radio Two and my choice, TalkSport. My Dad wanted to listen to Radio 2 because of the Saturday morning Sixties show that was on and we chatted about the fact that Sixties music changed once The Beatles emerged. In the early Sixties, my Dad went to see The Beatles a dozen times, often in The Cavern, but once in 1962, he said he saw them in St John's Hall, opposite Bootle Town Hall and there were less than a hundred people in there.

TalkSport were rightly focusing on the F.A Cup Final. They pointed out that Hull City's manager, Steve Bruce, was hoping to be only the third English manager in the Premier League era, to win the F.A Cup, the other two being Joe Royle of Everton and Harry Redknapp of Portsmouth. The Arsenal manager, Frenchman Arsene Wenger, was no stranger to the joys of managing a side to F.A Cup victory, having won it four times before. If he was to win it a fifth time today, he would equal Sir Alex Ferguson's record of five managerial F.A Cup victories. Arsenal have not won a trophy for nine years, a fact that has been often repeated recently, so not only would Wenger be ending the drought, he would be breaking (or at least equalling) an F.A Cup record in the process.

The drive down to Banbury was a leisurely one and the roads were not overly busy. The town and the station are only a couple of miles from the M40, so once we came off the motorway, we were parked up within a few minutes and with 45 minutes to wait before our train arrived, we wandered into a very pleasant looking Banbury town centre, so I could put my Scoop6 bet on. I later discovered my bet did not survive the first race, but as no one won the £10 million pot, I may put another £2 up next week and try for £12 million! The winner will definitely be someone who buys a ticket!

Our train from Banbury to Wembley Stadium left at half past twelve and was only half full. With the majority of Hull City fans heading down from the East side of the country and the majority of Arsenal fans already living in North London, there were just a scattering of orange and black Hull City tops and scarves at Banbury train station and no Arsenal fans in sight. The train journey was only an hour, through plenty of leafy suburbs, but although it did get busier as we got closer to Wembley, especially with Arsenal fans, most people were able to get a seat.

On arrival at Wembley Stadium we still had three and a half hours before kick off, so my Dad and I went to Pret a Manger for a coffee and a muffin. I text Alan and Phil to let them know where we were and also made contact with Richard Campion, the big Hull City fan who is close friends with my mate from Polytechnic, Jamie Lowe. About twenty minutes later, Alan, Jordan and Phil arrived, Phil proudly wearing his Arsenal top. They had arrived in London about ten o'clock and had spent a few hours having a look around. They had been to Camden Lock, Carnaby Street, Oxford Street and Bond Street, with Alan proudly showing me a photo of him outside the London Palladium. He also said he had collared a Norwegian TV crew on arrival at Wembley and given them the full fourteen round story. I wonder how good Norwegian translators are at deciphering Mancunian? Unfortunately we didn't get to see Richard though, he was in Edgware when I text then headed into the stadium soon after arriving at Wembley. We shared a few texts during the game, but he was in the lower tier and we were up in the heavens so there was no way we could meet up.

Before going into the ground, we went up to have our photos taken at the Bobby Moore statue. It was difficult to get a good photo though, as there were a load of drummers entertaining the crowd right by the statue, so after a couple of quick shots we headed down to the square by

Wembley Arena and Phil, Jordan and I had a quick pint of Stella, at a bargain Wembley price of £4.95!

The whole shopping area around Wembley Arena is fantastic now and there is even a play area for children. During the 1980s Cup Finals, there was very little around Wembley other than the odd old fashioned pub, a load of concrete and a mass of supporters, many of whom were tanked up and enjoying a bladder relieving wee at the side of Wembley Way. Nowadays, the atmosphere is more family orientated and the Hull and Arsenal fans mixed happily in the local shops, bars and restaurants.

About an hour before kick off we went into the ground. My Dad and I had opted to take the cheaper Hull City seats, leaving Alan and Jordan to join Phil in the Arsenal end. We knew we wouldn't be meeting up after the game, nor would we be meeting for another round, so it was a more emotional goodbye than usual, hands were shaken heartily and slightly awkward hugs were exchanged before we headed to our separate entrances. This is the end of a journey, but the start of a friendship, so plans are already afoot to do some other footballing adventure together.

My Dad and I walked through the Arsenal contingent to get to Entrance D with part of the Hull City contingent. They were in good voice as they queued and it was good fun trying to decipher some of the Hull City songs. Two of my favourites were the following gems :-
"His Nan is from 'ULL, His Nan is from 'ULL,
Liam Rosenoir, His Nan is from 'ULL !"
And,
"Don't sell McShane, Super Paul McShane,
I just don't think you understand,
That if you sell McShane,

Super Paul McShane,

You'll Have a F###ing Riot On Your Hands!"

The Allan McGregor one wasn't as good :-

"He saves to his left,

He saves to his right,

Allan McGregor,

He shags ten birds a night."

Anyway, once we got through the turnstile, we went on one escalator after another as we headed towards the top seats in the stadium. We were going so high, I was half expecting to see Willie Wonka at one stage and for him to welcome us into a glass elevator and for us just to float above the pitch for the duration of the game. I'm not great with heights so once we went in, to discover we were a few hundred feet above the pitch was a bit unnerving, as the tiers are really steep, but after a few minutes of sweaty palms, I grew accustomed to my new environment and started to enjoy the spectacular view.

Prior to kick off, Leona Lewis came out and sang 'Abide with Me' and 'God Save The Queen' and the Hull City fans sang 'Can't Help Falling In Love With You'. When my grandparents (my Mum's Mum and Dad, my Nan and Pop) had been married fifty years, they paid for the family to go on a Mediterranean cruise. One night, when we were all having a meal to celebrate their Anniversary, about twelve of the waiters came over, one with a guitar and serenaded them with 'Can't Help Falling In Love with You'. My Nan shed a tear, so that song always reminds me of them. My Nan died of cancer six years later, one of many reasons that I want to help Alan's fundraising for 'The Christie'.

Before we knew it, the game was under way, thirty years after my first Wembley F.A Cup Final, I was at my first without Everton (my sixth in total). Last time I had been at Wembley for an F.A Cup Final in 2009, Louis Saha had put Everton ahead after 25 seconds and I wasn't expecting another lightning start, but in the first ten minutes, Hull City got off to an absolute flyer.

We didn't see the first couple of minutes. Some people like to stand up at games even though they have a seat. It often happens in the first tier of a stadium, as the people on the front row are at eye level with the pitch, so can't see too well. To enable them to see better, they stand up which creates a domino effect behind them. Other times, people just stand up because they are excited. I presume the latter was the case with the couple in front of us, as we had a perfect birds eye view from a few hundred feet up, but when everyone sat down at kick off, they stayed standing. They were in their 40s, appeared like they had more than a few scoops, were draped in black and oranges sheets with hats with bells on. My Dad was pretty relaxed about spending the afternoon watching an orange sheet, I didn't want to stand as we had kids behind us, but I was just about to ask them to sit down, when the lady did spontaneously and a minute later her husband or partner followed. As he did so, Hull City had a corner.

Half the Hull City contingent moaned as Stephen Quinn hit a corner to Tom Huddlestone, who was standing outside the box. Huddlestone struck a shot first time, which wasn't fantastically hit and wouldn't have gone in, but on its way through to the goal, James Chester deliberately diverted the ball, past a wrong footed Fabianski and into the back of the net. Four minutes in and Hull City were ONE-NIL up!

Before the game, all our gang of five agreed that if Arsenal scored first they would run away with it, but if Hull City scored first, it would be very interesting. We had been given the goal the four neutrals amongst us wanted and the goal Phil, the Arsenal fan must have dreaded. I noticed the ten men, in plain clothes, that were sitting next to me and in the ten seats along were not reacting at all, then twigged they must have been Arsenal fans that could only get tickets in the Hull end. The rest of the supporters around me went wild other than the drunk couple in front of us, who just looked confused by the noise. A 14 year old a few rows down implored everyone to get on their feet.

"Come on everyone! This is 'ULL in the Cup Final and we're f###ing winning! Come on!"
Still no-one stood. I don't blame them. We were 300 feet up and it was steep. It felt safer sitting. The 'ULL fans could still shout and clap whilst sitting down.

Five minutes later, Hull City fans were in dreamland. Stephen Quinn wide on the left beat a man and put in a far post cross that Steve Bruce's son, Alex steered on to the post. Curtis Davies was first to the rebound and from a tight angle, put the ball back into the far corner of the night, before wheeling away in tongue poking delight! Only eight minutes had gone and it was TWO-NIL to Hull City!

Once again the couple in front of us looked around bewildered like Rosanna Arquette's character in Pulp Fiction.

"Hey man! What's all the noise for, man! We want peace, man! Not noise, PEACE!"
The 14 year old kid was off again.

"Come on you boring b###ards! Stand up and support 'ULL! This is our team! COME ON! Support 'em!"

Again everyone took no notice. The rest of the Hull City contingent were going too potty to care, other than my row of Arsenal fans who looked ashen faced.

Hull City had started fantastically and the Arsenal supporters were stunned but there was one big problem, there were still 82 minutes to go. Surely Hull City couldn't continue to play this well for another 82 minutes and Arsenal would now awaken from their slumber.

"What a start, Dad! I still can't see Hull winning though, can you?"

"If they can make it to half-time two-nil up they might," my Dad observed.

I totally agreed, however, it was Hull who initially remained in the ascendancy and a few minutes later another Alex Bruce looping header from a corner was going goalbound until it was headed clear by Kieran Gibbs. We have said in many previous games, that one moment changed the path of the game and in this F.A Cup Final, that Gibbs moment was the vital, path changing moment.

In the 17th minute, referre Lee Probert awarded Arsenal a free kick 25 yards out and Santi Cazorla struck a fine right footed curling shot, that flew past McGregor's hand outstretched fingers, skimming them along the way and into the back of the net. TWO-ONE.

The ten lads next to us, who were Arsenal fans in disguise, stood up and shouted 'Come on', but not 'Come on, Arsenal', so the surrounding Hull fans didn't know who they were urging on. The rest of the Hull contingent were still upbeat, shouting , "Steve Bruce, Steve Bruce, Steve Bruce.." in an encouraging mantra. At the other end of the stadium, the Arsenal fans came to life and recognised they were now right back in it. Arsenal fans have been subjected to the odd humiliating defeat when they were battered in the opening exchanges and continued to be battered for the rest of the game, Chelsea and Liverpool away spring to mind, but at 2-1, this no longer felt like one of those games. This felt like a 'great comeback' game. Replays showed McGregor had managed to fingertip the shot on to the bottom of the bar and the slightest of extra contact would have prevented a goal, but the extra contact hadn't happened and Arsenal were buoyed.

The rest of the first half could not continue at the same frantic pace as the first twenty minutes and the game settled down. Arsenal bossed the next 15 minutes and had several blocked shots and one attempt from Giroud that went wide, but then Hull stepped up a gear and created a chance for Tom Huddlestone who shot over from a well struck effort from just outside the box. When the half-time whistle went, TWO-ONE to Hull City seemed just about right.

At half time, I received a text from Phil saying,

"What a nightmare half for Arsenal," but in reality, it wasn't a nightmare half, it was just a nightmare opening ten minutes.

I also had one from Hull City fan, Richard Campion which simply said, "Nerves here!!!!"

During the interval, Terry Neill was invited on to the pitch to give his thoughts on the first half, as he has both played for and managed both Arsenal and Hull City. My Dad thought I had misheard the stadium announcer, as he couldn't remember Terry Neill representing Hull City only Arsenal. Internet checks revealed, however, he has played for and managed Hull City too. I was thinking that was an amazing statistic and then realised if Alan and I had been given our dream final of Manchester City against Everton, then Joe Royle could have been doing that role.

As I sat chatting to my Dad, I thought again of those Allan Stewart words of wisdom from the Scotland-Brazil World Cup game. Hull City fans needed to enjoy the half time break. I had a gut feeling that Arsenal would go on to win and the Hull fans needed to savour the feeling of leading in an F.A Cup Final at half-time as it may never get any better than this.

"Next goal wins," I said to my Dad.

"What do you mean?" my Dad said sounding confused, like he had missed a goal whilst staring at the draped orange blanket of the drunken hippy in front.

"I mean if Arsenal equalise, they will go on to win, but if Hull score a third, that will be that."

"You're probably right," my Dad agreed.

The drunken hippies had gone for a half time drink and when they returned they headed to seats a few rows back from the ones where they had sat in the first half.

"Are you sitting up there for the second half?" my Dad asked, thinking they had spotted two more enticing seats.

"Were we not sitting here in the first half?" the lady asked.

"No, you were down here," my Dad explained.

"Were we?"

They then staggered down a few rows and stood next to us. We then had to explain they were actually sat in front of us and then they awkwardly attempted to to climb over the seat. The lady managed to get one leg over but then lost all co-ordination and everyone surrounding her had to life her trailing leg up and over the seat.

"That pair will wake up tomorrow morning and think they are off to a Cup Final," I said to my Dad.

As the teams came out for the second half, the 14 year old in front was off again, like he was conspiring with the hippies to annoy everyone else!

"COME ON 'ULL!" he roared, "Stand up everyone! Support your club!"

To be fair to the lad, he was full of passion and excitement for his club and just wanted the rest of the Hull City fans to feel that same intensity. The fact our row had ten Arsenal fans and two neutrals probably didn't help his cause.

The second half started like the last 35 minutes of the first half had gone, with Arsenal having the lion's share of possession, but Hull breaking dangerously and having their own efforts on goal from time to time. Arsenal had a couple of penalty claims waved away, one of which looked like it could have been given when Cazorla was felled by Curtis Davies. Steve Bruce had been in his technical area for the whole game but when Cazorla's penalty claims were turned down, Wenger who had been shown on camera earlier in the game with a suit jacket on, arrived jacketless in the technical area for the first time, remonstrating wildly with the assistant referee and the fourth official. He looked like a man who felt his job depended on victory and perhaps it did.

After 56 minutes, all the Hull City fans broke out into a minute's applause to commemorate the 56 Bradford City fans that had died at Valley Parade on 11th May 1985. I had read about it on Twitter, so joined in for the full minute. Unfortunately, the Arsenal fans looked on, bewildered. It was a pity word had not spread to them too, as it would have been an even more powerful gesture if the whole stadium had participated.

Following on from that, Wenger took off Podolski and introduced Yaya Sanogo, who I felt had had a poor game against Wigan in the Semi Final. Phil told me before the game that Sanogo had been troubled with injury this season and had not really had the opportunity to find his form. Perhaps he will turn out to be a better player than he has shown so far. After thirteen games for Arsenal he has yet to score.

In the 66th minute there was another substitution and perhaps a decisive one, as the excellent Alex Bruce was replaced by Paul McShane. McShane is loved by the Hull City fans, but Bruce had been having the sort of game his father would have been proud of in his heyday and Hull could have done with his presence for the last 24 minutes. Chances were starting to come Arsenal's way more and more often as Hull City were starting to tire. When you retain possession well, like Arsenal do, the other team have to work very had to chase the ball down and the efforts of the Hull City team on a very warm May afternoon, were beginning to show.

In the 71st minute, Cazorla swung over a dangerous corner, Bacary Sagna who impresses each time I see him, outjumped his marker and from his header the ball hit another Hull City defender, James Chester, on the back and ricocheted towards goal. Laurent Koscielny managed to get in front of the keeper and prod the loose ball home into the net from six yards out like an accomplished centre forward rather than the centre back he actually is. TWO-TWO!

With twenty minutes left, there still looked like there were more goals in the game. "I hope someone scores," my Dad commented, "as extra time is normally cagey and not overly entertaining, so I want someone to win it in the ninety."
As he said this, I received a text of Phil that summed up his afternoon, which just said, "This is killing me!"

Steve Bruce soon sent Sone Aluko to replace Stephen Quinn, to inject fresh legs into a weary side.

In the final twenty, it could have gone either way but Arsenal were the team who were presented with the golden opportunity to grab a winner.A ball across the box from Sanogo fell to Kieran Gibbs seven yards out and despite having to beat the onrushing keeper, Allan McGregor, it looked easier to score than to miss, but he struck his left foot shot a little too well and it flew up and over the Hull keeper's bar. After that, McGregor, who had only returned to the team last week after a serious kidney injury sustained at West Ham, had to make two or three decent saves, one a particularly good one from Giroud, but after ninety minutes, it finished all square at 2-2. For the second time on the trot for us, extra time beckoned.

Before extra time got under way, my Dad and I discussed how lucky we had been. For twelve rounds, a draw would have resulted in a replay, another journey, another ticket and another expense, but all our initial twelve games were decided within ninety minutes. Once we reached Wembley where the games had to be decided on the day, both games have finished level after ninety minutes. Fate has definitely been sympathetic on my lack of monetary funds!

The first half of extra time saw Arsenal have a string of chances, none better than Giroud's after three minutes. Aaron Ramsey, the Arsenal midfielder was coming more and more into the game as it had gone on and when he dispossessed Curtis Davies, he curled across an inch perfect cross that was met by the onrushing Giroud who directed a strong header towards goal, but agonisingly for him and the Arsenal fans it cannoned off the bar and fell back to Davies who headed clear.

At half time in extra time, Wenger sensed his side had the fitness advantage and wanted to avoid penalties. Steve Bruce had made his final change after 101 minutes throwing on George Boyd for Liam Rosenoir, so Wenger played his final cards too, sending on Wilshere and Rosicky to replace Ozil, who had failed to sparkle, and Cazorla who had shown flashes of brilliance, but overall had not had his best game other than making telling contributions for the two Arsenal goals.

Three minutes into the second half of extra time, Hull City's David Meyler picked up the ball on the left hand side of his own half, twenty yards outside his keeper's box. Meyler delayed his pass and was robbed of the ball by Aaron Ramsey, who played the ball back to Bacary Sagna, then received the ball back from him and advanced down the right wing. He played the ball to Areta, but whilst Arteta was making a simple short ball to Wilshere, Ramsey began an intelligent sprint into the box. Wilshere played the ball in to Sanogo, who passed to Giroud, who cleverly backheeled to the onrushing Ramsey who, at full pace, flicked an inch perfect shot into the McGregor's left hand corner. The goal was a lovely move, but all stemmed from Ramsey's tenacity to win the ball back from Meyler. THREE- TWO to Arsenal.

It would have been totally understandable if Hull City's weary bodies had sagged and Arsenal had gone on to score a fourth, but Hull had given a spirited performance all day and continued to do so. They were to have two chances deep into extra time. The first seemed to happen in slow motion. There was some indecision in the Arsenal defence and the ball landed halfway between Sone Aluko, the Hull City substitute and Fabianski in the Arsenal goal on Hull's left wing. Perhaps not realising Aluko was a fresh legged, lightning quick substitute, Fabianski dashed from goal but Aluko beat him to the ball. Aluko had two choices, shoot from a tight angle or square the ball to one of two Hull City forwards who were running forward to support him. A pass could have been intercepted by an Arsenal defender, so Aluko opted to have a shot and it seemed to be heading goalwards but eventually ran across the goal, evading Gibbs who almost miscued it into his own goal.

Aluko even had time to have one more shot from the edge of the box. Fabianski was blinded by a cluster of players between him and the ball but showed good delayed reactions to dive low to his left and save. Minutes later, it was all over and Arsenal had ended their nine year trophy drought and become the 2014 F.A Cup Winners!

My Dad and I stayed around to watch the majority of the post-match celebrations and commiserations. As the Hull City players climbed the stairs to the Royal Box, my Dad noticed that the 14 year old lad who had been urging the crowd to support their team had gone home! "So much for him supporting his team," my Dad commented wryly.

The vast majority of Hull City fans who had been absolutely superb all game stayed on to acknowledge their side's valiant effort. They could not have given more.

Over in the Arsenal end, no-one was leaving as the Arsenal players climbed the stairs to lift the Cup.Club captain Thomas Vermaelen, an unused substitute on the day was the first to lift the new F.A Cup trophy. Their barren years were over and they now hoped a new era of trophy winning had begun.

FINAL SCORE : Arsenal 3 Hull City 2 (after extra time)

Scorers :- Arsenal – Cazorla, Koscielny, Ramsey .

> **Hull City – Chester, Davies.**

Our 'Speccies':- Calvin Wade, Alan Oliver, Richard Wade, Phil Cooper, Jordan Oliver.

F.A Cup Winners – Arsenal.

Epilogue - In The End There Was Light – Written Sunday 18ᵗʰ May 2014

After fourteen fantastic rounds of football and having witnessed sixty goals, our journey came to an end with Phil Cooper's Arsenal winning the F.A Cup. My Dad and I found a train waiting for us at Wembley Stadium and despite a 5 p.m kick off and extra time, we were back at his car in Wigan by midnight. I shook his hand warmly and thanked him for coming on this journey with me. Abiding with family tradition there we no hugs, but a huge amount of unspoken and undisplayed affection. My Dad's part in this story will stay with me forever.

I was back home in time to catch the end of the F.A Cup highlights on ITV and was disappointed to hear that they weren't deeming the game to be a classic. In my eyes, it was the best F.A Cup Final for a neutral since Coventry's 3-2 victory over Tottenham Hotspur in 1987. Granted there were mistakes, but for incident and excitement it could hardly have been bettered. Hull City played a huge part and despite feeling pleased for Arsene Wenger, I felt sorry for Steve Bruce. One of my former neighbours, Chris Beech, played for Bruce at Huddersfield and said he was a genuinely well liked guy by everyone at the club and he always comes across well on television. He was gracious in defeat, but couldn't help feeling one or two decisions had gone against them.

From a personal perspective the opening Chapters of the book questioned what this F.A Cup journey had in store. I wrongly described my life as "shitty" (or the financial side of it anyway), but over the last nine months things have picked up a lot and although by no means a rich man in financial terms, I am a rich man in so many other ways. I have my health, my family, my wife and my friends and through this wonderful F.A Cup experience, have found some fantastic new friends too. I didn't get to 13 stone 13 pounds like I had intended or to a 36 inch waist either, but I am heading towards it! Neither Brad or Joel have been picked up by Everton yet, but I won't love them any more if they are.

If one man epitomises the F.A Cup it is Arsene Wenger. In the opening Chapters, I said the F.A Cup was not the trophy it was, but I think this season it has had a resurgence. The same is true of Arsene Wenger. Neither the F.A Cup or Arsene Wenger were ready to be written off and I hope both have happy times in future years.

Finally, Bill Shankly once said football was more important than life and death. Through meeting Alan Oliver and his fundraising efforts for The Christie Hospital, I have come to recognise that in some instances that statement is true. When I arrived home last night, I had a text from Alan to say they had stayed to witness all the Arsenal celebrations and as a result missed the last train from Euston to Manchester so had gone to Victoria to get the last coach. It left London at half past eleven and was arriving in Manchester at twenty to six! At half past eight this morning, Alan rang me to say that he had had very little sleep, but was functioning on adrenalin as he had to be at the pub at ten o'clock ready to prepare for today's "Cancer Beats" musical event that was on from midday to midnight! Through football links he has raised £5000 for The Christie so far and I am hoping this book sells well enough to double that. If that additional money does one extra thing to help one cancer sufferer prolong their life, then football has, in a round about way, become more important than life and death to them.

29918552R00223

Made in the USA
Charleston, SC
29 May 2014